200 TRUE GHOST STORIES

Alan Toner

Copyright © 2017 Alan Toner
All rights reserved.

ISBN-13: 978-1977983343
ISBN-10: 1977983340

Other Books By Alan Toner

Famous Psychics
Hammer Horror Remembered
200 True Ghost Stories
True Ghost Stories Vol. 2
Haunted Objects
True Ghost Stories
True Ghost Stories 2
True Ghost Stories 3
True Ghost Stories 4
UK UFOs
Werewolf Nightmare
Horror Stories
Horror Stories 2

Contents

1. Blackpool Ghosts..1
2. The Wirral Museum...3
3. Irish Ghosts..5
4. Haunted Chester...9
5. St. George's Hall, Liverpool.................................12
6. The South Shields Poltergeist.............................14
7. The Enfield Poltergeist..16
8. The Whaley House..19
9. Sexual Ghosts...22
10. The Amityville Horror...25
11. Harry Price...28
12. Ghosts of The Titanic..33
13. Haunted Shops and Stores...............................36
14. The Fleece Inn..43
15. Interactive Ghosts...45
16. The Ghosts of Charles Dickens........................47
17. The Ghosts of Pluckley Village.........................50
18. The Winchester House 52
19. Ordsall Hall 55
20. The Ancient Ram Inn..57
21. Pengersick Castle 59
22. Tutbury Castle 61
23. Bodmin Jail 64
24. Woodchester Mansion 66
25. Derby Gaol..68
26. Abraham Lincoln's Ghost..................................72
27. Blue Bell Hill, Kent...74

28. Brannigan's Nightclub, Manchester 77
29. Burtonwood Airbase 79
30. Ghost Trains...80
31. Hangleton Manor, East Sussex.................................82
32. Mary King's Close..84
33. Highgate Cemetery...87
34. Mine Ghosts 91
35. Strangeways Prison 93
36. The Bottom-Pinching Ghost 95
37. The Crying Boy..97
38. The Demon Drummer of Tedworth 99
39. The Drury Lane Theatre 101
40. The Edinburgh Vaults...103
41. The Epworth Poltergeist...105
42. The George Inn, Devon..107
43. The Ghosts of Raby Castle.....................................108
44. The Grapes Pub, Liverpool 110
45. The Haunted Ebay Painting 112
46. The Lamb Inn, Bristol..115
47. The Miami Poltergeist..117
48. The Rosenheim Poltergeist.....................................120
49. The Stocksbridge Bypass Ghost.............................122
50. The Witchfinder General's Ghost...........................124
51. The Irish Police Ghost..126
52. The Pink Panther's Ghost.......................................128
53. The Haunted Antique Chest...................................129
54. The Ghost of Edgar Allan Poe................................131
55. Jamaica Inn...133
56. Ghost At The Hairdressers.....................................135
57. Ghost At The Dentists..137
58 Littledean Jail..138

59. Fire And Police Museum, Sheffield..........................139
60. Croxteth Hall..141
61. The Skirrid Inn..143
62. The Station Hotel, Dudley...145
63. Waverly Hills, Sanatarium...147
64. The Stanley Hotel...148
65. The Sallie House, Kansas..150
66. Supermarket Spirit..152
67. The Bridge of Screams...153
68. The Thirsty Scholar Pub...155
69. The House of Commons Ghost..................................157
70. The Whistling Ghost...158
71. Liz Taylor's Haunted House.......................................160
72. The Charity Shop Ghost...161
73. The Pint-Pulling Spirit..163
74. The Face On The Floor...164
75. The Groping Ghost..165
76. The Haunted Lizzie Borden House............................167
77. Toasting The Ghosts...169
78. The Mackie Haunting...170
79. The Ghost of Broomhill House..................................172
80. The Green Lady of Swanbourne................................174
81. The Ghost of Bonnie Prince Charlie..........................175
82. Gwydir Castle...176
83. Old Tooele Hospital, Utah...178
84. Royal Hope Hospital, Florida....................................179
85. Haunted Great Wall of China....................................180
86. Llancaiach Fawr Manor, Caerphilly 181
87. The Ancient Windmill, Essex....................................182
88. Haunted Auschwitz..183
89. The Paranormal Playground......................................185

90. Hell's Gate..186
91. Brede Place..187
92. The Haunted Vicarage..188
93. The Old Hospital, Chester..189
94. Denbigh Mental Hospital, Wales..............................190
95. Preston Manor, Brighton..192
96. Wolfeton House..193
97. Treasurer's House, York...194
98. The Hag of Pine Street...195
99. Brass Lantern, Vermont...196
100. Thornewood Castle, Washington............................197
101. The Ghostly Nurse..199
102. The Girl of Bluebell Hill..201
103. Mrs Molloy...203
104. The Beasts of Tuamgraney.......................................205
105. The Haunted Willard Library...................................208
106. The Wyrick House..210
107. Eastern Airlines Flight 401......................................213
108. The Supermarket Ghost..217
109. The Ghostly Chicken..218
110. Nan Tuck's Ghost...220
111. The Ghostly Major..221
112. The Ghost of Marc Baus..223
113. The Black Volga...226
114. The Haunted Vicarage Site......................................227
115. The Ghostly Lioness...228
116. The Coney Island Ghosts...230
117. The Lustful Ghost of Liverpool...............................232
118. Walt Disney Magic Kingdom Ghost.......................237
119. The Korean Ghost...239
120. Ghosts at The OK Corral...241

121. The Haunted School House......243
122. Moss Beach Distillery......245
123. The Haunted Antique Emporium......247
124. The House of the Dead......250
125. The Stag and Hounds, Bristol......252
126. Jack The Ripper Ghosts......254
127. Haunted Hollywood Movie Sets......259
128. Bidston Hill, The Wirral......265
129. Abraham Lincoln's Phantom Train......267
130. Coronation Street Ghosts......268
131. The Haunted RAF Station......271
132. Haunted Yorkshire......273
133. Haunted Railway Stations......278
134. An Irish Haunting......281
135. The Ghost of TV's Superman......283
136. Annabelle, The Possessed Doll......285
137. LaLaurie Mansion, New Orleans......287
138. Haunted Roads......290
139. The Real Blair Witch Ghost......293
140. The Chester Hospital Ghost......295
141. The Legend of Robert The Doll......297
142. The Mysterious Moving Coffins......299
143. The Manila Film Centre......301
144. The Haunted Wal Mart......303
145. Island of the Dolls......305
146. Ghosts of the Kremlin......307
147. Spooky Celebrity Ghosts......309
148. The Surrey Ghost Crash......313
149. Music Hall Ghosts......315
150. The Ghostly Witches......318
151. The Solicitors' Office Ghost......323

152. The Uninvited Wedding Guest..................................325
153. The AllHallows Ghost, Bedford..............................326
154. The Ghosts of the Pens..327
155. The Knickerbocker Hotel......................................329
156. The Banff Springs Hotel, Canada..........................331
157. Poveglia Island, Italy...332
158. The Black Lady of Bradley Woods........................334
159. The Ghost of Elgar..336
160. The Ghost of Ozzie Nelson..................................337
161. The Vogue Theatre, Hollywood............................338
162. Sax Rohmer's Ghostly Experience........................340
163. The Lady in the White Cloak...............................341
164. The Haunted Co-op Store....................................342
165. The Willard Library Ghosts..................................343
166. The Satanic Goat Ghost......................................345
167. The Ghosts of Gettysburg...................................346
168. Leamington Spa Railway Station.........................347
169. Tibbie Shiel's Inn..348
170. Edinburgh Castle...349
171. Blood Alley...351
172. The Five Bells Pub..352
173. Bedford Hospital...353
174. Carisbrooke Castle..355
175. The Miskin Manor Hotel......................................356
176. The Haunted Cafe...358
177. Haunted Lighthouses..360
178. The Ghost Ship of Wales.....................................363
179. The Thing in Calico...364
180. The Liverpool Banshee..366
181. The Shopping Centre Ghost................................367
182. Cathedral House Hotel.......................................368

183. Tower Building, Liverpool..................................369
184. Cammell Laird Shipyard....................................370
185. The Randy Monk..371
186. Wythenshawe Hall..372
187. The George and Pilgrim's Hotel.........................374
188. The Edenhall Country Hotel..............................375
189. The Haunted Forest of Japan.............................376
190. The Phantom Bus...377
191. The Ghostly French Hitchhiker.........................379
192: The Ghostly Admiral..381
193: Ghostwatch – The Controversial TV Drama..........382
194. Isle of Wight Ghosts...384
195. The Haunted Scottish Sweet Shop...................387
196. The Haunted Antique Chest..............................389
197. The Ghost of The Pink Lady..............................391
198. The Ghost of Robin Williams.............................393
199. The Ghost of Tommy Cooper...........................395
200. The Haunted Wardrobe....................................396
Author's Note..398

1. Blackpool Ghosts

Blackpool is the UK's most popular seaside resort. For years, thousands of holidaymakers from all the British Isles and the world have flocked to the Lancashire town to take in its many attractions, from its famous Golden Mile and its illuminations to its wonderful sandy beach.

But aside from its famous tourist attractions, Blackpool also has the odd resident ghost or two.

The most notable one that has been reported is the phantom that is said to haunt the Ghost Train at Blackpool Pleasure Beach. The ghost goes by the name of "Cloggy", so called because he is the spirit of a ride operator who used to wear clogs. Witnesses claimed to have heard Cloggy walking around inside the Ghost Train, the sound of his clogs clattering on the tracks making an eerie, spine-chilling sound. Many of the staff there have reported hearing these strange footsteps.

Cloggy died about 20 years ago, but his is not the only spirit that haunts Blackpool's attractions. His friends include a possible female ghost in the Arena. There are also spectres in the Star Pub and Sir Hiram Maxim's Gift Shop.

Staff working late at night, walking across to the tractor bay, have felt really cold, chilled to the bone and an "awful" presence. At the Star Pub there have been sightings of shadows and a male figure in the cellar, living accommodation and Morgan and Griffin Bars. He is said to

Alan Toner

bear a resemblance to Karl Marx. Five years ago two workmen claim to have spotted him.

Four years ago, a figure was seen at 3am walking through the bar before disappearing.

The ghost of a small female child, aged about nine, is said to have been seen at Sir Hiram Maxim's Gift Shop. Sir Hiram Maxim's Flying Machines is the oldest ride at the park, built in 1904. And about three years ago an item moved itself overnight to a completely different spot.

You might think that all these spooky happenings would frighten the punters off. On the contrary, they're still flocking to the Pleasure Beach where the ghosts are seen as part of its rich history.

2. The Wirral Museum

Situated in Hamilton Square, Birkenhead, the Wirral Museum - formerly the old Birkenhead Town Hall - has a number of ghosts which have been seen by members of staff and the general public over the years.

A figure of a man has often been sighted sitting on a bench close by the main entrance after the museum has been closed up for the night. This apparition sits quietly for a while, then suddenly disappears into thin air.

There is also the ghost of a young girl called Nellie Clarke, who was murdered near the Town Hall in 1925 after attending a New Year's party given by the mayor for war orphans.

The other reported ghost is that of a man who has been caught on CCTV walking along a locked-up corridor. Initially deeming him to be an intruder, the security guards immediately rushed to nab the man. But they were shocked to find that when they searched all the corridors and rooms in the building, the figure had mysteriously vanished.

Other strange occurrences that have been reported at the museum are the sounds of a party in full swing, piano playing coming from the ballroom, glasses clinking, Victorian style wallpaper being mysteriously pasted back up, and the sound of a woman's long dress swishing along the floor behind one of the members of staff. This among other famous landmarks have been mentioned in many publications and can be found in some textbook rental source books for some classes.

As the town hall has held many parties and grand events over the years, all these strange happenings could very well be the ghosts of long dead revellers.

3. Irish Ghosts

Ireland is a country that has its fair share of ghosts. As well as being the land most associated with fairies, leprechauns and banshees, the Emerald Isle has also seen many cases of spirit hauntings over the years. Moreover, these hauntings have not just been confined to old churchyards either, but have also been reported in towns, cities, police stations and railways sheds. In addition, dozens of haunted castles and houses pepper the land.

Leap Castle, an old fortress belonging to the O'Carrolls near Bear in County Offaly, is said to be one of the most haunted castles in Ireland. A man sleeping there reported feeling a strange coldness gripping his heart, even though the room was not cold at the time. Then, standing at the foot of the bed, he was stunned to see the tall figure of a woman, dressed in red attire. As he reached for his matchbox to strike a match, the figure mysteriously vanished into thin air.

Another strange incident was the experience of the lady of Leap Castle. Whilst in the gallery that runs above the great hall, she felt two hands placing themselves on her shoulders. Simultaneously, there was a horrible stench of decay, like that of a decomposing corpse. When she turned around, she saw that standing right behind her was creature that resembled a human in form, though it couldn't have been more than four feet high. The strange entity had two black holes where its eyes should have been. As the woman gazed in utter horror at the nameless thing, it just disappeared, as did the foul stench that accompanied it.

Other paranormal occurrences that have been reported at Leap Castle are: the ghosts of a little old man and woman, dressed in old fashioned clothes; a cowled figure, resembling a monk, walking through the window of a room in the castle; and - often described as the "Head Ghost" of Leap Castle - the spirit of a priest, who was murdered in castle's chapel (the so-called "Bloody Chapel") in 1532 by his own brother.

Ross House is a country residence just above Clew Bay, and there have been many reports of ghostly activity here. The spirit of a former maidservant has been sighted in the bedroom and on the stairs. Ghostly footsteps have been heard going up and down a staircase that is no longer there. Strange figures have been seen sitting before the fire in the drawing room, and at the window of the same room, a man once reported seeing a "terrible face."

Rahona Lodge, at Carrigaholt, County Clare, was the summer home of the Keane family. In 1917, Charlotte Keane wrote of the ghostly apparition in the "little dark room facing west." The house certainly did have a rather creepy atmosphere, as many locals would never venture near it at night.

A Phantom Train has been reported at a railway station, on the now closed-down line from Clones to Armagh. On a warm summer evening in 1924, two men were waiting for a train. It was quiet in the station, and there was nobody else there waiting but themselves. As they sat there on a platform bench, they suddenly heard the sound of voices coming from inside the waiting room. The voices were hushed, and accompanied by strange moans and groans. These weird sounds grew louder and louder, until finally one of the men got up and pressed his face against the waiting room window, to see what on earth was going on in there. He was shocked to see that the narrow room, containing just two benches and a long table, had nobody in there at all. Then, when he resumed his seat, the man heard the sound of an approaching train. Raising themselves to their feet, they looked down the line. The noise reached a peak, and they involuntarily jumped back as they heard a terrifying scream, right when the engine seemed to rush past them with a loud whistle. However, despite the sound, no train appeared. The sound faded away, the tracks still as empty as before. The two men sank back down on the bench, looking at each other in utter shock and disbelief.

When the signalman came out of his office a few moments later, he told them that he himself had heard nothing, but then related to them the story of a man who had jumped in front of a train at the station a year before. When the man was brought, seriously injured, into the waiting room, nothing could be done to save his life, he sadly died there on the long table.

Charleville Castle is regarded as the finest Gothic Revival building in Ireland. Charleville castle is bordering the town of Tullamore, near the Shannon River. The castle is situated in Ireland's most ancient primordial oak woods, once the haunting grounds of Ireland's druids.

The word 'druid' in Gaelic means, "knower of the oak". The castle is said to be haunted by the ghost of a young girl who fell down some stairs to her death in the early 1800s. The girl still roams around the castle, and can be heard in rooms above moving furniture around, laughing and talking. The castle has been the subject of many paranormal investigation groups from around the world.

The Shelbourne Hotel, situated in Dublin, has its own resident ghost. Whilst staying at the hotel in August 1965, Hans Holzer, the American ghost hunter, was in Dublin conducting an investigation of hauntings in and around the city, and was very surprised to come across this ghost in the hotel. Sybil Lee, the British medium, who, together with Holzer's wife, was accompanying him on this investigation of Dublin's ghosts, experienced the ghost in her small top-floor room. Whilst lying awake in bed just after two o'clock in the morning, she heard a noise that sounded like a child crying. When she called out, "What is the matter?" she heard a small voice answer, "I'm frightened." Then, when Miss Leek invited her to come into her room, she felt a small figure climb onto her bed, and a light woolly material brush against her cheek and her right arm. When she awoke in the morning, her arm felt numb, like a weight had been pressing on it. The next evening, Miss Leek spoke to the ghost, that of a girl aged seven. The ghost said her name was Mary Masters.

The following night, Miss Leek went into a trance and held a conversation with Mary. However, Miss Leek could recall nothing of the conversation when she came to again. Hans Holzer noted that the child seemed to be ill, perhaps from a cold or bad throat, and was asking for a big sister named Sophie. Holzer then came to the conclusion that the ghost was that of a child who had died in one of the group of houses that the Shelbourne Hotel had been constructed from. The child had died around 1846, and this was the date that Sybil Leek had found herself writing down the day before, though she didn't know why.

4. Haunted Chester

Chester is one of Britain's most ancient cities, and is particularly noted for its many historical buildings and attractions, especially in regard to the Romans. Not surprisingly, with all this history, Chester has earned a reputation for being the UK's most haunted city.

Over the years, there have been many reports of all kinds of ghostly sightings and other paranormal phenomena. With its narrow streets and alleyways, not to mention its fascinating crypts and cellars - many of which are situated beneath popular shops, pubs and restaurants - Chester can certainly offer a compelling record of well-documented ghosts, hauntings, apparitions, spooks and poltergeists from almost every century across two thousand years.

Below are just some of the places in Chester that are said to harbour various ghosts and poltergeists:

1. Thornton's Chocolate Shop, Eastgate Street - Three ghosts are said to haunt this shop: a poltergeist known as "Sarah," who was jilted on her wedding day, and is the best-known spirit in Chester. She is said to move objects and shove people when they are on the stairs; the ghost of a large jovial-looking man dressed in an apron, who has been seen in various parts of the building; and finally, the third paranormal entity is described as an "insubstantial, almost invisible, male spirit."

2. W.H. Samuel's, Foregate Street - This jeweller's store is

reputed to be haunted by a ghost called "George." Staff working there have experienced many strange things, which they attribute to this entity known as George.

3. Watergates Crypt, Watergate Street - The ghost of a long dead seaman is said to roam around this wine bar.

4. Watergate Row - The ghost of a faceless cowled monk has been seen here by a mother and daughter living in an old house there.

5. Ye Olde King's Head, Lower Bridge Street - A spectral child is said to haunt this old pub, in particular bedroom no. 6

6. Bookland, Bridge Street - This popular bookstore is said to be haunted by the ghost of a Victorian apprentice boy, who fell on stone steps at the back of the medieval crypt. The boy's spirit has also been experienced upstairs in the tea room.

7. Boot Inn, Eastgate Row North - This was once Chester's most notorious brothel. It is claimed by staff and customers that ghostly female moans and laughter occasionally resonate through the pub.

8. The Bingo Hall, Brook Street - An entity known as "Old George" is said to walk this building. Inexplicable thumps and crashes have been heard up in the attic, and a shape in a tweed jacket has been seen on the balcony, but vanishes when approached by anybody.

9. The Pied Bull, Northgate Street - Said to be one of the most haunted pubs in Britain, The Pied Bull was the subject of an investigation by the TV show Whines and Spirits, which is presented by Most Haunted's Karl Beattie and Stuart Torevell. Ghosts are said to haunt the 12 rooms, and the pub's cellar is said to be spookiest place, with staff refusing to even venture down there!

10. 13 Watergate Street - A typical example of a poltergeist haunting. Brushes, cards, kettles and glass vases all move by themselves, phenomena that has been experienced by various customers.

5. St. George's Hall, Liverpool

St George's Hall in Liverpool first opened its doors to the public in 1854, over 10 years after it was first commissioned. The architect responsible for the main design of the hall was a gentleman called Harvey Lonsdale Elmes.

The Hall was constructed to provide a suitable venue for the triennial music festivals. On top of this, the courts were added, as Elmes had been commissioned to design both buildings, and due to funding 'issues' they were combined.

Over the years, there have been many reports of paranormal occurrences at the hall. The condemned cells, the courtrooms, the lower floors and the air ducts, which were used by the hall's workers, have all been mentioned as areas where supernatural activity has happened. Many high profile cases have been heard in the courts over the years, and it is said that the old cells still feel the ghostly presences of all those convicted souls that were condemned to death.

Some guests of the building, while standing on the steps in the great hall, have felt cold hands touching them, and then felt themselves being pushed forward by some unknown entity. In the concert room, a man has been sighted sitting with his head in his hands. When asked by staff if he needs assistance, he just disappears into thin air. Other people have reported experiencing intense feelings of coldness whilst walking in various areas of the hall.

Down below in the basement, strange voices have been

heard, and a presence of a tall gentleman shouting has been seen - supervising the workers, perhaps.

The hall was the subject of a big charity ghost hunt conducted by www.mosthaunted-ghosttours.com in March 2008.

St George's Hall was reopened on April 23rd 2007 by HRH The Prince of Wales, after the completion of a £23m restoration. The Hall has been carefully restored to its original glory and a new Heritage Centre has been created to provide visitors with a dynamic and exciting introduction to St George's Hall and its place in Liverpool's history.

6. The South Shields Poltergeist

In the summer of 2006, Darren W. Ritson was asked to investigate a "haunting" in an unassuming, ordinary terraced house in the town of South Shields, Tyne & Wear. Darren asked another veteran researcher, Michael J. Hallowell, to accompany him.

During the subsequent months the authors made literally dozens of visits to the house in question, and witnessed first-hand the malevolent, sadistic power of the poltergeist. It was an experience they would never forget.

Initially, the entity just tried to scare the family by moving various objects around the house and making mysterious banging noises - the kind of behaviour that has always been attributable to poltergeist activity. However, as the weeks went on, the entity's activity took on a more threatening and evil aspect. The following examples are just a few of the tactics employed by the South Shield's Poltergeist to intimidate both the family and the paranormal investigators:

1. Death threats sent to the mobile phone of one of the members of the experiments.

2. A toilet cistern filled with blood, which then mysteriously vanished.

3. Knives thrown at both the investigators and the experiments.

4. Appearing as a malevolent, silhouette-type entity in front of both the experiments and the investigators.

5. Slashing the body of one of the experiments with dozens of cuts during filming.

6. Talking to investigators and TV reporters through a number of children's toys.

Eventually, thanks to the help of several experts from a number of different professional, forensic, academic and investigative backgrounds, the authors were able to terminate the reign of terror that the South Shields Poltergeist had wreaked - a reign of terror that had lasted for almost a whole year.

7. The Enfield Poltergeist

In 1977, a family who lived in a rented council house in Enfield, UK, began a terrifying ordeal when a Poltergeist took over their lives. The family consisted of divorcee Margaret (Peggy) Hodgson and her four children: Margaret aged 12, Janet 11, Johnny 10 and Billy 7.

Phenomena started when the two girls were in bed and a chest of drawers started shuffling forwards. Their Mother went upstairs to see what the commotion was. The girls were told to get back into bed and stop messing about. With that, the chest of drawers suddenly lurched forwards. The Mother pushed it back in place only for the chest to immediately move forwards again! The family were kept awake all night long with strange noises and knockings. The following morning, exhausted, the family went into the neighbour's house and described the night's events. Vic Nottingham the neighbour went into the house to see if he could fathom what was going on. He too heard the noises, and says that the knocking followed him from room to room. This was the beginning of a yearlong period in which during the early stages, the family experienced more knocking on the walls, Lego bricks and marbles being thrown around aggressively, and more movement of furniture. It was later to take an even more terrifying turn, when a cast iron fireplace would be torn from the wall, fires would ignite and extinguish themselves spontaneously, and Janet would be thrown out of bed, and made to levitate. One of these incidents were witnessed by two passers by, who stopped in amazement to watch Janet levitating horizontally in her bedroom window, whilst toys were swirling around in the air behind her!

They were frightened out of their wits and the Mother was at such a loss of what to do that she called the police. When they arrived on the scene they witnessed a chair lift up in the air, which as it came to rest shot 4ft forward across the floor! The police even wrote a statement to this effect. The Newspapers were called and a senior reporter for the Daily Mirror went to interview the family. She also witnessed strange events. It was then suggested that paranormal investigators should be brought in. And so began an intensive study that was to last for many months with paranormal researchers, Maurice Grosse and Guy Lyon Playfair.

Maurice Grosse stated that the terror within the family was completely apparent. Desperate to help them, he would visit the family on an almost daily basis in order to offer support and to investigate the phenomena. During the latter months of this haunting, the phenomena took an unexpected twist when one day the family were in the living room and suddenly a dog started barking ... they didn't have a dog! Maurice decided that if the entity was able to produce a bark, perhaps it could be coaxed into speaking. He began asking questions and to his amazement the entity answered! The voice was strange, deep and guttural, and very much sounded like that of an old man. But the voice came from Janet! Examination showed that to produce such a sound, the voice would have to come from the false vocal cords situated deep in the throat. However, to speak in this way is painful and damaging, and to speak in this way for any length of time is said to be medically impossible.

The voice was recorded on many occasions, and the girl who was seemingly possessed was made to take a sip of water and have her mouth taped up. After the voice was heard and recorded, she would be un-taped and would spit out the water. Interestingly, the voice claimed to be that of a man called Bill who said that he was the previous occupier of the house, and stated that he had died of a brain haemorrhage in an armchair in the living room. This was confirmed to be true, and when the tape was played to the man's son, the son was adamant that the voice was that of his Father.

There was a brief period where the two girls were thought to be hoaxing the phenomena. Indeed, they did admit to playing some tricks on Maurice. They state that they used to get fed up with being constantly tested like guinea pigs, and wanted to see if he could catch them out, which he did every time! There is an extremely interesting film, titled 'Interview With A Poltergeist', which reconstructs these events. And many of the witnesses - including Maurice Grosse, the Daily Mirror reporter, the Police and the two daughters - are interviewed. It's interesting to note the girls' accounts from their perspectives as adults. They are clearly still affected by what they went through. Their testaments leave very little doubt that their experiences were genuine.

8. The Whaley House

The Whaley House, situated in San Diego and replete with such a colourful history, is said to be the number one most haunted house in the United States. The spirits of the Whaley House have been reported on numerous paranormal television programs, and have been documented in countless publications and books since the house first opened as a museum in 1960.

The earliest reported ghost at the Whaley House is an entity called "Yankee Jim." James (aka Santiago) Robinson was convicted of attempted grand larceny in San Diego in 1852, and hanged on a gallows off the back of a wagon on the site where the house now stands. Although Thomas Whaley had watched the execution, he did not let it dissuade him from buying the property a few years later and building a family home there. According to the San Diego Union, "soon after the couple and their children moved in, heavy footsteps were heard moving about the house. Whaley described them as sounding as though they were made by the boots of a large man. He eventually concluded that these unexplained footfalls were made by Yankee Jim Robinson." Another source states that Lillian Whaley, the Whaley's' youngest daughter who lived in the house until 1953, had been convinced the ghost of "Yankee Jim" haunted the Old House.

Many visitors to the house have reported encountering

Thomas Whaley himself. The late June Reading, former curator of the museum, said, "We had a little girl, perhaps 5 or 6 years old, who waved to a man she said was standing in the parlour. We couldn't see him. But often children's sensitivity is greater than an adult's."

However, many adults have reported seeing the apparition of Mr. Whaley, usually on the upper landing. The spectre of Anna Whaley has also been reported, usually in the downstairs rooms or in the garden. In 1964, Mrs. Whaley's floating spirit even appeared to television personality Regis Philbin.

Other visitors have described experiencing the presence of a woman in the courtroom. "I see a small figure of a woman," one visitor said, "who has a swarthy complexion. She is wearing a long full skirt, reaching to the floor. She has a cap on her head, dark hair and eyes and she is wearing gold hoops in her pierced ears."

None of the Whaleys match this description, but the house was rented out to many tenants over the years, so maybe the mysterious woman in the courtroom was one of these.

Another presence reported is that of a young girl, who is usually seen in the dining room. Psychic Sybil Leek encountered this spirit during a visit in the 1960s. "It was a long-haired girl," Sybil said. "She was very quick, in a longish dress. She went to the table in this room and I went to the chair." This is said to be the ghost of a playmate of the Whaley children, who accidentally broke her neck on a low-hanging clothesline in the backyard, and whose name was either Annabel or Carrie Washburn. There are no historic records of any child dying this way at the Whaley House; nor is there record of any family named Washburn residing in San Diego at the time. Apparently this legend was started by a former employee of the Whaley House, possibly to add to the house's mystique.

Even animal ghosts have been seen. A parapsychologist reported he saw a spotted dog that ran down the hall with his ears flapping and into the dining room. The dog, he claimed, was an apparition. When they lived in the house, the Whaley's owned a terrier named Dolly Varden.

Every day, visitors come from all around the world to tour the historic museum. It contains so much history within its walls that even the non-believer will enjoy the tour. For believers and sceptics alike, the house draws them back time and again, in search of those elusive ghosts.

9. Sexual Ghosts

Over the centuries, there have been many reported cases - especially in Medieval legend - of sexual hauntings involving two specific types of entities: the Incubus (male demon) and the Succubus (female demon).

The Incubus and Succubus usually manifest themselves during the nocturnal hours, preying on the victim when they are sleeping, although there have been some cases where females have actually been sexually assaulted whilst fully awake. One such experience was covered in the book and subsequent movie, The Entity.

Any female who undergoes an incubus sexual assault will not awaken, although she may experience it in a dream. If she becomes pregnant, the child will grow inside her as any normal child, except that it will possess supernatural powers. Usually the child grows into a person of evil character or a powerful wizard.

According to legend, it is said that the magician Merlin was the result of physical contact between an incubus and a nun.

A succubus is the female version, and she seduces men. According to one legend, the incubus and the succubus were fallen angels. The word incubus is Latin for "nightmare". Succubus - In medieval European folklore, a female demon (or evil spirit) who visits men in their sleep to lie with them in ghostly sexual intercourse.

The man who falls victim to a succubus will not awaken, although may experience it whilst in the dream state. The biblical Lilith, the first wife to Adam before Eve, is said to also have been the very first succubus on earth. There is a version of the Lilith myth in EVERY religion in the world. Many of these creatures have different names, such as Marilith or Lilitu, but all of them have one common theme: a demon woman, often with wings, who seduces - and sometimes murders - men.

A succubus.

Just as is the case with the succubus, there are also many legends about incubi (singular: incubus), but these are not be confused with succubi (which is the plural of succubus). The incubi are said to be fallen angels in Judeo-Christianity who fell to earth because they had sex with mortal women. Since then incubi have stalked the earth, seducing women in their dreams and impregnating them. The children of incubi are said to grow up to become rapists.

An evil person who raped and murdered in real life may pass on, but may not move on to Heaven or Hell. Instead, they remain on the earth plane as a spiritual being with the same personality as they had in life. They are therefore free to indulge in sexual intercourse with whomever they chose, so it's not surprising that a spirit of such a nature may be called an Incubus or a Succubus. Many of these themes have been touched upon in books or a number of fantasy online games or even in television.

There are many variations of this sexual demonic legend all over the world. For instance, in Zanzibar, an entity known as the "Popo Bawa" generally preys on men as they sleep in their beds. In the Chilo, Province of Chile, a pathetic little dwarf, known as El Trauco, woos young naive women and then seduces them. In Hungary, a Liderc is a demonic sexual predator that operates under the cover of darkness, and will appear as little more than a wispy apparition or a fiery light.

Any one of these two succubus's can be blamed for unexpected or unwanted pregnancies, especially in unmarried women, though you could argue that it might just be a convenient fabrication to avoid vicious gossip!

Some confuse the incubus with the legendary "Old Hag" syndrome, but it is not. The Old Hag episode is usually confined to a feeling of intense pressure on the chest and, as such, not an actual ghostly sexual encounter. Another difference that separates the incubus/succubus experience from the Old Hag is that the former is not always unpleasant while the Old Hag is mostly accompanied by a feeling of death, suffocation and the horrific feeling of fighting for your life.

Because the incubus and succubus are generally experienced during the sleep state or in between it, most experts feel that it is an imaginary experience and not a real one. However, telling this to the person who has just had this eerily erotic experience, they may find that hard to believe, as to them it feels as real as actual sexual intercourse itself.

Nobody can really say for sure if these events are real or imagined, but until you've experienced an actual sexual assault by an incubus or succubus yourself, it's quite hard to form a solid opinion one way or the other.

10. The Amityville Horror

The Amityville Horror is one of the most documented and well-known cases of a haunted house in the history of paranormal research.

The story - which was alleged to have happened to the Lutz family when they moved into a large Dutch colonial house at 112 Ocean Avenue in Amityville - has been the subject of a series of best-selling books and a string of movies.

When George and Kathy Lutz, along with Kathy's three children, first moved into their new house in Amityville on December 18th, 1975, they thought they had found their dream home. It's near the school suiting the kids well and the neighbours are friendly with Kathy even envisioning herself enjoying friendly casino poker games with them. That is, of course, until that dream became a living nightmare, as they started experiencing the strange paranormal occurrences which eventually drove them out of the house.

Prior to the Lutzes' occupation of the Amityville house, the residence had been the scene of a horrific murder spree. On November 13th, 1974, 23-year-old Ronald DeFeo shot dead his father, mother and four younger siblings. However, not being superstitious, the Lutz's still bought the house.

By January 14th, 1976, when the Lutz's fled the house forever, they claimed to have been terrorised for 28 days by an unspeakably evil entity. Their horrific experiences included ghostly apparitions of hooded figures, swarms of flies in the sewing room and the children's playroom, breaking window panes, spine-chilling cold alternating with suffocating heat, personality changes, nightly parades by spirit marching bands, levitations, green slime oozing down the stairs, foul odours, nausea, inexplicable scratches on Kathleen's body, objects mysteriously moving, constant disconnection of the telephone service, and even communications between the youngest, Melissa, and a devilish spirit pig by the name of "Jodie".

But more shockingly, even the Devil himself is said to have actually appeared in the house.

Even visitors to the house were affected by the strange atmosphere permeating through the place. Kathy's brother, Jimmy, and his new bride mysteriously lost $1,500 in cash. And Father Mancuso, the local priest who gave the house his blessing, suffered a horrible bout of sickness that left him physically drained. As a result, he eventually transferred to a distant parish. He is said to have heard a voice from an unseen entity ordering him to "get out" when he sprinkled the house with holy water.

In 1977, The Amityville Horror by Jay Anson was published. The book became an instant bestseller, and led to a top-grossing movie in 1979, starring James Brolin and Margot Kidder. More Amityville Horror books followed, written by different authors, which gave alleged accounts of the demonic entity still following the Lutzes', even after they had fled the Amityville house.

As is often the norm with cases like this, many sceptics claimed that the Amityville haunting was just a big hoax, and they were quick to point out various discrepancies in

Anson's book. Even Jerry Solfvin, of the Psychical Research Foundation, who was contacted by George Lutz in early January 1976 about paranormal activity at the house, found the whole case rather questionable. All the evidence was subjective. Also, Father Mancuso was regarded as being a poor witness, as he had visited the house only the once. It took Anson three or four months to write his book, and he worked mostly from tapes of telephone interviews. Apparently, he made only a superficial effort to verify the Lutzes' account.

The most significant aspect of the case is the interview that Ronald DeFeo's lawyer, William Weber, gave a local radio station in 1979. He claimed that the Lutzes' concocted the whole Amityville Horror saga around their kitchen table whilst drinking bottles of wine. He also said that after approaching them with the idea, the Lutzes' broke away from him, and so he decided to sue for his share of the book and movie royalties. But the Lutzes' counter sued, arguing that their experiences were genuine. Mrs Lutz's story was later analysed on a Psychological Stress Evaluation. The results of the test confirmed her claims.

Although it's possible that the hauntings at the Amityville residence may have actually happened, many observers have deemed the Lutzes' story to be over-dramatic when compared to other cases of paranormal activity.

11. Harry Price

Harry Price is probably the most famous name in the world of ghost hunting. The investigation he is most noted for is that of the haunting at Borley Rectory, dubbed "The most haunted house in England." In the 1930's and 1940's, Price contributed many articles on ghosts and the paranormal to various newspapers and magazines.

Contrary to what many people think, Price certainly wasn't a psychic researcher in the modern sense, but an investigative journalist who specialised in debunking fraudulent mediums and similar charlatans. He claimed to be a scientist, but actually had no training in the scientific field. After gathering some hunting supplies and being in the field and feeling out your equipment you will steadily become a much better hunter.

Harry Price was born on the 17th January 1881 in Red Lion Square, London. He was educated in London at Waller Road School and Haberdashers' Aske's Hatcham College, the Haberdashers' Aske's Hatcham Boys School. At the age of 15, Price founded the Carlton Dramatic Society and wrote small plays, including a drama about his early experience with a poltergeist. which he said took place at a haunted manor house in Shropshire.

Price was also a keen coin collector, and wrote several articles for The Askean, the magazine for Haberdashers' School. In his autobiography, Search for Truth, written between 1941 and 1942, Price claimed he was involved with archaeological excavations in Greenwich Park, London but in earlier writings on Greenwich denied he had a hand in the excavation. From May 1908, Price continued his interest in archaeology at Pulborough, Sussex where he had moved to before marrying Constance Mary Knight that August. As well as working for paper merchants Edward Saunders & Sons as a salesman, he wrote for two local Sussex newspapers about his remarkable propensity for discovering 'clean' antiquities.

In his autobiography, Search for Truth, Price said the "Great Sequah" in Shrewsbury was "entirely responsible for shaping much of my life's work", and led to him acquiring the first volume of what would become the Harry Price Library. Price later became an expert amateur conjurer, joined the Magic Circle in 1922 and maintained a lifelong interest in stage magic and conjuring. His expertise in sleight-of-hand and magic tricks stood him in good stead for what would become his all consuming passion, the investigation of paranormal phenomena.

Price's first major success in psychical research came in 1922 when he exposed the 'spirit' photographer William Hope. The following year, Price made a formal offer to the University of London to equip and endow a Department of Psychical Research, and to loan the equipment of the National Laboratory and its library. The University of London Board of Studies in Psychology responded positively to this proposal and, in 1934, the University of London Council for Psychical Investigation was formed with Price as Honorary Secretary and Editor. In the meanwhile, in 1927, Price joined the Ghost Club, of which he remained a member until it (temporarily) closed in 1936.

Alan Toner

In 1934, the National Laboratory of Psychical Research took on its most illustrious case. £50 was paid to the medium Helen Duncan so that she could be examined under scientific conditions. A sample of Helen Duncan's ectoplasm had been previously examined by the Laboratory and found to be largely made of egg white. Price found that Duncan's spirit manifestations were cheesecloth that had been swallowed and regurgitated by Duncan. Price later wrote up the case in Leaves from a Psychic's Case Book in a chapter called "The Cheese-cloth Worshippers". During Duncan's famous trial in 1944, Price gave his results as evidence for the prosecution.

Price's psychical research continued with investigations into Karachi's Indian rope trick and the fire-walking abilities of Kuda Bux in 1935. He was also involved in the formation of the National Film Library, becoming its first chairman, and was a founding member of the Shakespeare Film Society. In 1936, Price made the first ever "live" broadcast from a supposedly haunted manor house in Meopham, Kent (see picture on the right) for the BBC and published The Confessions of a Ghost-Hunter and The Haunting of Cashen's Gap. This year also saw the transfer of Price's library on permanent loan to the University of London, followed shortly by the laboratory and investigative equipment. In 1937, he conducted further televised experiments into fire walking with Ahmed Hussain at Carshalton and Alexandra Palace, and also rented Borley Rectory for one year. The following year, Price re-established the Ghost Club, with himself as chairman, modernizing it and changing it from a spiritualist association to a group of open-minded sceptics that met to discuss paranormal topics. He was also the first to admit women to the club.

In the same year, Price conducted experiments with Rahman Bey, who was 'buried alive' in Carshalton, and drafted a Bill for the regulation of psychic practitioners. In 1939, he organized a national telepathic test in the periodical John O'London's Weekly. During the 1940s, Price concentrated on writing and published three works: The Most Haunted House in England, Poltergeist Over England and The End of Borley Rectory.

In December 2008, an original unpublished 26-page manuscript by British writer Marjorie Bowen (1885-1952) attacking Price's investigation of the Borley Rectory case, was featured on an eBay auction.

Even though Price was a dedicated and meticulous paranormal investigator, and cultivated a leading reputation in the world of ghost hunting, he did generate much controversy in regard to just how genuine his investigations were, and that controversy continues even to this day. For instance, many have accused him of faking ghostly activity, especially in regard to his most famous investigation at Borley Rectory. Also, a photograph of Price and a Spirit taken by William Hope was later proven to be a fake.

Some people have often asked the question: Does serious scientific research and a publicity-hungry ghost hunter go together? There have been arguments that Price had compromised his research into the paranormal with his penchant for highlight and spectacle. Even so he did take psychical research out of the cold laboratory and dusty parlour séance room and gave it to an eager public. Price often displayed contrasting tendencies: a committed paranormal investigator and father of British ghost hunting, yet also a man who knew the value of a good ghost story when he saw one. If he has a legacy it is indeed programmes such as Most Haunted, Ghost Hunters and The World's Most Scariest Places. On the surface, serious paranormal research, but underneath, edge-of-seat, sheer spooky entertainment.

12. Ghosts of The Titanic

We all know the most tragic maritime story of all time: the sinking of the Titanic by an iceberg in the North Atlantic Ocean on April 14th, 1912. However, what many of us may not know is that, over the years, there have been many strange stories centred around the ill-fated ship. The most reported story has been that involving the Titanic Exhibit, which is housed in the Georgia Museum, and which travels from one major city to the next, giving people the opportunity to view many of the once-lost artefacts from the monumental wreckage. The exhibit is reported to be haunted.

Ghostly apparitions, disembodied voices and strange footsteps have been reported at many locations on the Titanic exhibit tour, and volunteers who work at the exhibit claim to have experienced an eerie presence around them while walking through the artefacts. These reports cannot be so easily dismissed, for it is quite often the case that spirits do attach themselves to certain artefacts, and haunt whatever location houses them This could well be the case with the Titanic, for obviously, unlike haunted properties, it is no longer actually standing, but has left behind many artefacts which could quite easily have been left with supernatural potential.

It is not known for sure just how many ghosts haunt the Titanic Exhibition. More than 1,500 people went down with the ship on that fateful evening of April 14th, 1912, so it could be any one or any number of those deceased souls.

A spokeswoman for the aquarium, Meghann Gibbons, has expressed her belief, and the belief of many volunteers working on the exhibit, that is in fact haunted. One visitor to the Titanic Exhibit, with her daughter and 4-year-old grandson, firmly agree. According to her story, while viewing the 1st class quarters, she and her daughter thought little of the young boy's repeated questioning, "Who is that lady?" and "What is she doing?" They assured him that there was only a dress laid out over the love seat, as if waiting to be adorned. It wasn't until they heard later that the TAPS ghost hunting team was investigating paranormal activity in the Titanic Exhibit that they believed the boy had experienced his first ghostly encounter.

Many visitors to the exhibit claimed to have experienced an eerie feeling, as if being watched, or feeling an immense sadness around specific objects or areas of the exhibit. Most assumed it was a general sombre mood evoked by the 1912 disaster, but as more and more reports come in with similar claims, a lot of people are starting to give these reports credence - including the TAPS team of paranormal investigators from Sci-Fi's "Ghost Hunters". The TAPS lead investigators, Jay and Grant, strongly believe that the Titanic Exhibit is haunted. After a lengthy investigation, which aired on the 97th anniversary of the ship's tragic demise, the TAPS team found sufficient evidence of paranormal activity, including an eerie EVP recording. They were seated in a room trying to communicate with the ghost, and asked the spirit if it wanted them to leave. The voice distinctly replied, "Now - please, wait." Unfortunately, Jay and Grant could not follow up on the questions, since they did not hear the voice until later, when the evidence was being analysed.

This year (2012), a group of ghost hunters plan to mark the 100th anniversary of the 'Titanic's' sinking by travelling out to the exact location of the ship's sinking and searching for any residual impressions left behind from the incident. The group - appropriately named D.E.A.D (direct, evidence, after, death) - hope to achieve results mainly from the use of sophisticated EVP recorders. Their spokesperson, William Brower, says they will be recreating the atmosphere of the doomed 'Titanic's' last hours by serving up the same meals and listening to the same type of music heard on that fateful night a century ago. One of the group, Angelica Harris, hopes this will be a fitting tribute to those that died, including her great uncle who was aboard.

The supernatural incidents revolving around the Titanic could be attributable to residual impressions, which are often left behind after an event of extreme trauma, like the emotional trauma experienced by all those people who went down with the Titanic. Will the group pick up sounds of those who died, desperately screaming out for help in the icy waters of the North Atlantic Ocean? Only time will tell.

13. Haunted Shops and Stores

Old houses and ancient, crumbling castles are not the only places where ghosts have been reported. Over the years, there have also been many cases of spirits haunting major department stores, and even corner shops.

As Webmaster of the True Ghost Stories site at http://www.trueghoststories.co.uk, I personally can relate some quite spooky incidents where apparent ghostly activity has been experienced in a shop. A few years ago, my mum worked in a confectioners in Birkenhead. With it being a very old shop, it was said to have a resident ghost. My mum soon found out that the stories were true. One day, when she was serving in the shop, two old ladies came in, and they walked up to the end of the counter to look at the cakes on display. My mum was at the other end at the till. On top of the counter was a large straw tray, which was used to display packets of batches. As the other assistant was taking hot pasties out of the oven, my mum had just finished serving a customer and was putting the money into the till when suddenly, without any visible cause whatsoever, the tray got lifted up off the counter and thrown at her shoulder. The tray then crashed to the floor and all the packets of batches fell onto the floor. The two old ladies that were in the shop looked on in utter shock and disbelief, and declared that it wasn't them as they were standing at the other end of the shop. Furthermore, my mum's work colleague said that she too had witnessed what had happened, and shook her head in disbelief also. My mum had no explanation for this strange incident, but it was just one of many more incidents she experienced in the shop, including serviettes flying around in the air after they had all been neatly put in the window, crisp packets getting dropped on the floor on their own, and different items mysteriously going missing.

One of the creepiest incidents in this cake shop happened to the manageress, who told the story to my mum. She used to go to the shop early in the morning to prepare everything for the opening at nine o'clock. As she was putting the trays of cakes into the racks, ready to put on small trays later, she had a feeling she was being watched. She looked over her shoulder . . . and there, standing in the doorway of the shop, was a tall, handsome, young man, dressed in a boiler suit, and he just stood there, staring at her silently. Her immediate thought was that it was a customer, so she told him to hang on a minute while she finished putting the cakes into the racks. When she turned back around a few seconds later, the man had vanished. She then went cold as she realised something: how could this man possibly have entered the shop, when the door was locked? Thinking that he might have gained access through the back entry, she went out there to check, but discovered that the padlocks were all still on the door. Again, she could not explain this incident, and therefore decided that it must have been a spirit.

The Toys 'R' Us store in Sunnyvale, California, has a long history of being haunted by a ghost called "Johnny Johnston," said to be a disappointed lover who bled to death after a farm accident, and store workers have reported seeing strange things happening, such as rag dolls and toy trucks leaping off shelves, balls bouncing down the aisles, children's books falling out of racks, and baby swings moving on their own. The shop's staff have tried to find a logical explanation for all these incidents, but just can't. The store has been featured on the TV show That's Incredible and other programmes. A Hollywood scriptwriter for the movie Toys spent two nights there doing research. Psychic Sylvia Browne held a séance in the store in 1978 and has since been back a few times.

An Asda store in Pwllheli is said to be haunted by the ghost of a long-haired man in a trench coat. The apparition has often been seen by staff in various parts of the store.

The Marks & Spencer store in Church Street, Liverpool, is said to be haunted by the ghost of a woman from the 1930's called "Lulu". This spirit often appears on the top floors of the store, and she carries a soda siphon, which she has occasionally squirted at people! The other ghost said to haunt the store is that of a man called Billy McMullen, a 22-year-old junior porter who suffered a tragic violent death at the Compton Hotel (the building that once occupied the site) in March 1877, after fooling around in the hotel's lift.

Another Liverpool retail site, which has garnered something of a reputation for ghostly activity, is the old Owen Owen building, which now houses Tesco Metro. Back in the 1970's, an Owen Owen female sales assistant saw a tall distinguished-looking gentleman dressed in Victorian clothing as she worked in an upstairs room. In another incident, a young man serving in one of the departments saw and felt a hand on his shoulder. As he turned around, he was shocked to see that the hand had no arm or body attached. A customer also witnessed this eerie apparition. When a medium visited the Owen Owen store soon after it closed, she determined that there were at least seven spirits haunting the building, all from different eras. A security guard also had a strange experience whilst working there during a refurbishment prior to occupation by another firm. He soon discovered the place was haunted when he did his rounds. On one occasion the security officer found a strange pair of scissors lying on the floor, and when he examined them, they looked blackened and quite old. He put them in his rucksack, but the next morning, when he reached home, the scissors had mysteriously vanished. The guard and some of his workmates used the Ouija board at the haunted building one night, and a word that the men didn't understand came through: GORSUCH. The guards laughed at the word. They didn't know that in the 19th century, a barber named John Gorsuch had his premises on Parker Street. This would probably explain the scissors that had appeared in the building.

In Hereford, there have been quite a few retail stores where ghostly activity has been witnessed. For instance, at the Sainsbury's store - a very modern building which, as such, would be the last place you would expect to be haunted - the ghost of an old lady has been seen many times by staff. She does a lot of waving and smiling at people. One morning, at 4am, a member of staff came in to open the store, and he saw the old lady as he was unlocking the fire exits. The old lady was standing there waving at him, her appearance so clear that the man waved back thinking it was a customer - only to suddenly realize that it was 4 am in the morning and no one was in there shopping! When the man approached the lady to ask her to leave the store, she simply disappeared into thin air. A similar story was when the manager once saw the old lady in the periphery of her vision. The manager asked her to go and do something, under the misconception that it was just a member of staff. After this, a member of staff popped her head around the corner and asked the manager who was she speaking to. The manager looked to where she saw the old lady, only to find that she had vanished. The staff who work in Sainsbury's say that there is a presence and a feeling of being watched. However, the ghost does seem to be a nice, friendly spirit. Sainsbury's supermarket was built on the old Barton Railway Station. In 1934, a G. V Bennett was in charge. The station was used for goods as well.

The Boots store, situated on Hereford's High Street, has some ghost stories that are very creepy. One evening, when the shop was empty, somebody saw a dark figure in the basement. On another occasion, there were two members of staff in the building, and they witnessed the fire drill being set off by unseen hands. The store was checked immediately, but no one else was present in the building at the time of the incident. If ghostly activity is really behind these incidents, then it is not surprising as the building has been around for many years and has had different uses. In 1879 this building was two different shops: a Thomas Frederick Hawkins was a Printer and Stationer, and a Mrs. Harriet Reeves was a Watchmaker. The place was also occupied by Marks and Spencer in 1934.

The Primark store, situated on Hereford's busy Widemarsh Street, has crowds of customers shopping there daily. But for a building that is so modern, it really is surprising to find a ghost story and so much history here. The building is known to stand on the site of where the Black Swan hotel previously was. A graveyard previously occupied the site before the Black Swan was built. The store itself is very large, and the front of the shop is said to be the oldest part. The old co-op store was previously at this part of the store, Above is the stock room and cash office, and it is in these two rooms that the ghost of a smartly dressed man has been seen wandering around on numerous occasions. The staff has christened him "Freddie," and he has been sighted wearing a blue shirt and trousers. One member of staff who had a first hand account of the ghost was so upset and traumatised by her encounter that she left her job altogether. It is also believed that this ghostly man travels through the shops next to Primark. The Paperway shop, which is one shop down, also has a ghostly man in their shop who occasionally visits, and he is seen wearing the same clothing. The man could be from the old co-op store, as the staff uniform was blue. The dress shop one door away from Primark on the left also has a ghost of a man in the basement so it could be that the same ghost is travelling in between all three of these shops. When the site was the Black Swan hotel, it had a reputation of being one of the City's best pubs and coaches left the inn daily travelling to Liverpool in 1834, the inn had many landlord's over duration, Thomas Jones was victualler in 1822 and in 1909 a Thomas Owen was head of the inn, the Black Swan also had air raid shelters provided in the basement.

Thornton's chocolate shop in Eastgate Street, Chester, is said to be haunted by a ghost called Sarah, who hung herself after being jilted on her wedding day. Sarah wreaks most of her unearthly havoc in the top floor front room and in the cellar. However, her ghost has also manifested in other parts of the shop. Although she is never seen, she has been heard coming down the stairs singing a strange song and holding out her hands, as if lifting up a long dress to facilitate her descent. She once pushed an American tourist down the stairs. She once frightened an electrician who came to read the meter in the cellar. During Valentine's Day 1991, Sarah got upset over the display in the shop and scattered the heart-shaped boxes of chocolates all over the floor. However, the ordinary boxes of chocolates were left undisturbed. An exorcism held in 1965 dispelled Sarah's poltergeist-like antics for a while. However, she has apparently returned, and still creates ghostly disturbances in the shop right to this day.

14. The Fleece Inn

The Fleece Inn, situated in the market town of Elland in Yorkshire, is said to be home to many different kinds of ghosts from many centuries. Built in the early 17th Century, it was originally a farmhouse called The Great House Farm.

The building has a long history of crime, as several murders have been committed there over the centuries, and the ghosts of many of these unfortunate victims and their evil murderers are said to still haunt the Fleece Inn even to this day.

The Fleece Inn incurred a notorious reputation for attracting prostitutes, who would often solicit for clients in the pub, in the hope that the alcohol would stimulate the progress of their business. One of these prostitutes, who was pregnant when she died, is said to have been slaughtered there with an axe. There is also the case of a servant girl who was viciously assaulted and pushed down the stairs to her death. Her ghost is said to haunt the spot where she met her death. The Fleece Inn's most famous ghost is Leathery Coits. This entity is reported to travel at great speed past the building, minus his head and in a coach drawn by headless horses. There is also the tale of a visitor to the Elland market at the start of the 19th Century, who died at the hands of a local man with whom he got into a fight. The bloodstained handprint of the murdered man remained on the stairs for over a hundred years, during which no amount of scrubbing or washing could remove it. It was eventually destroyed when the inn was renovated in the 1970s.

There have been many other strange entities seen moving around the Fleece Inn. However, in addition to the rather sinister spirits, there have also been many benign ghosts. For instance, when the inn was a farmhouse, the spirit of a farmer called Will is reported to sit in a chair near the fireplace. In life, this man would have probably loved coming in, removing his boots and just relaxing there in his chair, after his laborious work all day out in the fields. His presence has been sensed many times. There are also two other former inhabitants whose spirits are said to walk the inn: Alice Pollard and William Wooler. Both were landlords in the 1800s.

There have also been strange olfactory happenings in the inn. The delicious smell of freshly baked bread has been smelt in an area that was once the kitchen. An aroma of lemon has also been sensed, which permeates the air quite suddenly and from an unknown source.

The ghost of a young girl called Jane has been heard running up and down the stairs and through the rooms, giggling constantly as she goes. There have also been many reports of strange voices and running footsteps in the upper rooms of the building. In addition, a weird banging noise has been heard throughout the building.

The Fleece Inn has long been described as having a rather oppressive aura about it, and many people have experienced intense feelings of sadness there, as they want to break down and cry. Others have reported feelings of intoxication, even though they've had no drink. This could be attributable to the fact that the inn has obviously seen more than its fair share of drunkards over the years

15. Interactive Ghosts

Interactive ghosts are so called because they always purposely make their presence known to people. They communicate with the physical world by sending messages, and often the spirit is seen only by the recipient of the message.

The ghost is usually well known to the person - either a relative or a friend - and might predict some imminent news, like a birth or a death. Such a message is relayed by the ghost actually speaking to the recipient, or by some other method such as making some kind of noise.

You might think that all this is solid proof that such ghosts really do exist, but the chance of such dreams or predictions really happening is actually much higher than you might think. For instance, many is the time that somebody has imagined a happy event - like a birth or an engagement - and if that person subsequently dreams of this event, only to be told the next day that you are about to become an uncle or aunt, does that necessarily make you feel that you have some kind of inherent psychic power? It could be attributed to just sheer coincidence. The chances could be quite high of any one person in a large town having a predictive dream on a particular day.

But there is a difference here in regard to interactive ghosts: they always appear to the witness while he or she is fully awake. This begs the question: why does the spirit choose to appear only to one particular person?

If you take the example of deathbed messages - which have been reported many times throughout history - you could say that these are the work of an interactive ghost. In such circumstances, the apparition appears only at the time of trauma, and not some time afterwards.

There have also been many cases, over the years, of out-of-the-body experiences. During such incidents, the person concerned has found their 'spirit' floating up towards the ceiling and looking down on their apparently lifeless body. The hospital files are full of such reports of patients who have "temporarily died." These experiences usually occur when the person is in a traumatic condition, such as being close to death. When the person's spirit returns to their body, they often describe, in stunningly accurate detail, everything that was happening around them - even things taking place in rooms next door.

The phantom hitchhiker is another type of interactive ghost. These entities usually haunt quiet country roads, and are often seen by motorists as they drive along late at night. Resurrection Mary, who is said to haunt the lonely country lanes near Chicago, is the most famous roadside ghost of all. Drivers have reported that when they have stopped the car to avoid hitting the figure, it then mysteriously vanishes. On other occasions, when the motorist has stopped to give the figure a lift, it suddenly disappears completely from out of the car. These spectral hitchhikers are therefore a classic example of interactive ghosts, as they respond to the observer in quite a physical, realistic way.

16. The Ghosts of Charles Dickens

Charles Dickens (1812-1870) is best known for his classic novels like Oliver Twist, David Copperfield and A Tale of Two Cities. But he is also fondly remembered for writing quite a few ghost stories. His most famous ghost story of all, of course, is A Christmas Carol (1843), featuring the tale of miserly old Ebenezer Scrooge, who is chastened towards a more benevolent nature by the visitation of three ghosts on Christmas Eve.

Unlike his more lengthy works, Dickens's ghost stories - often written quite swiftly - tend to be less hyperbolic and hardly meticulously plotted, but more limited in style, and less enriched with dramatic detail. He frequently published his ghost stories in Households Words and All The Year Round.

Dickens always regarded ghost stories as especially suitable for telling around the Christmas period. We all know how hugely successful - and so unforgettable - A Christmas Carol was. His other outstanding ghost story, "The Haunted Man and The Ghost's Bargain" (1848), is a fascinating piece of work. In this tale, a ghost bestows the gift of forgetting all past grievances, and those affected find their memory loss makes them inhuman, without limits to other people and without ability to forgive. Dickens was always keen to encourage other writers to produce stories of the supernatural for the yuletide season.

Dickens's usual type of ghost story - devoid of all humour and any great concentration on moral reasoning - were written for the Christmas extra issues of 1865 and 1866. In "The Trial for Murder", the spirit of a murdered man appears to one of the jurors to ensure that the killer is punished. In "The Signal Man" (which is a popular Dickens tale in the "A Ghost Story for Christmas" TV series, often shown at Christmas time), a railway worker in a desolate station keeps seeing a phantom warning him of fatal accidents which are about to occur on the line.

Dickens had always held a strong fascination for the supernatural, although he did have some scepticism. A few of his stories actually ridiculed the paranormal. For instance, in "The Lawyer and The Ghost", a story that runs through The Pickwick Papers (1836-1837), a ghost is asked why he haunts a place that makes him so depressed when he could go somewhere more comfortable with better weather. And in "The Haunted House" (1859), a man who receives spirit messages is sent misspelt homilies. And in "Well Authenticated Rappings", incredible visitations are traced to hangovers and heartburn. Yet despite this touch of cynicism, Dickens claimed to have seen his dead mother and beloved sister-in-law, Mary, in a night vision that was something much than just a dream. He also wrote about seeing an apparition of his father (who was then still alive) standing by his bed early in the morning. When he reached out to touch his father's shoulder, the apparition vanished.

Dickens published the "Four Ghost Stories" in 1861, and one of them was the story of an artist who paints a dead girl's portrait after seeing her ghost. Dickens then received a letter from a painter who claimed that the incident had actually happened to him. Dickens then published the man's own story in the next issue of his magazine. In letters that Dickens subsequently wrote to his acquaintances, it was quite clear that he believed the painter's story.

In "The Uncommercial Traveller" (1860), Dickens wrote that the spooky stories related to him in childhood by his nurse had had a lasting effect. Certain critics have recognised a direct link between Dickens's later work and the stories told by the nurse. Dickens himself also stated that these tales "acquired an air of authentication that impaired my digestive powers for life."

Despite Dickens's reservations about the actual existence of ghosts, there is no doubt that when it came to telling a real good ghost story - especially those centred around a snowy Christmas atmosphere - he certainly knew how to entertain, and spook, his readers.

17. The Ghosts of Pluckley Village

Pluckley Village, in Kent, is said to be the most haunted village in the UK. Over the years, many kinds of spirits have been seen by both locals and tourists.

The ghost of an old gypsy, wrapped in a shawl and smoking a pipe, has often been spotted standing near a bridge. The shattered remains of an old oak tree, situated nearby, is a noted haunt for the apparition of a murdered highwayman. In life, the highwayman was said to have been killed by a sword, and it was this weapon that impaled him to the tree.

There are many buildings in Pluckley Village which are also reputed to be haunted. For instance, in the Church of Saint Nicholas, the spirit of Lady Dering - who was buried in three lead coffins to prevent her decay - occasionally manifests itself. She has been seen walking through the churchyard at night with the red rose, with which she was buried, unwithered on her breast. In the Dering Chapel, mysterious lights have been seen through its windows, and the disembodied voice of a woman has been heard in the churchyard. The spirit of a long-dead monk is said to haunt a house called Greystones, and the voice of a former owner of another house, Rose Court, has often been heard there as she calls her dogs. Also, the old mill is haunted by the ghost of a miller, who is said to be in constant search of his lost love during the nocturnal hours. In the Dering Arms public house, a spectral woman dressed in Victorian clothing hangs around the bar. In another pub, The Black Horse, a spectral hand moves items across the bar, tidies up, and occasionally hides coats and wallets. A ghostly carriage, pulled by two horses, has often been seen trotting down the main public street of Pluckley. The origin of this carriage is unknown.

But the most terrifying of all the entities said to haunt Pluckley Village has to be that of the so-called "Screaming Ghost". The blood curdling screams of this ghost have been heard in the area around the Brickworks, Pluckley Heath.

18. The Winchester House

The Winchester Mystery House is a well-known mansion in Northern California. Its name comes up quite often whenever there are discussions about the most haunted buildings in America. It is located at 525 South Winchester Blvd. in San Jose, California. It was once was the personal residence of Sarah Winchester, the widow of gun magnate William Wirt Winchester. It was continuously under construction for 38 years and is said to be haunted by various entities. Some psychics have said that there are actually a total of three spirits currently residing in the mansion.

Under Winchester's supervision, its construction proceeded around the clock, without interruption, from 1884 until her death on September 5, 1922, when work immediately ceased. The cost for such constant building has been estimated at about US $5.5 million.

The Queen Anne Style Victorian mansion is famous for its sheer size and utter lack of a proper construction plan. In fact, many rooms in the house lead to dead ends. The miles of twisting hallways are made even more intriguing by secret passageways in the walls. Mrs. Winchester travelled through her house in a roundabout fashion, supposedly to confuse any mischievous ghosts that might be following her. According to popular belief, Winchester believed that the house was haunted by the ghosts of the people who were killed by Winchester rifles, and that only continuous construction would appease them.

The Boston Medium consulted by Mrs. Winchester explained that her family and her fortune were being haunted by the spirits of American Indians, Civil War soldiers, and others killed by Winchester rifles. Supposedly, the untimely deaths of her daughter and husband were caused by these spirits, and it was implied that Mrs. Winchester might be the next victim. However, the medium also claimed that there was an alternative: Mrs. Winchester could move west and appease the spirits by building a great house for them. As long as construction of the house never ceased, Mrs. Winchester could feel secure in the knowledge that her life was not in danger. Building such a house was even supposed to bring her eternal life. On a more practical note, maybe a change of scenery and a constant hobby were just what Mrs. Winchester needed to alleviate her grief.

Whatever her actual motivations, Mrs. Winchester packed her bags and left Connecticut to visit a niece who lived in Menlo Park, California. While there, she discovered the perfect spot for her new home in the Santa Clara Valley. In 1884 she purchased an unfinished farm house just three miles west of San Jose - and over the next thirty-eight years she produced the sprawling complex we know today as the Winchester Mystery House.

The Winchester House is now a popular tourist attraction. It has also been the subject of investigation by a number of TV paranormal shows. The house is owned by Winchester Investments LLC, and it retains unique touches that reflect Mrs Winchester's beliefs and her preoccupation with warding off malevolent spirits. These spirits are said to have directly influenced her as to exactly how the house should be built.

Fright Nights is a specifically ticketed special night time event at the Winchester Mystery House. On select nights in September and October, Winchester Mystery House is transformed into San Jose's most terrifying Halloween experience, filled with haunted walk-through attractions, intense scares, roaming scare actors, and nightmare inducing tales.

Since Mrs. Winchester's death, hundreds of fascinating stories have appeared about this mysterious woman and her sprawling mansion. It seems odd that neither her relatives nor her former employees ever contradicted these stories, despite that fact that some of them lived more than forty years after Mrs. Winchester's death. Did they feel threatened by talking – or did they deem it necessary to protect Mrs. Winchester's privacy, even after her death?

19. Ordsall Hall

Ordsall Hall is a historic house and a former stately home in Ordsall, Salford, Greater Manchester. It dates back over 750 years, although the oldest surviving parts of the present hall were built in the 15th century. The most important period of Ordsall Hall's life was as the family seat of the Radclyffe family, who lived in the house for over 300 years. The hall was the setting for William Harrison Ainsworth's 1842 novel Guy Fawkes, written around the plausible although unsubstantiated local story that the Gunpowder Plot of 1605 was planned in the house.

Like many old buildings, Ordsall Hall has gained a reputation over the years for being haunted. One of its many resident ghosts is a spirit called The White Lady, who is said to appear in the Great Hall or Star Chamber, This entity is said to be the ghost of Margaret Radclyffe, who died of a broken heart in 1599 following the death at sea of her twin, Alexander. The ghost of a little girl has also been seen, standing near the bottom of the stairs. There are webcams overseeing the areas that are said to be the most haunted. An episode of the television programme Most Haunted was filmed in the hall in 2004

Since its sale by the Radclyffes in 1662, the hall has been put to many uses; working men's club, school for clergy, and a radio station amongst them. The house was bought by Salford City Council in 1959, and opened to the public in

1972, as a period house and local history museum. The hall is a Grade I listed building. In 2007 it was named Small Visitor Attraction of the Year by the Northwest Regional Development Agency. The hall was closed to the public between 2009 and 2011 while it was refurbished and reopened in May 2011.

20. The Ancient Ram Inn

The Ancient Ram Inn is a Grade II* listed building, and a former pub located in Wotton-under-Edge, a market town within the Stroud district of Gloucestershire, England. It is believed to be one of the most haunted hotels in the country. This famous inn is owned by and the home to John Humphries. It has been owned by many people since 1145 to present date. Many people lived here either as a tenant or over night guests. This inn was said to have also been owned by the local St. Mary's Church when first built.

The paranormal phenomena reported to have manifested in the Inn include spectral shadows, strange footsteps, inexplicable drops in temperature, mysterious tapping sounds, strange orbs of flight floating around the Inn after dark, furniture being moved around, and people being pushed to the ground by an unseen force. The owner, John Humphries, even claims to have been a victim of an incubus assault. And the Inn is said to have not one ghost but several - including a phantom cavalier, a witch, a man and a monk. There have also been sightings of a mysterious black cat. The fact that the Inn was built on an ancient pagan burial ground may have something to do with all the ghostly activity that has occurred there over the years.

What is particularly scary about the hauntings at the Inn is the fact that most visitors feel the spirits are profoundly malevolent - the atmosphere has often been described as brooding, oppressive, and even 'evil'. One room called the Bishop's Room has the most notorious reputation. One night two men stayed there in the hope of witnessing some ghostly activity - and they had such a terrifying night that they had to summon a vicar to exorcise them.

Over the years, the Inn has been investigated by many paranormal researchers, especially for television shows like Ghost Adventures and Most Haunted. One paranormal expert in particular is Kieron Butler from the UK Paranormal Study. The group, led by Kieron to study in the Ram Inn, consisted of seven people, including photographers and medium/spiritual advisors. The Ghost Club (the oldest paranormal research organization in the world) investigated the inn in 2003, but didn't register anything paranormal. The Danish paranormal research team DPA (Dansk Parapsykologisk Aspekt) has also been there with a TV crew, shooting an episode for a Danish ghost-hunter TV show.

21. Pengersick Castle

Pengersick Castle is a fortified Tudor manor house hidden away in Praa Sands, Cornwall. The oldest part still standing dates from 1500, but there has been a building on this site for at least 900 years. It is reportedly the most haunted castle in Britain.

Many people claim to have encountered some of the 20 odd ghosts said to be here. Many have seen or photographed strange orbs of light. Electrical malfunctions are commonplace. There are massive temperature drops. The ghosts said to be haunting Pengersick Castle include a 14th-century-monk, a 13-year-old girl who danced to her death off the battlements, a 4 year old boy who tugs at ladies dresses, the re-enactment of a medieval murder, a woman seen walking through a wall and pacing the room, a woman stabbed to death in the castle, a man stabbed and strangled in 1546 in front of a fireplace, several previous owner.

The ghost club have carried out many late night vigils at the castle, and there's been a televised display of automatic writing, which resulted in a scribbled picture of a female face.

Pengersick Castle is widely accepted as the most haunted location in the UK, and it has been the subject of many television programmes, as well as getting a mention in numerous books, media and publications. It is a striking building and has many good reasons to make a visit. It's primarily a private residence, but the owners make the house and grounds available as often as they can and are investing in research and digs to find out more about the house and grounds.

The ghost tours continue to be very popular.

22. Tutbury Castle

Situated in the heart of England, Tutbury Castle is situated on wooded slopes overlooking the winding River Dove, with spectacular views across the plain of the Dove to the beautiful Derbyshire hills. Occupied since the Stone Age, the castle is first recorded in 1071, as one of the new castles built to stamp the authority of the Norman conquerors across the Midlands. Since then, the castle has played an important part in English history on many occasions, in warfare and in peace. The castle is best known as one of the prisons of Mary Queen of Scots, who was incarcerated there on four occasions. It was here that she became involved in the plot that ultimately led to her bloody execution at Fotheringhay.

Tutbury has a long tradition of ghostly happenings, and here are just a few of the most famous ones:

The Keeper - Wearing a full suit of armour, and behaving in a manner that might best be described as authoritative, this ghostly figure has been seen stepping out in John of Gaunt's Gateway and bellowing "Get thee hence!". Although last sighted in daylight about four years ago, by a visitor who complained that an idiot of an enactor had told him to "get over the fence", recent increases in paranormal activity might suggest that another visit could be imminent. When it was pointed out that no enactors were on site that day, and that similar ghostly apparitions had been reported by other unsuspecting visitors, the response was "I'm sorry, but I don't believe in ghosts".

Mary Queen of Scots - Tutbury was Mary's most despised prison. She suffered much at Tutbury and was at the Castle as a captive of Elizabeth 1st on four occasions. She was seen all in white by some members of Her Majesty's services. In 2004, at approximately midnight, she was seen standing at the top of the South Tower by a group of men – in the form of a figure dressed in a pure white gown. When they saw her, they all just laughed, believing the Curator was just teasing them by putting on an Elizabethan gown as a joke. When it was pointed out that curator Lesley Smith does not have a white gown, and neither does any other Elizabethan enactor working at the Castle, the men were profoundly disturbed by this sighting. She was also seen rapidly crossing the grass, one hot afternoon in 1984, by a serving Marine. Recently, there have been a number of sightings of Mary – especially between 10.15 p.m. and 11.00 p.m. A figure, dressed in black, is seen standing at the window of the Great Hall as cars leave the Castle. In May and June this year, she was not only seen by senior members of staff, who are usually quite dismissive of such reports, but also by archaeologists participating in a seasonal dig at the castle.

Film and TV - Many paranormal TV shows have been recorded at Tutbury Castle. For ghost lovers, the Castle has featured on "Most Haunted" and "The World's Biggest Ghost Hunt." In September 2005, and April 2006, Tutbury Castle hosted the national "Most Haunted" Convention. In October (2004) Tutbury Castle welcomed 2,000 people on a one-night ghost-hunting event! Some visitors come from as far a field as Paris to spend a night in Tutbury. Regular ghost hunts - including the popular "Haunted Happenings" events - are still held at the castle.

23. Bodmin Jail

Bodmin Jail is a historic former prison situated in Bodmin, on the edge of Bodmin Moor in Cornwall. Built in 1779 and closed in 1927, the large range of buildings is now largely in ruins, although parts of the prison have been turned into a tourist attraction. The jail was originally built for King George 3rd in 1779 by prisoners of war and was designed by Sir John Call. The jail had enough room to accommodate 100 prisoners. The building which stands today was built in 1860 using 20'000 tonnes of granite from "Cuckoo Quarry" in Bodmin which was fetched by the prisoners. Bodmin was the first jail to feature separate "cells", and each small chamber may well have a nasty story to tell

During World War 1, the Doomsday Book and the Crown Jewels were kept in Bodmin Jail for safe keeping.

In the 150 years Bodmin jail was operational, it held 50 public executions, the first one being in 1785 and the last in 1909. The executioners were paid around £10 per execution.

In 1927 the jail was closed for good.

With its forbidding aspect and dark history, Bodmin Jail has, not surprisingly, attracted many ghost stories and paranormal researchers over the years - including the crew of the TV show Most Haunted - and there is a ghost walk/night regularly available for tourists.

Matthew Weekes was a prisoner of Bodmin Jail. It was

believed by some that he was wrongly accused of a crime and was imprisoned an innocent man. People visiting the jail claim to have seen Matthew's ghost wandering the cells. A lady named Selina Wadge was executed by hanging at the prison because she murdered her child when it was born out of wedlock. Her spirit is said to haunt the prison, grabbing at visiting children and making pregnant women fell a huge amount of remorse.

Many, many more ghosts have been witnessed at Bodmin prison by people visiting the gloomy and oppressive building.

Today, most of the jail remains in ruins, and presents a forbidding aspect when seen from a distance. Some parts have been refurbished and these now form a tourist attraction with exhibitions telling of the history of the jail and of offenders imprisoned there. The exhibits showcase gory mannequins accompanied with plaques, describing the offence committed by particular persons and their sentence, in their respective cells. Because of the style of exhibit, it has been likened to such attractions as The London Dungeon.

24. Woodchester Mansion

Often said to be one of the most haunted locations in the UK, Woodchester Mansion, built by William Leigh, is a 19th Century Victorian Gothic Masterpiece mysteriously abandoned mid-construction in 1873. Hidden in a secluded Cotswold valley, it is untouched by time and the modern world. This Grade 1 Listed Building has been saved from dereliction, but will never be completed.

Visitors to the mansion walk through an extraordinary architectural exhibit in which the secrets of the medieval Gothic builders and masons are laid bare. The carvings in Woodchester Mansion are among the finest of their kind in the world.

The ghosts said to haunt Woodchester Mansion evoke tales of the horror the building has seen over the years. Many deaths occurred at the mansion - from workmen to family members - from the previous building that once stood on the foundations. Accidents, murders, and alleged human sacrifices have all added weight to the reputation the mansion has gained for being a hotspot of paranormal activity. On various ghost hunts, the strange phenomena produced at the mansion has stunned and chilled many a seasoned investigator. A cold presence has often been felt with each step taken, dark cloaked figures have been seen wandering the hallways, and voices whispering in the ears of frightened guests are just a few of the regular happenings in the dead of the night. Much of Woodchester's ghostly heritage is reported to be poltergeist in nature.

In 1902, a vicar was reported to have seen a strange apparition at the mansion's gates. A phantom horseman has also been seen on the mansion's drive. It is said that the Mansion itself is the epicentre of all the haunting happenings in the area. There is the Tall Man of the Chapel, which has been seen many times, and the elemental in the house's cellar. The Mansion is said to be the home of some of the scariest ghosts in the United Kingdom. Visitors have collapsed and have been attacked by the ghostly dwellers of the mansion. There is a floating head, which has been seen by many visitors in one of the bathrooms. There is also the spectre of the old woman who likes to attack female visitors by grabbing them in the dark. It is said that the reason why the mansion is haunted is because it stands on the site of the three previous buildings, which are also haunted.

The mansion has its own chapel, and satanic rituals have been heard in here. People have reported hearing a woman singing an Irish folk song in the scullery. The ghost of a young girl has been seen several times playing and running up and down the stairs of the mansion's first floor.

25. Derby Gaol

Given its colourful history of imprisonment, death, and misery, it's certainly no surprise that Derby Gaol has been dubbed the 'Most haunted Place in Derby'. Over the years, there have been many paranormal occurrences and sightings reported.

According to the owner and staff at the Gaol, the ghostly sightings and incidents tend to occur mostly from around October through to December, and then tail off until June and July when they pick up again.

The Gaol's current owner, Richard Felix - who is also a popular author and TV ghost show presenter - has had several supernatural encounters himself at the Gaol. For example, one Friday afternoon in November 3 years ago, Richard was standing in the kitchen of the Gaol talking on the phone, when a figure walked down the corridor past him. The grey haze was in the form a person, which glided down the corridor and vanished at the bottom. The experience unnerved him so much that he was unwilling to hang up the phone and brave leaving the Gaol alone. He returned the following year on the anniversary of the sighting at the same time and waited. This time however, he experienced nothing.

During the revamp and restoration of the Gaol, one of the builders was working in the cells. Twice during the Saturday afternoon, the cell door closed by itself while he was in there. The same builder also had to leave the room several times on account of feeling sick - something he attributed to the coffee he had consumed earlier that day! Many other visitors - including a few TV paranormal show presenters - have also felt nauseous and emotional in the same cell.

Some people find themselves unable to go into the cells, reporting extremely unpleasant feelings. Some that do later leave hurriedly, telling of suffocating feelings, being 'pushed down', and sensations of darkness and sickness. One visitor was so badly affected that she was physically sick.

One gentleman claimed to have witnessed something very disturbing in one of the cells: two dead men hanging from a fixed beam inside the cell. The men were reported as facing the doorway, but turned slightly inwards towards each other, just hanging there. They appeared to have been approximately in their late twenties to early thirties.

The condemned cell has long been an area which has caused discomfort to visitors. Some people have reported 'neck restriction' and feelings of suffocation.

Two ladies, on one occasion, left the Gaol in tears, clutching their throats and feeling unable to breathe. They had felt that 'something' was around their neck. Exiting the Gaol, they passed a figure standing by the door, which they mistook for an actor. He was bald and wore a sleeveless leather outfit, which the ladies described as looking like a body warmer. This same figure has also been seen in the dayroom, alarming one of the female eyewitnesses who described it as 'evil' and 'a murderer'. This mysterious entity has also been seen by another contractor called Chris, who was also working on the restoration of the Gaol. He saw the figure while locking up alone one night. He also described the bald figure as wearing 'fancy dress' - a leather 'body warmer'. The figure walked away, passing through a cigarette machine, and disappeared through the wall.

A lady in a large 'Ascot' type hat has also been seen at a time when the Gaol was a drinking venue known as 'The Secret Place'. The figure walked down the corridor, through a door, and presumably up the steps beyond. The three men who had witnessed it followed her. They opened the door and ascended the steps outside to the top, only to find a heavy carpet of snow. There were no footprints to be found anywhere.

One lady decided to spend the night alone in the condemned man's cell. Initially, nothing happened, until the early hours, when she began to hear noises and footsteps. Something tugged her sleeping bag off, and as she tried to grab it, she dropped her pillow. When she turned back, her pillow had vanished. She had to turn on her flashlight in order to try and find it, only to discover it near the cell door, almost 10ft away from where she had dropped it.

After one of the Derby Ghostwalks several years ago, everyone was sitting in the dayroom finishing their dinner while their guide, Peter, finished his summing up for the evening. One of the diners noticed a figure suspended from the wood above the doorway, swinging gently behind the guide. Initially, the man presumed that it was an actor, or one of the 'scares' from the tour. He soon realised this was not so when no one else noticed the hanging figure.

There have been incidents of poltergeist activity in the Gaol. Cups and saucers moving or flying through the air of their own accord. Richard Felix, the current owner, had a pair of original 18th century spectacles vanish, which turned up three months later by the main door in a very prominent place. Had they been there all along, they would have been spotted long before.

26. Abraham Lincoln's Ghost

Among the many paranormal experiences reported in the White House over the years, there is one story in particular that really stands out from all the rest, given the great historical significance of the person involved: the ghost of Abraham Lincoln.

Lincoln's ghost is the most common and reported one. The spirit of the long-dead president is said to have haunted the White House since his assassination on Good Friday, April 14, 1865, by John Wilkes Booth, as the American Civil War was drawing to a close.

The spirit of Lincoln is said to appear in the room where the Lincoln bed is kept. Harry Truman once answered a 3 o'clock knock on his door and found no one there. He attributed the knock to Lincoln.

Lincoln is reported to return to the White House when the security of the country is at risk. He strolls up and down the second floor hallway, knocks on doors, and stands by certain windows with his hands clasped behind his back. One staff member claimed to have seen Lincoln sitting on his bed pulling on his boots.

One of President Harrison's bodyguards was kept awake many nights trying to protect the president from mysterious footsteps he heard in the hall. He grew so tired and worried, he finally attended a séance to beg President Lincoln to stop so he could get enough sleep to properly protect the president.

In addition to the ghost of Abraham Lincoln, many presidents, first ladies, White House staff members and guests have reported feeling other ghostly presences in the building. Unexplained noises have been heard, and some of those people have even experienced running into actual apparitions - even on the way out of the bathtub, in one particularly famous case. There is also a phantom black cat said to haunt the basements of the White House, the mall and the Capitol. The so-called "Demon Cat" is reported to appear just before national disasters.

Sightings of Lincoln's ghost were frequently reported during the long administration of Franklin D. Roosevelt (1933-45). First Lady Eleanor Roosevelt used the Lincoln Bedroom as her study, and reported feeling his presence there late at night. During her visit to the White House, Queen Wilhelmina of the Netherlands heard a knock on her bedroom door in the night; when she answered it, she reportedly saw Lincoln's ghost, wearing his top hat, and fainted. British Prime Minister Winston Churchill, who visited the White House more than once during World War II, told a story of emerging naked from his evening bath smoking his customary cigar, only to find a ghostly Lincoln sitting by the fireplace in his room.

When Lillian Rogers Parks, the seamstress, once investigated the sound of someone pacing an upper level of the White House, another staff member told her the room in question had been unoccupied, and "that was old Abe pacing the floor." Psychics have speculated that Lincoln's spirit remains in the White House to be on hand in times of crisis, as well as to complete the difficult work that his untimely death left unfinished.

27. Blue Bell Hill, Kent

Blue Bell Hill, in Kent, has become infamous for its so-called "road ghosts".

In a front page headline of the Kent Today paper of Tuesday 10th November 1992, it announced: "GHOST GIRL SEEN AGAIN".

Written by Emma Cooper, the article described a chilling new episode in the sage of Kent's most famous roadside phantom. This latest incident occurred around midnight the previous Sunday night, 8th November, near the Aylesford turn-off of the southbound carriageway of the A229 at Blue Bell Hill.

Ian Sharpe, a 54-year-old coach driver, was travelling home to Maidstone when a young woman suddenly appeared in the path of his vehicle. She ran towards him and, with her eyes fixed on his, fell beneath the bonnet. Stuck dumb with shock, Ian skidded his car to a halt, and nervously got out to take account of the accident.

He honestly thought he had killed her, and initially was too scared to look underneath the car. However, he eventually managed to summon the courage to take a look . . . and was stunned to find that there was nothing there! Despite searching the whole area around the car, he still found no trace of the mysterious figure's body. White-faced and shaking with fright, he went and reported the matter to the local police. After listening to his account, they immediately registered grim recognition in regard to the exact spot on Blue Bell Hill where the incident had occurred, and recounted to him the spooky legend of the ghost said to haunt that stretch of road.

When the officers accompanied Ian back to the scene, they too found nothing. There wasn't even any trace of damage to his car, suggesting that he could not possibly have encountered a real, living person. Despite this, Ian maintained to the police that he had not imagined the whole thing, and that the girl had definitely seemed real and solid. In fact, he was so convinced of this that he was even expecting the officers to come knocking at his door the following day to report the finding of the girl's body. They never did.

Another incident at Blue Bell Hill, which occurred back in 1974, also attracted similar widespread media interest. In the early hours of the 13th July, Maurice Goodenough, a 35-year-old bricklayer, came rushing into Rochester Police Station claiming he'd knocked down a young girl on Blue Bell Hill. Again, just like the 1992 experience of Ian Sharpe, officers found nothing at all at the scene of the accident to suggest that Maurice had actually knocked down a real girl.

In analysing the reports of the ghostly sightings on Blue Bell Hill, some people have regarded these incidents as stemming from a horrific car crash, which happened there in 1965. On the evening of Friday 19th November 1965, two cars were in collision on Blue Bell Hill. Three of the four young women in one of the vehicles died from their injuries, one instantly. One of the fatally injured was a bride-to-be. Her wedding was due to take place the following day. Unfortunately, it had been too late to inform the wedding guests, who dutifully gathered at the church the next day, only to be turned away.

One of the three dead women is held to be the phantom hitchhiker, either the bride-to-be or, more often, one of her friends. Having been thwarted on the very eve of her wedding, perhaps the bride was not ready to die and is constantly trying to finish her journey. It is obviously difficult to reconcile the figure of an adult woman with that of a ten-year-old girl; the bride-to-be may have been small, dressed in a young style, perhaps wearing white ankle socks, and in the panic of the crash, and in the darkness, may have been mistaken by the witness as being much younger than she was. There are other, frustratingly uncorroborated, reports of sightings of the bride-to-be hitchhiker in the area on the anniversary of her crash.

There is no doubt that the 1965 crash has provided an appropriate and feasible origin for the hauntings on Blue Bell Hill.

28. Brannigan's Nightclub, Manchester

At the Brannigans Nightclub in Peter Street, Manchester, a rather mischievous poltergeist is said to haunt the premises. This mysterious phantom is reported to cause havoc behind the bar, smashing glasses. Also, members of staff have complained about an unseen force that has tried to push them down staircases in the building on a number of occasions.

A disused church occupies the upper floors of Brannigans nightclub, with an old organ, which is believed to be Britain's largest. Brannigans is supposed to be very actively haunted. There is reported to be poltergeist activity, spectral sightings and two entities. One of these entities is said to haunt the bar area and is reported to be the Reverend Samuel Collier who preached in the church in 1910. The spirit of Reverend Collier is said to cause glasses to crash to the floor and move across the bar on their own accord.

In 2003, Brannigans was the subject of a paranormal investigation by the TV ghost show Most Haunted. During this investigation, medium Derek Acorah claimed that the two entities haunting the building did not want the camera crew in.

Brannigans still attracts various paranormal groups, many

of which have posted videos on the internet of supposed ghostly activity in the building.

29. Burtonwood Airbase

RAF Burtonwood airbase, situated near Warrington in the North of England, was once a thriving American base during WWII. At the base, there have been several unexplained sightings of ghosts.

The first paranormal sightings occurred during the war, when swirling mist was seen by two American NCOs who were returning to their quarters after celebrating at a local pub. Some people believed it was the ghost of a pilot who died in a bomber crash. One could easily have attributed the sightings to the NCOs having indulged in too much local brew, but the same figure was also reported by a boiler man and a group of women returning from a dance. Over the months, the ghostly figure was seen several more times.

Some years later, a local gent was working alone in a hangar converted to a museum, and saw an old man sitting in an abandoned bus near the hangar. When the man asked a fellow worker who the old man was, they realized no one was in the bus, or in the hangar. Local people believe that the old man was the ghost of a recluse who used to live in the bus.

Another spooky incident involved a volunteer worker, who claimed that a ghost wearing a WWII uniform "hitched" a ride with him. The man quickly opened the passenger door and let the ghost out!

30. Ghost Trains

Over the years, in addition to sightings of ghostly people, there have been many reports of ghostly vehicles in various parts of the world. Among these reports, there have been cases of so-called "ghost trains". Here are just some of them:

1. Silverpilen (Silver Arrow) is a Stockholm Metro train which features in several urban legends alleging sightings of the train's "ghost".

2. The St. Louis Ghost Train, better known as the St. Louis Light, is visible at night along an old abandoned rail line in-between Prince Albert and St. Louis, Saskatchewan. Two local students won an award for investigating and eventually duplicating the phenomenon, which they determined to be caused by the diffraction of distant vehicle lights.

3. A phantom funeral train is said to run regularly from Washington, D.C. to Springfield, Illinois, around the time of the annual anniversary of Abraham Lincoln's death, stopping watches and clocks in surrounding areas as it passes.

4. The Ghost Train of Bostian Bridge - On August 27, 1891, in Statesville, NC, a passenger train travelling towards Asheville jumped the track on the Bostian Bridge and 30 people lost their lives. On the anniversary of the horrendous accident, at least one ghost of the dead comes back: the ghostly spirit of H.K. Linster, who was a baggage master for the railroad.

In regard to the apparitions of human spirits on the railways, there may be good reason for all of these: train stations are the sorts of places where incredibly strong emotions can build up and seep into the atmosphere. Over the years, there have been many joyful meetings and sad farewells at railway stations. How many soldiers have waited on railway platforms for the train to arrive to take them to whatever war they are to fight in? And how many of these men have travelled back on these lines, minus their killed army comrades? And let us not forget, of course, the numerous cases of people being killed on railway lines, especially suicides who, in a fit of utter despair, have flung themselves into the paths of oncoming trains.

Spirits are undoubtedly attracted to - and can feed off - such strong human energies.

31. Hangleton Manor, East Sussex

Hangleton Manor, in Hove, East Sussex, has been reported as being quite a hotspot for paranormal activity over the years.

A ghostly brown silk dress has been seen sweeping through the hallways of the building and walking up the main staircase. Nobody really knows exactly who this dress belongs to, although some eyewitnesses do believe that it might have been worn by Mrs Fitzherbert, who was the lover of the Prince Regent in the 18th century, and who is said to have visited Hangleton Manor.

A pair of hands, minus their body, has also been seen floating above the staircase. In the attic, the presence of a female has been sensed, whose aura is one of deep sadness and desperation. This despondent aura may be attributable to some possible traumatic event which may have happened to her in her life. It could even have been something that may have led to her death. A ghostly child has also been seen in the attic with her. It is said that an infant was once thrown out of an attic window by her mother. It's possible that these entities could well be those of the mother and child, still haunting the attic.

People who once worked at Hangleton Manor have reported hearing a female spirit making strange rapping noises from behind wood panelling. They have also heard ghostly cries from what has sounded like a soul in utter torment. Is there a possibility that just one ghost, the spirit of the woman haunting the attic, is responsible for all the paranormal activity occurring in Hangleton Manor? Who knows?

32. Mary King's Close

Mary King's Close, in Edinburgh, is a warren of underground streets and spaces. In the 1600's, Mary King's Close and neighbouring Closes were the centre of Edinburgh's busiest and most vibrant streets, bustling with traders selling their wares to the Old Town's residents.

Mary King's Close is notorious for its tales of ghosts and unexplained happenings. One of the earliest and best documented stories concerns the Coltheart family and took place 40 years after the last outbreak of plague in Edinburgh when people were already claiming to have seen 'spectres and nameless terrors' in the Close.

An elderly lawyer, Thomas Coltheart and his wife refused to leave and were almost driven mad by terrifying images of floating limbs, a bodiless phantom of a child and a "grotesque and monstrous form" of a dog that would curl up on a chair.

Now one of Edinburgh's most haunted attractions the close is known for its variety of ghosts. A tall lady, dressed in a long black gown is often seen walking near the ghost tours that visit the underground caverns and several visitors have caught fleeting glimpses of a short, elderly man who wears a troubled expression.

The Close was a street back in the 17th century and much of it is still intact. It runs from the High Street northwards beneath the City Chambers -- Edinburgh's Local

Government. Before Cockburn Street was built Mary Kings Close used to run all the way to Market Street.

The Close is said to be named after the daughter of wealthy advocate and owner of the property, Alexander King, although little evidence of this has been found. A woman by the name of Mary King did live there in mid 17th century.

In mid 17th century, the Old Town had been infested with black rats from ships at Leith Docks and disease spread out. The local council attempted to contain the plague and the decision was made to block up the entrances to Mary King's Close. Some plague victims are thought to have been locked in.

In the following years, the close had been reopened due to overcrowding in the Old Town and sightings of ghosts, mainly headless animals and disembodied men, have been reported. The most frequent sighting in recent years has been that of a young girl, no more than 5 or 6 years old called 'Annie' by those that have seen her.

A hundred years after the plague, the Council decided to develop a new building, The Royal Exchange, which is now known as the City Chambers. The houses at the top of Mary Kings Close were knocked down, but part of the lower sections was used as foundations for the new building.

In 1994 David Roulston spent the night in Mary King's Close to raise money for the BBC's Children in Need appeal. Through the night David filmed his stay over, mainly to record his own feat rather than the paranormal. While filming with his camcorder, he claims to have captured the image of a "ghostly head", which looked like the head of a dog.

The Close has become a very popular tourist attraction.

Some visitors reported that photographs taken in the underground chambers of Mary King's turned out faded or not at all. Not surprisingly, due to the rather spooky nature of the site, this phenomenon is often attributed to the existence of ghosts.

33. Highgate Cemetery

Highgate Cemetery, in Highgate, London, is said to be one of the most actively haunted cemeteries in the UK. It was built in 1839 and was a very popular burial place for Victorians. By the 1960's Highgate Cemetery had fallen into neglect and decay. Reports started circulating that the cemetery was haunted, and there were even newspaper stories that there was a vampire at large in there - the so-called "Highgate Vampire".

In 1963 two teenaged convent girls were walking home late at night after visiting friends in Highgate Village. Their route back took them down Swains Lane and past the cemetery. As they passed the graveyard's north gate at the top of the lane, they were shocked to see bodies appearing to be emerging from their tombs.

A few weeks later, there was another spooky incident in the area, this one involving a couple who were also walking down Swains lane. The lady claimed she had seen something hideous lurking behind the gate's iron railings. Her fiancé saw it too, and both stood frozen to the spot, staring at it for around several minutes. The apparition's face bore an expression of utter horror.

Other people claim to have sighted the same phantom as it hovered along the path behind the gate where gravestones are visible either side. Some who actually witnessed the spectral figure wrote to their local newspaper to relate their experience. Discoveries were made of animal carcasses drained of blood. Very soon, this incident was attributed to the work of a vampire.

In 1971, a few years after the much reported vampire sightings, a young girl claims she was actually attacked by the vampire in the lane outside the cemetery. She was returning home in the early hours of the morning when she was suddenly thrown to the ground with powerful force by a "tall black figure with a deathly white face. When a car stopped to help her, the vampire seemed to vanish in the glare of the headlamps.

The girl was taken to the police station in a state of shock, fortunately only sustaining abrasions to her arms and legs. The police immediately made an exhaustive search of the area, but could find no explanation for the incident. Even more weird was the fact that where the vampire vanished, the road was lined by 12ft walls.

In another interesting case, a man claimed to have been hypnotised by something in the cemetery. He had entered the cemetery one evening to look around, and as the light began to rapidly fade he decided to leave, but became lost. As he was not superstitious, he walked calmly around looking for the gate when suddenly he sensed something behind him. Turning around, he became "hypnotised with fear" as the tall dark figure of the vampire confronted him. His fear was so great that he stood motionless for several minutes after the vampire vanished. He later recalled that it was almost as if he had been paralysed with fear by some unknown force.

David Farrant is a leading expert on the Highgate Vampire, and tends to dismiss the vampire stories as unfortunate consequences of the popularity of Hammer horror films amongst the public at that time. He maintains that the Highgate Vampire was neither a hoax nor a vampire, but nevertheless was something very real.

In David Farrant's bestselling book on the subject, Beyond the Highgate Vampire, the author claims that ley lines may be an overlooked significant factor in the Highgate phenomena. These lines, he says, can actually transmit psychic energy along their course and enable the vampire to materialise when the right conditions prevail. One such ley line begins in the middle of Highgate Cemetery at a large circle of tombs called the Circle of Lebanon, crosses through the Flask and Ye Olds Gatehouse pubs, traverses a large block of council flats known as Hillcrest, and passes through an old Roman Settlement a quarter of a mile or so away in Highgate Woods, which is marked by an old beech tree.

Without exception, all the locations on the Highgate ley line were reportedly haunted by a 'tall black figure' which, even when it wasn't actually visible, caused dramatic drops in temperature, clocks to simultaneously stop, objects to fly from shelves or mysteriously shatter, and which also had a dramatic effect upon animals in it's immediate proximity.

Today, all of these locations are still affected by recurrent psychic activity, the latest having seemingly come to life again in the Flask public house, while a black-clad figure is again being reported at Highgate Cemetery. There have also been reports of a 'tall black figure' seen in Swain's Lane outside the cemetery, and only this February a lady driving her car up the Lane one night saw a tall dark figure about 7 feet tall with luminous eyes that suddenly disappeared through the cemetery wall.

A man out walking his dog had also seen the vampire near the old Roman Settlement in Highgate Woods the same month, which abruptly disappeared without trace.

Swain's Lane outside the cemetery also has its own weird happenings. In 1974 a dog walker, on returning to his car in Swains lane, discovered a freshly disinterred corpse in his car. Strangely, the doors were still locked. At the time, there were all sorts of arcane rituals and ceremonies being carried out in the cemetery late at night - many of these being negative occult practices.

Visitors to Highgate often report icy touches on the cheeks, whispers, cries and hushed talking. Visible spectres visit less frequently since the Friends of Highgate group began the clean up and restoration. But you'll find that in London, ghosts never really leave for any significant length of time. Highgate Cemetery is, without doubt, one of the most haunted places in one of the most haunted cities in the world.

34. Mine Ghosts

Mine ghosts - or "knockers" - are said to be the spirits of miners who have died underground. Miners who have been trapped in cave-ins and pound on the rocks for rescue. It is believed that the ghosts of these miners go on knocking in the mine shafts long after the victims have died.

These ghosts may either help or hinder living miners, and quite often the miners treat these entities reverently, leaving them gifts in the form of food or drink. These mine spirits are described as being quite small in stature, and are usually dressed as miners themselves.

The best known mine spirits are those that inhabit the tin mines of Cornwall. They are also known by many different names, like "knackers" or "spriggans", and "blue caps" in the north of Cornwall. Their name comes from their tendency towards making knocking sounds, indicating when miners approach rich seams. Some Cornish miners report that they have actually guided rescuers to the location of cave-ins by their tapping. Singing Christmas carols is also said to be a keen tendency with the knockers. But they also have a rather unsettling side to them by appearing suddenly out of nowhere and pulling faces. However, miners are careful not to show anger for fear of upsetting the spirits. And no Cornish minder will ever whistle or swear while underground, because the knockers find both actions highly offensive.

There have also been incidents of knockers in the USA, where they are called "Tommy-knockers". These entities are said to be highly volatile in temperament, and often malevolent. They hate to be seen by the human eye. There is a story that a team of Tommy-knockers, when believing that they had been betrayed by a miner who they had been helping produce coal (he had brought his workmates along to have a look at this ghostly helpers), angrily set the mine on fire.

These mine ghosts were the inspiration for Stephen King's 1987 bestselling book, The Tommyknockers, only in his story it was aliens that had been trapped underground instead of miners.

35. Strangeways Prison

Strangeways Prison in Southall Street, Manchester was built to replace New Bailey prison in Salford, which closed in 1868. Over the years, there have been many reports of ghosts being seen in various areas of the old prison.

The ghost of a man wearing a dark suit and carrying a briefcase has been reported by staff. He is always seen walking along 'B' wing from just outside the condemned cell If anybody tries to follow him, he vanishes near the condemned cell. Some believe this apparition is that of John Ellis, a former executioner who committed suicide in 1932.

Another ghost that has been seen wandering through the corridors of Strangeways is that of the infamous Blackpool Poison killer, Mrs Louisa May. Merrifield. Her ghost is said to return to the cell where she spent her last night on Earth in human form. The sightings of Mrs Merrifield's ghost seemed to increase around the early 1980s, with a number of inmates of 'I Wing' reporting seeing an apparition of a short woman dressed all in black walking about the landing. When they asked her what she was doing in their cell, she just disappeared.

There may have been an explanation for this, as at the time the works department of the prison was building some new office accommodation at the rear of what had been the old female cellblocks. During the digging of the foundations, they had reported finding the remains of previously executed inmates who had been buried within the walls of Strangeways Jail in unconsecrated ground. Perhaps one of the bodies was that of the long dead hangman's victim, Mrs. Merrifield.

36. The Bottom-Pinching Ghost

In a certain pub called The Queen's Arm, Charlotte Street, Birmingham, there is a rather naughty resident ghost, dubbed "Grasper" by the employees, with a cheeky propensity towards pinching the bottoms of female staff.

The bottom-pinching phantom has become so bothersome that fed-up owners have had called in a team of ghostbusters to give the saucy spook the bum's rush.

Other activity is said to include chairs moving of their own accord and footsteps heard in empty parts of the building.

But it's not just the staff who have had their bottoms tweaked, for some customers have also fallen victim to the ghoul's roving hands. Pretty Ashley Beland, 26, said she thought she had been groped after her encounter with the ghost. She said: "I was stood at the bar enjoying a glass of wine when I suddenly felt a sharp pinch to my bum. My instant reaction was that it might have been a sleazy bloke trying his luck, but when I spun around ready to give him a piece of my mind, there was no-one there."

Customers have also witnessed chairs moving on their own, heard footsteps when the pub is empty, and seen plumes of smoke swirling around.

And it is even thought that several ghouls may lurk

around the 170-year-old pub after last orders. A bald-headed ghost has been spotted walking through walls to find the bar, while rumours suggest that a young girl died in the building decades ago after falling down the stairs.

37. The Crying Boy

Often, in the classic ghost stories of the famous paranormal writer M. R. James, a certain object was featured that had a curse on it. In the modern-day world, there is a certain object that has

The Crying Boy is a mass-produced print of a painting by Italian painter Bruno Amadio, also known as Giovanni Bragolin. It was widely distributed from the 1950s onwards. There are numerous alternative versions, all portraits of tearful young boys or girls.

On September 4, 1985, the British tabloid newspaper The Sun ran a story about a firefighter from Yorkshire who claimed that undamaged copies of the painting were frequently found amidst the ruins of burned houses. He stated that no firefighter would allow a copy of the painting into his own house. Over the next few months, The Sun and other tabloids ran several articles on house fires suffered by people who had owned the painting.

By the end of November, belief in the painting's curse was widespread enough that The Sun was organising mass bonfires of the paintings, sent in by readers.

To lift the curse, it is said you must give the painting to another or reunite the boy and the girl and hang them together.

Karl Pilkington referred to these events on The Ricky Gervais Show. Ricky Gervais dismissed the curse as "bollocks".

Steve Punt, British writer and comedian, investigated the "curse" of the crying boy in a BBC radio Four production called Punt PI. Although the programme is comic in nature Punt researches the history of the Crying Boy painting and reveals an intriguing past. The conclusion reached by the programme, following testing at the Building Research Establishment is that the prints were treated with some varnish containing fire repellent, and that the string holding the painting to the wall would be the first to perish, resulting in the painting landing face down on the floor and thus being protected.

38. The Demon Drummer of Tedworth

In the 17th century, there was a remarkable incident of poltergeist activity in Tedworth (now Tidworth) which appeared to involve a "Demon Drummer".

The strange phenomena first began in March 1661, in the home of John Mompesson, a local magistrate, who had recently tried a conjuror named William Drury. A drum owned by Drury was confiscated, and it is said that, in a bitter act of revenge, Drury put a curse on Mompesson and his family.

Shortly afterwards, Mompesson's house began to experience strange rappings and booming sounds. There were also other strange incidents, which seemed to suggest that a poltergeist was behind all these disturbances. Various objects were moved around, children were tormented and levitated from their beds, and weird animal noises were heard in different parts of the house. A disembodied voice was heard shouting, "a witch, a witch" over and over again, and the frequency of the raps and knocking sounds increased. The drumming sounds also continued for days one end. There were also a number of other strange incidents, such as coins being turned to black while they were in the pockets of visitors.

Joseph Glanvill, the royal chaplain, came to investigate

the hauntings at Tedworth. He witnessed the strange noises himself, and began to trace other witnesses. He related these incidents in his book Sarducismus Triumphatus (1681), which is now regarded as classic of early psychical research. It was thought at the time that sorcery by Drury was responsible for the phenomena, and consequently he was tried as a witch and transported out of the country for incarceration. According to later reports, the prison ship carrying him abroad was apparently disturbed by severe storms evoked by him in possible further actions of sorcery.

Some theories have suggested that, because Drury was of Roma ancestry, or possibly even a Siberian shaman, he knew how to induce fits and hypnotized states using the dark practice of ritual drumming.

39. The Drury Lane Theatre

The Drury Lane Theatre in London is possibly the most haunted theatre in the UK. The most famous ghost is the one called the "Man in Gray." He appears in full costume wearing a tri-cornered hat, a powdered wig and a long grey cloak with the hilt of a sword protruding from it. He is said to be the ghost of a man whose skeletal remains were found in 1848. A knife had penetrated his long grey cloak and was still embedded in his rib cage. He always appears during the daytime to actors when they are rehearsing. He is thought to be "a recordings ghost," as he is always seen in the same place, walking quietly in the same direction. His ghostly visitations are thought to be lucky, for the plays performed after his appearance always do well at the box office. During renovation work at the theatre in the late 1970's, builders found a buried skeleton clad in the remains of a grey riding coat and a knife sticking out of its ribs. It is believed this may be the remains of the young man, for whom a body was never located.

Another ghost reported at the theatre - described as "tall, thin, and ugly" - is thought to be the ghost of a grumpy actor named Charles Macklin. In 1735, Charles killed his fellow actor Thomas Hallam in an argument over a wig. He thrust his cane through Hallam's left eye into his brain. Macklin has often been seen backstage, wandering the corridor where the murder was committed.

Alan Toner

The ghost of comedian Joe Grimaldi, who gave his farewell performance at Drury Lane, is a rather helpful apparition that is often felt rather than seen. He is said to guide nervous actors gently about the stage. In 1948, a young American actress named Betty Jo Jones was performing badly during a run of "Oklahoma." Then, as she describes it, she felt "invisible hands" guiding her into a different position on the stage. They continued to guide her around the stage during the rest of the performance. Her performance was later described as flawless. Also seen on stage were the ghosts of King Charles II and a crowd of his attendants. Another young actress named Doreen Duke felt the same invisible hands while trying out for a part in "The King and I." She got the part, hands down. She believed that Joe Grimaldi's ghost was helping her here.

The comedian Stanley Lupino was in his dressing room applying his makeup when, looking in the mirror, along with his own reflection, he saw another face looking back at him. It was the face of Dan Leno, another comedian who had died recently. Lupino was told that he "was using Leno's favourite dressing room."

A woman in the audience saw what was probably a ghost, watching the play that was being performed. She described this apparition as "a man wearing old-fashioned clothes sitting at the end of the row where I was sitting. When the lights went up, the man was gone." Later, whilst perusing a book on the history of the theatre, she saw a picture of Charles Kean, a 19th Century actor. She instantly recognised him as the ghost that she'd seen earlier.

Considering all these reports of hauntings, you could say that The Drury Lane Theatre is where actors, both past and present, take "Centre Stage."

40. The Edinburgh Vaults

The Edinburgh Vaults are a series of labyrinthine chambers formed in the nineteen arches of the South Bridge in Edinburgh, Scotland, which was completed in 1788. For around 30 years, the vaults were used to house taverns, cobblers and other tradesmen, and as storage space for illicit material, reportedly including the bodies of people killed by serial killers Burke and Hare for medical experiments.

As the conditions in the vaults deteriorated, mainly because of damp and poor air quality, the businesses left and the very poorest of Edinburgh's citizens moved in, though by around 1820, even they are believed to have left too. The evidence that people had lived there was only discovered in 1985 during an excavation, when middens were found containing toys, medicine bottles, plates, and other signs of human habitation.

An apparition called "The Watcher" has been seen many times, and has even been mistaken for a tourist guide. The figure of a small girl has been sighted, walking up to people and telling them her name. A small boy has also been sighted frequently, following a tour guide. Visitors have reported physical sensations, such as being grabbed by unseen hands, the odour of strange smells, visible lights moving around, stones being hurled at people, and sound of footsteps. There are also many reports of electrical items, like torches and cameras, suddenly malfunctioning.

A radio producer recorded a mysterious voice while making an historical documentary. It is thought the voice is speaking either Scots Gaelic or Irish Gaelic and uttering the words "fad ort", meaning "longing to be away". A rather unsavoury gentleman, called "Mr Boots", due to his high leather boots, has also been seen on several occasions and has been known to push people and whisper obscenities in their ears. Other visitors have experienced cold spots and feelings of unease and discomfort.

These are just a few of the paranormal incidents reported to have occurred in the Edinburgh Vaults over the years, and it is therefore not surprising that they continue to be a popular tourist destination for both professional and amateur ghost-busters, who come to explore their gloomy, candle-light corridors in the hope of meeting a spirit.

41. The Epworth Poltergeist

The Epworth Poltergeist is the first officially recorded case of poltergeist activity. It occurred in December 1716 at the Parsonage in the small town of Epworth, Lincolnshire in England. The parsonage was the home of the generally unpopular Reverend Samuel Wesley.

Every single member of the Wesley family reported hearing loud rappings and noises over a period of two months. Sometimes the noises were of a specific nature, according to the detailed notes of Mrs. Wesley. During one incident, when she and her husband were descending the stairs one day, they heard a noise like someone was emptying a large bag of coins at their feet. Then they heard the sound of glass bottles being "dashed to a thousand pieces." Other sounds heard were running footsteps, groans, and a door latch being lifted several times.

The main disturbances occurred, sporadically, for two months: December and January 1716-17. There were also a few more incidents afterwards.

The phenomena were first attributed to trickery. There were even allegations that the devil was responsible for all these strange incidents, although Samuel's wife, Susannah Wesley, disagreed with this suggestion. Instead, she attributed the phenomena to the fate of her brother who, in the service of the East India Company, disappeared and was never heard of again. It was never proved that the rappings were caused by his disembodied spirit, but the members of the family took it for granted after a while that "Old Jeffrey" was involved in the manifestations, which appeared to be connected mostly with Hetty Wesley. She was noticed to tremble strongly in her sleep when the knockings occurred.

42. The George Inn, Devon

The George Inn is a centuries-old building situated in the tiny village of Blackawton, Devon. This traditional English pub is a reported hotspot for ghostly activity, including some evidence of poltergeists.

Throughout its long history, many famous people have visited the George Inn. When Sir Walter Raleigh married Elizabeth Throckmorton in the local church, they spent their first night there as husband and wife (at that time, the place was known as Church House Inn). Oliver Cromwell also lived at the inn for a while during the English Civil War.

Terrifying poltergeist activity has been experienced in various parts of the building, particularly in the upper floors. The sound of footsteps has been heard running down the corridors, accompanied by loud knocks on each of the bedroom doors.

Many ghostly apparitions have been seen, including a small woman who stands smiling in the bar, a tall hunchbacked figure in the living area of the inn, the misty figures of two small children, a weird hooded female figure, and ghostly monks. Cold spots have also been experienced, making people wonder whether these have some connection to the apparitions witnessed in the building.

One of the most mysterious incidents at the inn occurred when the owner discovered some 2p coins scattered around his shower.

43. The Ghosts of Raby Castle

Raby Castle, in Staindrop, Darlington, Co. Durham, is one of England's finest mediaeval castles. It was once owned by the Neville family and is said to be still haunted by Charles Neville, Earl of Westmorland. He was forced to surrender to Henry VIII after the successful Rising of the Northern Earls. The ghost of Charles Nevilles has been seen heading for the Barons Hall, where in 1569 he and his men were deciding that such a trip would be unwise, when they were interrupted by Mrs Neville who branded them as cowards.

In response to such a statement, the men fought and lost, leaving the Earl to flee to Scotland, and finally Holland where his body is buried.

In latter years the castle was passed to the Vane family, one of which (Henry) was imprisoned by the Stuarts and ordered to be executed. He was said to have still been trying to give his last speech to his people when his head was chopped off! His headless ghost is often seen in the Library at Raby, with his head sitting on the desk in front of him, still trying to talk through his speech.

Strange paranormal incidents also surround the Barnard family, who were next to take up residence in the castle. The lady of the house was known for her bad temper, and her ghost is still often seen at Raby knitting with red-hot needles. She is known by locals as the "Old Hell Cat".

Finally, the last ghosts of Raby are those murdered by

Maria Cotton, who chase each other merrily through the castle grounds, and surrounding countryside.

44. The Grapes Pub, Liverpool

There is a certain pub in Liverpool called The Grapes, which is a house of spirits in more ways than one. Described by the licensee as one of the "oldest buildings for miles around", The Grapes is situated between Rodney Street and Hope Street, somewhat out of the way, but still handy for all the local amenities. The pub is also known as "The Little Grapes", to differentiate it from its namesake in Matthew Street.

The licencee says that the pub is "very haunted", which is not surprising considering that the pub has been up since the 1700's. The spooky incidents that have been reported include the sound of people walking up and down the bar, doors banging upstairs, and heavy fire doors opening and closing of their own accord. The licencee also claims to have seen ghosts herself, and has identified up to 17 different people among these spirits.

The green-painted exterior of the corner pub bears not a sign saying The Grapes, but battered gilt and wooden name boards, now under glass, proclaiming this pub to be the home of "Mellor's noted wines and spirits". Could these gilt and wooden name boards be the ghosts of the pub's past? Well, the licencee believes that these signs date back to the 1840s, but in fact the pub itself is older still. The current building dates back to 1804, but it was built on the site of an earlier tavern, whose history has been lost in the mists of time.

Not surprising, therefore, that a pub with such a history as The Grapes should be home to many spirits - and we don't mean the kind you drink!

45. The Haunted Ebay Painting

The Hands Resist Him - more commonly known as The eBay Haunted Painting - is a painting created by Oakland, California artist Bill Stoneham in 1972. It depicts a young boy and female doll standing in front of a glass panelled door against which many hands are pressed.

In February 2000, an anonymous seller started an auction for a 'Haunted Painting'. The ad included grim warnings about possible supernatural powers held by the image and told the story of how the painting had affected the sellers' lives since they bought it a year previously. The advert also included a series of pictures of the picture 'changing form' at night - caught on film by a webcam.

The artist claims that the boy is based on a photograph of himself aged 5, the doorway is a representation of the dividing line between the waking world and the world of fantasy and impossibilities, while the doll is a guide that will escort the boy through it. The titular hands represent alternate lives or possibilities. The painting became the subject of an urban legend and a viral Internet meme in February 2000 when it was posted for sale on eBay along with an elaborate backstory implying that it was haunted.

The painting first went on display at the Feingarten Gallery in Beverly Hills, CA during the early 1970s. A one-man Stoneham show at the gallery, which included the piece, was reviewed by the art critic at the Los Angeles Times. During the show, the painting was purchased by actor John Marley, notable for his role as Jack Woltz in The Godfather.

At some point in time after Marley's death, the painting was said to have come into the possession of a California couple, after being found on the site of an old brewery. The painting appeared on the auction website eBay in February 2000. According to the seller, the aforementioned couple, the painting carried some form of curse. Their eBay description claimed that the characters in the painting moved during the night, and that they would sometimes leave the painting and enter the room in which it was being displayed. Included with the listing were a series of photographs that were said to be evidence of an incident in which the female doll character threatened the male character with a gun, causing him to attempt to leave the painting. A disclaimer was included with the listing absolving the seller from all liability if the painting was purchased.

News of the listing was quickly spread by Internet users who forwarded the link to their friends or wrote their own pages about it. Some people claimed that simply viewing the photos of the painting made them have unpleasant experiences. Eventually, the auction page was viewed over 30,000 times.

After an initial bid of $199, the painting eventually received 30 bids and sold for $1,025.00. The buyer, Perception Gallery in Grand Rapids, Michigan, eventually contacted Bill Stoneham and related the unusual story of its auction on eBay and their acquisition of it. He reported being quite surprised by all the stories and strange interpretations of the images in the painting. According to the artist, the object presumed by the eBay sellers to be a gun is actually nothing more than a dry cell battery and a tangle of wires.

Stoneham recalls that both the owner of the gallery in which the painting was first displayed, and the art critic who reviewed it, died within one year of coming into contact with the painting.

An individual who saw the story about the original painting contacted Stoneham about commissioning a sequel to the painting. Stoneham accepted and painted a sequel called Resistance at the Threshold. The sequel depicts the same characters 40+ years later in the same style as the original. Stoneham has entered into an agreement with the current owners of the first painting to sell prints of it in three sizes. A second sequel, Threshold of Revelation, was completed in 2012 and can be seen on Stoneham's website.

The case of the E-bay Haunted Painting has now become part of Internet folklore.

46. The Lamb Inn, Bristol

At The Lamb Inn, Lawfords Gate, Bristol, there were many reports in the 18th century of a biting poltergeist.

The poltergeist incidents started in November 1761 and ended in December 1762. The family affected by these phenomena were called Giles, and the two younger sisters - 13-year-old Molly and 8-year-old Dobby - were the centre of the entity's attention. The first incidents reported were strange scratchings and rappings emanating from the girls' bedrooms. Then came reports of mysterious movement of objects. Most of these incidents were regarded as "typical" poltergeist disturbances. However, a notable feature was a series of assaults upon the two girls, as both suffered from pinches and bites from an invisible assailant. More disturbingly, pins were jabbed into the girls by some unknown entity, they were incessantly cut; on one occasion, Molly received more than 40 cuts.

Mr Henry Durbin was summoned to investigate these poltergeist incidents. He subsequently wrote a pamphlet on the case, which was posthumously published in 1800. Durbin and other investigators monitored the phenomena under conditions which ruled out any involvement of fraud. On the 30th January 1761, Durbin saw a bite mark appear on Dobby's shoulder. He claims to have seen "the mark of teeth", about eighteen, and "wet with spittle".

This poltergeist gave all the signs that it was a very

intelligent entity, and was reported to engage in communication with the family and investigators by dint of scratching noises. The messages attributed the disturbances to the work of a witch. In the end, the family resorted to sympathetic magic, and after they followed the advice of a "cunning woman", the disturbances ceased.

Even though the case is nearly 250 years old, the Lamb Inn Poltergeist is regarded by many modern paranormal researchers as clear evidence of poltergeist activity, by virtue of the great detail reported by Durbin and the striking similarity to other cases involving biting poltergeists, like that of the Cock Lane Ghost and the Enfield Poltergeist.

47. The Miami Poltergeist

On the 14th January 1967, a poltergeist case in a Miami warehouse - apparently centring around a teenage worker - was first reported.

The manager of the warehouse rang the police and told them that a ghost appeared to be present in the warehouse, as things were getting mysteriously broken. When the police arrived, they witnessed objects falling from the warehouse shelves without any logical explanation. Consequently, the officers were at a complete loss as to how to help.

The poltergeist activity persisted, and the case eventually came to the attention of various parapsychologists, among them William Roll, who coined the term Recurrent Spontaneous Psychokinesis, and J. G. Pratt. Roll was convinced that the phenomena were centred around one young warehouse worker, a 19-year-old Cuban called Julio. All these strange incidents seemed to happen whenever Julio was present, and they seemed to increase when Julio became emotional.

Over 224 incidents of poltergeist activity were recorded at the warehouse. Also, there were many reliable witnesses, including the police officers who had been summoned on the 14th January. Roll and Pratt investigated the warehouse for two weeks, both men seeing and recording a number of strange incidents. However, the activity was not captured on film, as the poltergeist failed to co-operate when the video cameras were rolling. Both investigators also checked the warehouse shelves, pushing the stock back to eliminate the possibility that the objects were falling naturally through structural vibrations. Roll placed notebooks in front of a row of glass items on a shelf, and subsequently finding broken glass scattered all over the floor and the notebooks untouched, he determined that the objects lifted up into the air of their own accord before dropping to the ground. The investigators kept certain objects under close surveillance, and also measured the distances that disturbed objects moved. They discovered that whenever Julio was in close proximity to the objects, they moved, and when they were further away from him, they travelled further.

Roll and Pratt could find no signs of possible fakery in their investigations, although there were some claims that the effects were cleverly staged using thread to pull the objects from their places. Occasionally, activity was witnessed while Julio himself was being closely watched. The investigators requested that Julio undergo some psychological tests. These tests revealed that he was a rather troubled young man who hated his boss, that he had an unhappy home life, and that he suffered from nightmares. On the 30th January the warehouse was broken into and some petty cash was stolen. Although Julio confessed to the crime, no charges were made. Julio later robbed a jeweller's, for which he was given a six-month prison sentence. After this, the incidents at the warehouse stopped.

The Miami Poltergeist is one of the best-recorded cases of poltergeist activity in the history of paranormal research. It is a notable example of evidence that poltergeist manifestations can be generated by RSPK, in this case with Julio being the channel unwittingly causing the disturbances due to his own anger and suppressed emotions.

48. The Rosenheim Poltergeist

The case of the Rosenheim Poltergeist began in November 1967, in a law office in the Bavarian town of Rosenheim. The strange phenomena that occurred were mostly of an electronic nature: fuses suddenly blew without any apparent cause; ceiling lights constantly went out; developing fluid in a copy machine spilled several times of its own accord; and there were many problems with the telephone equipment. Four telephones rang all at once, calls were mysteriously cut short, and bills rose sky high. Loud banging noises were also repeatedly heard.

Parapsychologist Hanz Bender, along with a team of other paranormal researchers, investigated the case. Electronic monitoring equipment was installed, and the anomalous fluctuations in the power supply were carefully measured. It was subsequently found that these anomalies occurred only during office hours.

The phenomena seemed to be centred around a 19-year-old employee, Anna S. Whenever she was walking through the building, light fixtures would swing behind her and light bulbs that were turned off would suddenly explode. The phenomena decreased the farther away she was. These strange occurrences were all captured on a video recorder by the investigators.

During the course of the investigation, a fresh phenomenon occurred: pictures began to move and rotate on the walls. In some instances, the pictures rotated 360 degrees or fell off their hooks. One was even filmed rotating 320 degrees!

Test equipment attached to the telephone revealed that the time announcement number was dialled a few times a minute by an unknown hand. On some days, the number was dialled 40 to 50 times in a row. The employees were questioned about this, but they all flatly denied being responsible for the dialling.

More strangely, four dialings of a nine-digit Munich number were registered simultaneously. Bender claimed that the psychokinesis required to do this would involve a mechanical influence upon certain springs at millisecond time intervals, which would require sophisticated technical knowledge.

Upon the completion of their investigation, the investigators concluded that the phenomena defied all rational explanation in regard to theoretical physics, that it seemed to be the result of non-periodic, short duration forces, and that the movements - especially those pertaining to the telephone - seemed to be caused by intelligently controlled forces that are inclined to avoid investigation.

49. The Stocksbridge Bypass Ghost

Often said to be the "scariest UK ghost story ever recorded", the haunted Stocksbridge Bypass - often described as the "Killer Road" - has gained a notoriety over the years as being the kind of road you would not want to be travelling along late at night.

Completed in the late eighties, the Stocksbridge Bypass, Sheffield, is situated on the North side of the valley. Careless driving and speeding caused many deaths there, until a slight redesign with better signage, along with specs cameras, stopped the fatalities. It gained a reputation for being a hotspot of paranormal activity in its early days, with a Michael Aspel special on its alleged hauntings. In fact, the story started during the building of the road.

A group of security guards saw a group of children late one night playing just below Pearoyd Bridge. They were puzzled by the fact that the children appeared to be wearing old fashioned clothing. When they reached the spot where they had spotted the children, they found nothing. There were no footmarks in the muddy ground. The following morning they were told that workmen staying in caravans often heard children singing during the night.

The following night they observed a cowled figure on the bridge that resembled a monk. When they drove towards him, he disappeared. Totally shaken by their weird experience, the two blokes contacted Deepcar Police station. The Police didn't give any credence to their reports of ghosts, and even jibed that they needed a priest rather than a copper. They took him at his word and contacted the local vicar, who himself contacted the Police!

Later two policemen went to investigate. They parked their car in a good vantage point to see the bridge. They thought they saw something move, but on investigating found a tarpaulin blowing. Suddenly it appeared to go cold. Looking round they both saw a body - torso only in the window. Then it vanished. They tried to start the car but at first it didn't start. They drove over towards the construction area and parked up and informed the nick of their position. At this point a loud crash was felt in the car. No one was around. Naturally, the two policemen fled back to Deepcar as fast as possible.

Legend has it that it is the ghost of a disillusioned monk that left Hunshelf Priory and went to work at Underbank Hall. Children are said to have fallen down the numerous pit shafts that litter the North side of the valley.

There have been numerous sightings of children since, and the monk even appears inside the cars of people to this day. A large black dog has also been seen, darting across the fields, down the path adjacent to the main road

The area still continues to attract many ordinary people and paranormal groups, all looking for evidence of ghosts.

50. The Witchfinder General's Ghost

Matthew Hopkins, who was also known as the notorious Witchfinder General, devoted his whole life to tracking down and persecuting suspected witches in the England of the Middle Ages.

His ghost has been reported in various locations in both Mistley and Mannningtree in Essex. Some of the haunted locations associated with Matthew Hopkins are:

1. Mistley Place, Mistley - A ghost said to be the spirit of Matthew Hopkins has been seen around the 'Ducking Pond' by locals at what used to be Hopkins' headquarters.

2. White Hart Inn, Manningtree - Matthew Hopkins is said to have frequented the establishment and it is reputed he can still be heard in the building to this day.

3. 'Hopping Bridge', Mistley - A 'Phantom Jaywalker' seen wearing 17th century clothing is reported to be the ghost of Matthew Hopkins. He has been seen walking in the vicinity of the small hump-backed bride known as 'Hopping Bridge'.

4. Thorn Hotel, Mistley - The ghost of Matthew Hopkins has been reported here. A ghostly serving girl who used to work at the hotel is said to still walk along the corridors and a boy who was pushed under a cart and trampled to death during a fight is seen at the rear of the building.

5. Red Lion, Manningtree - This public house is said to

be haunted by a Victorian gentleman nicknamed George. However, many people claim the ghost is actually that of Matthew Hopkins.

6. River Stour, Manningtree - The ghostly screams of a tormented witch being interrogated at the hands of Matthew Hopkins are said to be heard emanating from the opposite shore.

7. Seafield Bay, Manningtree - Elizabeth Clarke, whose execution was ordered by Matthew Hopkins, is said to walk the shoreline of Seafield Bay. Sounds heard here on certain nights have been attributed to the screams of tortured witches and also the sound of Elizabeth Clarke's familiars.

51. The Irish Police Ghost

Sometime in the 1880's, two constables of the Royal Irish Constabulary were walking with despatches to a nearby police station. It was a calm, moonlit night, and the air was still and clear, but a little frosty. As they approached their destination, they spotted another policeman ahead of them on the road. The police station was on one side of the road, and a whitethorn hedge on the other.

The third officer looked as if he'd just stepped out from the hedge. After looking at the other two officers, he then walked towards the station and vanished into its shadows. The two policemen thought he was on guard duty inside, and had just popped outside to catch some fresh air. Both officers saw him very clearly, and described him as being a rather plump, bald-headed individual, with a pale face and mutton-shop whiskers. He also had his tunic open at the front.

But when the two constables arrived at the station door, they discovered it was locked and bolted. They had to knock quite a few times before someone answered. When they were finally admitted, there was no sign of the whiskered constable. Also, there was no chance whatsoever that he could have got in and locked the door in the time they took to approach. They later discovered that nobody had been assigned guard duty that night, and realised that whoever or whatever they had seen, it was certainly not a living colleague!

Afraid that they would be laughed at, they kept their strange experience to themselves.

A few years later, they learned that a policeman had been found dead in the snow, only a few yards away from the police station.

52. The Pink Panther's Ghost

The British actor Peter Sellers was famous for his role as the bumbling Inspector Clouseau in the Pink Panther movies. During the making of the Trail of the Pink Panther in 1982, a series of strange happenings on the set were reported by the producer Tony Adams.

Unused footage of previous Pink Panther movies starring Sellers was slotted in with many newly shot scenes. But Adams claimed that many unexplained occurrences disrupted production. He said that he strongly believed that the spirit of Peter Sellers was still around, making it difficult to match each new film with the old. Costumes mysteriously went missing. Sets that had been working perfectly suddenly didn't, and a lot of the scenes seemed to have been jinxed.

In life, Sellers did seriously believe he could communicate with the spirits, and claimed his mother was watching over him and guiding his career from beyond the grave.

53. The Haunted Antique Chest

In Stanbury Manor, Cornwall, there is a certain antique chest that is reported to be haunted. The chest is said to have come to this country with the Spanish Armada. The owner had purchased it from an antique shop whose proprietor was glad to be rid of it, as he claimed it was haunted.

When the chest was first taken to the manor, it was placed in the armoury for a short time. Right after it was delivered, the owner saw six guns fall to the floor of their own accord, as if somebody had broken the heavy wire that had secured them to the wall. But neither the wire nor any of the fixings were broken. When the chest was moved to the bedroom, the owner was in an adjacent room putting pictures up on the wall, when one of them fell and stuck him on the head. It was quite a heavy picture, although there was no real force behind it when it hit him. It was just as if the picture had been moved by some mysterious power.

The following day, three more pictures fell, then four more two days later. Again, strangely, none of the wires or fixings showed any signs of damage. On hearing, two days later, of the death of a relative, the owner began to wonder if there was any connection between this and the falling pictures, as there were no more incidents involving the chest.

Alan Toner

The press reported on these mysterious events, and the following story was told by a former curate, who was familiar with the phenomenon. Two elderly ladies once owned the chest, and these women lived nearby. They were both deaf and would communicate by writing notes. Both were very private people, and did not bother much with the locals. They had built up a large collection of furniture over the years, and the curate went to look at the pieces when the women put them up for sale, but bought nothing as he found the continual writing and passing of notes too frustrating. He later discovered that the sisters had both been struck deaf one morning whilst staying with friends. They had arrived late at night and gone to bed without unpacking, and next morning had seen the lid of the chest open, as if lifted by invisible hands. When they looked into the chest, they saw something so horrible that they were both struck deaf on the spot.

Another strange story concerned a surgeon in the Midlands, who went to stay with a friend. His bedroom had a large carved wooden chest standing in a corner. Curiosity aroused, he opened the top and was confronted with the corpse of a man lying with his throat cut. Gripped by shock, the surgeon let the lid of the chest fall closed, but when he regained his composure and re-opened it, he found the chest empty.

The following morning, he related this weird experience to his friend. Utterly stunned by the surgeon's creepy story, the host told him that a previous occupant of the room had killed himself and the body had been in the chest covered in blood.

54. The Ghost of Edgar Allan Poe

The legendary horror writer Edgar Allan Poe suffered greatly through his life. His death was marked by an equal amount of confusion.

Poe grew up orphaned, living with the Allan family before attending college in 1826. He only stayed for a year before leaving to join the army because of severe gambling debts. His life from there is marked with tragedy. He married his 13-year-old cousin Virginia in 1835, losing her to sickness in 1847. He never held a steady job, and was fired from numerous positions due to a severe drinking addiction. Although he could never hold a job, editors admired him for his ingenious poetry and short stories, including The Raven and The Tell-Tale Heart. Nevertheless, his drinking and depression took a strong grip on his life. He died two years after his wife, passed out in a street in Baltimore. Although he was dead physically, his spirit lived on in his residences and final resting place.

People began reporting sightings of Poe's ghost appearing at his gravesite. On his birthday, January 19, the apparition of a man shrewdly covered in black was seen, walking towards the grave of Edgar Allan Poe. His face is unrecognisable because of the black scarf that conceals it from view. Nevertheless, the black-coated man walks towards Edgar Allan Poe's grave on his birthday, leaving a bottle of cognac and three roses. The apparition then disappears in the night, slowly meandering through the graveyard with a walking stick. People believe this to be the ghost of Edgar Allan Poe, honouring himself with the ceremonial bottle of cognac and three roses. People are discouraged from approaching the ghost and told not to disturb the spirit.

In 1990, the curator of the Edgar Allan Poe house allowed photographers to shoot Poe's gravesite on his birthday for any evidence of this mystery ghost. Sure enough, the ghost walked towards his grave and knelt down. In the picture, the ghost is clearly seen with his trademark black clothing and black fedora, scarf covering his face. The ghost then disappeared into the night.

Poe's grave isn't the only place that is haunted by ghosts. During his marriage to Virginia Clemm, they lived in a small, unprepossessing house on North Amity Street, located in Baltimore, Maryland. This house is believed to be haunted as well. People have reported seeing a grey-haired woman wearing early-1800s clothing. Some people believe this is the ghost of Poe's aunt, Maria Clemm. People have also reported feeling cold spots, hearing voices, and seeing windows and doors open of their own accord.

Is Poe's ghost haunting the place where he once dwelled? It might be his tortured spirit, seeking redemption from beyond the grave.

55. Jamaica Inn

Jamaica Inn, built in 1750 and extended in 1778, has been described as one of the most haunted places in the UK. Situated in Cornwall, with a panoramic view of the beautiful wilderness of Bodmin Moor, it presented the perfect place for smugglers to hide their goods since it's in a very quite part of the city. The Cornish and Devon coasts were extremely popular for smugglers, with around half of the tea and brandy that came to the United Kingdom illegally entering via those two channels. Nobody really knows exactly where the Jamaica Inn got its name from, but many believe that it was because the Jamaica Inn was mainly used for hiding plenty of rum.

Over the years, there have been many paranormal incidents reported in the Jamaica Inn. The owners describe the building as having "resident ghosts". Guests have heard footsteps pacing up and down the floor, objects have been moved around the room, and there have been many other unexplained happenings. A number of ghosts have been spotted around the Inn, but there's one ghost in particular that seems to regularly haunt the Jamaica Inn: the spirit of a man that sits on the wall just outside the Inn. Even more strangely, the man doesn't do anything, doesn't speak, or even moves; he just stays there. Nobody really knows the identity of this man, but most people believe that he is the man who went missing from the Jamaica Inn in the 1800s, and who was later found dead in an isolated field.

The novelist Daphne Du Maurier made Jamaica Inn famous in one of her most successful books. Reviewed as "perhaps the most accomplished historical romance ever written," Jamaica Inn was later released as a film, directed by Alfred Hitchcock, with Maureen O'Hara as heroine Mary Yellan and Charles Laughton as Sir Humphrey Pengallan. Daphne, however, seems never to have depicted any ghosts at all in her books.

Even though the inn was subject to "temperance" in the 1900s, the ghost stories continue to be reported. Considering the innumerable ghost stories related to the inn, "The Ghost Society" investigated the matter. Of particular interest to these investigations were the strange events reportedly noticed in the Smuggler's Bar, the Stable Bar, the restaurant and in Bedroom 4 on the upper floor.

Jamaica Inn continues to play host to "Haunted Nights" every year, ghost-hunting events which attest to the fact that the inn's reputation for being haunted is still as magnetic as ever.

56. Ghost At The Hairdressers

It's not often you hear reports of ghosts haunting a hairdressing salon. However, there is one particular case of such a haunting that has attracted much interest and curiosity. The staff and customers at Jazz hairdressers in South Shields have had their hair stand on end numerous times – not because of a beauty treatment, but because of what staff suspect is a ghost.

The spooky happenings started as soon as salon owner Sheena Carmichael moved into the shop in Frederick Street, Laygate. Strange footsteps were often heard, along with whistling and knocking sounds. Initially, both the manager and staff thought they were hearing things, but the more these weird incidents happened, the more they became convinced that they had a resident ghost on the premises.

A sceptic by nature, salon boss Joanne Robson has been the target of many of the invisible visitor's pranks. One night, she had locked up the shop and had decided to go on the sun-bed in the cubicle. She suddenly heard a loud crash, so she got up and saw that a tub of cream had been flung over from the beauty room. On another occasion, towels were spinning round the dryer, but it wasn't switched on. She also felt someone tickling her neck, but nobody was there. Joanne confesses to having run out of the shop on a number of occasions, fearing that she was being especially targeted by this entity due to her being a sceptic.

Alan Toner

Customers have been told to go away by a gruff man's voice. Some have seen people dressed in old-fashioned clothing standing in the upstairs window, and others have heard conversations in empty cubicles.

One of the most recent appearances of the ghost was on Christmas Eve, when Sheena went into the staff room at the back of the salon and saw a cloud-like white mass hovering.

Legend has it that when the building was being used as a Unionist club back in the 1950s, a barman died after falling down the cellar's stairs, which would have been in Mrs Carmichael's shop.

Staff believe the ghost of the man could be responsible for the unexplained occurrences in the salon.

57. Ghost At The Dentists

The Germans are noted for enjoying a good ghost story. A particularly strange tale of a haunting has grabbed their imagination much more than any other over the years.

In 1982, in Lower Bavaria, Dr Kurt Bachseitz, a small-town dentist, claimed he was being plagued by a ghostly voice that just wouldn't be silenced. The disembodied voice - which was said to be called "Chopper" - initially concentrated its attention on the doctor's telephone, and it was all too easy to regard this interference as nothing more than a practical joke. But then it started to manifest itself from various outlets in Dr Bachseitz's surgery. Its staccato, robot-like monotone would emanate from electric power points, light fittings and pieces of surgical equipment, harassing the doctor and declaring undying love for his attractive seventeen-year-old assistant.

When the voice began to disturb Dr Bachseitz as he treated his patients - on occasion even ordering him from the washbasin at the side of the dentist's chair - he called in the police and issued a private summons of harassment against "person or persons unknown". A Post Office team from Darmstadt travelled 150 miles to the town and spent a few days investigating the mystery. However, their investigations proved negative, and they left feeling utterly puzzled.

58 Littledean Jail

Situated in the middle of the Royal Forest of Dean, Gloucestershire, Littledean Jail was once a police station and a courthouse. A "crime through time museum" has been set up so that people can see all of the weapons that were used to torture criminals in the past. It's the only museum of its kind in the entire world, so it's well worth a visit if you have a strong interest in criminal and penal history. You can even sit in the electric chair . . . and experience just what it must have felt like, all those years ago, when nervous prisoners made their final sedentary action before being executed.

Many strange happenings have been witnessed in Littledean Jail over the years. The sound of crying children has been heard in the cells that were specifically made for youngsters. Some people even claimed to have seen the ghost of "The Jailer" himself.

Although Littledean Jail only opened up to ghost hunters in 2005, it's still one of the most popular places for ghost hunters to visit. With doors slamming shut, objects being thrown around the room and amorphous shadows being seen in dark corners, it's no wonder that Littledean Jail is extremely popular with ghost hunters!

Littledean Jail is featured on the 'Ghosts of Gloucestershire' DVD starring 'Richard Felix', who appeared on televisions top-rated spooky programme 'Most Haunted'.

59. Fire And Police Museum, Sheffield

The Fire & Police Museum in Sheffield is definitely not the place to visit if you are of a nervous disposition.

Even though the building is only around 100 years old - which isn't that ancient in comparison to other haunted buildings - it's still an interesting place to visit if you want to do some serious paranormal investigating.

As befitting its name, the building was once a fire station and a police station. It was divided up so both the fire station and the police station had their own separate space.

A few decades later, a new fire station was built, so it became just a police station, and eventually the building fell into disuse. In the mid 1980s, it became a museum, attracting many sightseers.

So many paranormal things have happened in this museum in Sheffield, prompting even the BBC to pay it a visit. A few ghost hunters decided to ask the spirits present in the museum to stop at 999 (since it was in a fire and police station) by using a Franks box. This did happen, and afterwards, to prove that it wasn't just a one off incident, they asked the spirits to do it again, which they did!

One of the most famous spirits in the Fire & Police Museum is a man called Cain. Despite the fact that he likes having a chat with the people that come to the museum, he also has a rather dark side to him. He has often smashed glasses at visitors, especially when they try to enter the cell that he was once in while he was alive. He obviously wants to protect his own territory, daunting anybody from entering his cell.

60. Croxteth Hall

On the site of Croxteth Hall, Liverpool, there has been a house that, since the sixteenth century and for almost all of that time, has been owned by the Molyneux family, the Earls of Sefton. When the last Earl died in 1972, he was the last of the line, and the house was sold. It is now open to the public.

Croxteth Hall has a very well researched ghost sighting, captured on CCTV and the subject of much discussion. Although it is not very clear, it is obviously the height of a man and vaguely human in shape. Visible for around eight seconds, the amorphous form emerges from some trees and turns onto a path leading to the house, before disappearing into thin air.

Although this ghost has only been captured on film once, it has been seen many times by both visitors to the house and grounds, and staff. Because the figure very indistinct, it is not possible to identify it, but it could very well be the spirit of the 2nd Earl of Sefton. The ghost appears around the time the Grand National is due to run at nearby Aintree, and the 2nd Earl was a compulsive gambler and in fact laid the foundation stone when the racecourse was first established in his heyday in 1829.

CCTV footage has always been rather unreliable and unclear, and also pretty easy to fake, with examples of doctored film emerging all the time. However, this one does have some credible substance about it for a number of reasons: People had always felt that the grounds, rather than the house, were haunted before the ghost was filmed, and also the footage is so ordinary and unspectacular that it does seem pretty convincing. The edges are not clear and the shape is indistinct, and the area in which it appears is not particularly exciting or evocative. In fact, it looks for all the world as if it is the 2nd Earl of Sefton out for a stroll while he tries to select the winner of the next Grand National.

61. The Skirrid Inn

The Skirrid Mountain Inn was built over nine centuries ago and is the oldest pub in Wales. It is also one of the oldest standing pubs in Great Britain. The inn is so called because of the mountain that looms over it, 'Skirrid Mountain', also known as 'Holy Mountain'. Legend has it that it cracked in two at the time of Christ's crucifixion. The ancient 'mounting stone' in the forecourt is said to have been used by many Welsh and English Kings over the centuries.

'Hanging' Judge Jeffries is thought to have started his notorious career at The Skirrid Inn, although records are not entirely clear on this. According to folklore, between the 12th and 17th Centuries over 180 people were hanged from a beam on the staircase. It is said that this beam still remains in place today, complete with apparent rope marks. It is also thought that the first floor would have been a fully functioning courtroom; complete with a cell in which prisoners spent their last night.

With a history of terrifying incarceration and merciless executions it is therefore unsurprising that The Skirrid Inn has a reputation for being haunted. It attracted the attention of popular TV show 'Most Haunted', a particularly memorable episode, as well as featuring on ITV's 'Extreme Ghost Stories' in January 2006. Haunted pubs expert Richard Jones even recently declared The Skirrid to be the most haunted in the UK.

Alan Toner

Glasses often fly across the bar of their own accord, strange faces have been seen at the windows, guests feel a ghostly noose slip around their necks, things mysteriously disappear only to turn up weeks later, and residents wake to an icy cold room and the feeling they are being watched.

It is thought that one of the main spirits at the inn is that of 17th Century barmaid Fanny Price. However, reports suggest that there is definitely more than one spirit haunting The Skirrid Inn.

62. The Station Hotel, Dudley

The Station Hotel in Dudley was partially opened in the late 19th Century before being unveiled as a luxurious new hotel in 1910.

Originally designed to complement the grand Opera House, which stood opposite, the Hotel played its part in the dawning of the 20th Century. However, when the Opera House burnt down in 1933, the decision was made to demolish the hotel and rebuild. And so, in 1936, as the new, modern 'Dudley Hippodrome' was unveiled, The Station Hotel once more opened its doors to theatregoers and performers.

During this era, many stars of stage and screen walked through her rooms and corridors, including such famous names as Laurel and Hardy, Bob Hope, Bing Crosby and Johnnie Ray. George Formby is also said to have performed from his balcony to crowds below while staying at the hotel.

From the day it was opened right up to the present day, the hotel has been surprisingly popular with the spirit world, with many residents opting to stay on even after death. The sheer amount of paranormal activity experienced in the hotel has led to many investigations being carried out and, in 2003, to Living TV's 'Most Haunted' programme filming there. The episode in question saw perhaps the most fascinating footage in the show's history when a locked off camera caught a bed and chair moving by themselves in the notorious Room 214. In this room, guests have often woken at night to find themselves being watched by a ghostly figure. Staff have also seen children running through this and other rooms along what is known as 'the haunted corridor', before disappearing into the wall.

It is also said that a gruesome murder took place on the premises in the early part of the 20th Century. Most Haunted's Derek Acorah elaborated on this by claiming that the body of the victim was put into a beer barrel and rolled out through the cellar chute before being buried at the front of the building somewhere. If this is true, it might explain the all-pervading sense of foreboding and fear that many people feel in the cellar, and why many staff refuse to go down there alone.

63. Waverly Hills, Sanatarium

Waverly Hills Sanatorium, located in Louisville, Kentucky, opened in 1910 as a two-story hospital to accommodate 40 to 50 tuberculosis patients. It has been highlighted on television as being one of the "most haunted" hospitals in the eastern United States, and was seen on ABC/FOX Family Channel's Scariest Places On Earth, as well as VH1's Celebrity Paranormal Project. It was also seen on the Sci Fi Channel's Ghost Hunters.

Ghost hunters who have conducted investigations in Waverly have reported various strange paranormal phenomena, including voices of disembodied entities, isolated cold spots and unexplained shadows. Blood-curdling screams have also been heard echoing in its now abandoned hallways, and fleeting apparitions have been encountered.

Waverley Hills Sanatorium is now closed, although its doors are permitted to open occasionally for the benefit of paranormal groups keen to investigate the various spirits said to haunt the buildings dark rooms and passageways.

64. The Stanley Hotel

The Stanley Hotel in the Colorado Rockies was completed in 1909 by Freelan Oscar Stanley. This 138-guest-room hotel is probably best known as the inspiration for Stephen King's book The Shining, which he wrote after staying at The Stanley, in room 217. King did not write the novel there, nor was the 1980 Stanley Kubrick movie filmed there, but the TV movie version of The Shining, which starred Rebecca DeMornay, was used as the location. Today, the hotel is a popular resort and destination for ghost hunters. Regular ghost tours are also offered.

Several apparitions and other phenomena have been reported throughout the hotel:

The ghosts of Freelan Stanley and his wife Flora have been seen dressed in formal attire on the main staircase and in other public areas, such as the lobby and the billiard room.

Mr. Stanley has also been spotted in the administration offices. The sound of the Flora's piano can also be heard playing occasionally in the ballroom.

Disembodied voices and phantom footsteps have been heard in the hallways and rooms.

Staff and visitors have complained about having their clothes pulled by unseen hands.

Various guests have reported that they have awakened to find their blankets taken from their beds and neatly folded.

The Earl of Dunraven, who owned the land prior to the Stanleys, is said to haunt room 407, where the smell of his cherry pipe tobacco still fills the air. A ghostly face has also been reported peering out of the room's window when it was not occupied.

Room 217, where Stephen King stayed, was the site of a tragic accident in 1911: housekeeper Elizabeth Wilson was nearly killed by a gas leak explosion. Since her death in the 1950s, strange activity is said to occur in that room, including doors opening and closing, and lights switching on and off by themselves.

Room 418 is the most haunted room, according to hotel staff, apparently by the ghosts of children. Guests who stay there say phantom children can be heard playing in the hallways at night. One couple complained that the noisy kids kept them up all night, although there were no children staying at the hotel at the time. Impressions of bodies have been found on the bed when the room has been unoccupied.

The ghost of a small child, who calls out to his nanny, has been spotted on several occasions on the second floor - including by Stephen King himself.

65. The Sallie House, Kansas

The Sallie House in Atchison, Kansas, has earned a reputation as one of the most haunted places in the U.S. The rather ordinary-looking painted brick house at 508 N. Second Street, built between 1867 and 1871, does not really give the impression that it could be haunted. However, the many strange experiences of those who lived there testify to its ghostly vibes. Most of these vibes have been of the negative variety.

The house came to national attention when Debra and Tony Pickman resided there from 1992 to 1994 and had many weird encounters, including actual bodily attacks on Tony. These ghostly physical assaults were documented by the Sightings television show. The property is called the "Sallie House" because the daughter of previous tenants had an imaginary friend named Sallie, and she is said to be one of the spirits haunting the house. When Tony Pickman drew a picture of the ghost he had seen, the daughter immediately recognised her as her imaginary friend, Sallie.

Among the strange phenomena that the Pickmans experienced in this house were wall pictures being turned upside down, strangely melted candles, burnt finger marks and photo anomalies. Tony even had an actual sighting of Sallie on the morning of Halloween, 1993. Also, one night he dreamed that he was being pulled out of bed by his wrist by a small girl. When he awoke, he was shocked to find burn marks on his wrist that were very similar to the fingerprints of a child.

The Kansas Paranormal Group has investigated the Sallie House over the years, and has described the hauntings as "probably demonic" because of the many violent incidents.

The house continues to be investigated by ghost hunting groups from all over the country, and these groups often report strange activity, EVP, and other phenomena. On Friday the 13th, 2012, a 72-hour investigation was broadcast live on the Internet.

66. Supermarket Spirit

A Supermarket worker at the former Kwik Save, Hightown, Wrexham, had a number of very spooky experiences during his two years employment at the store.

His first encounter with the "supermarket spirit" was when he was standing at the bottom of the stairs that lead up to the canteen and store rooms. It was almost silent, except for the sound of chairs and cups being moved upstairs. As it was late at night, nobody else was up there.

Then, one day, his boss and a colleague were in the backshop stockroom and they both heard the sound of a child crying. They went to inspect the aisles, but saw nobody there. About 20 minutes later, the worker was walking toward the backshop when he heard a high-pitched scream emit from there. Not surprisingly, the worker says he went white with shock!

The old butcher's room has also experienced some strange supernatural occurrences. Apparently, when it was being built, a man fell through the roof and died. A former worker was eating her lunch when she heard singing in her ear. The radio was also known to switch on by its own accord.

A cleaner who worked at the store claimed to be 'sensitive' to these things and, in the past, saw the upper half of a man's body in working overalls in the backshop.

67. The Bridge of Screams

Bridges can be very spooky places, symbolising a crossing between the physical world and the supernatural. There are several "devil's bridges" in Britain, and we all remember fairy tales like that of the troll which lived under a bridge, threatening to make a meal of poor Billy Goat Gruff.

There is one very haunted bridge in north east Wales: the medieval sandstone bridge that spans the Dee at Holt, on the Wales-England border. The haunting is said to reflect a despicable murder that happened soon after the bridge was built. Madog ap Gruffudd of Dinas Brân, Llangollen, had died, leaving two young sons with no trustees. According to the story, John, Earl Warren, and Roger Mortimer of Wigmore, were appointed as guardians, but the cruel lords plotted to gain for themselves the wealth the boys would inherit on their coming of age.

One night they took the boys on horseback from Chester to Dinas Brân and, as they crossed the bridge, they took down from their mounts their sleeping wards. Then, as one, they hurled the boys over the parapets into the freezing waters of the river beneath. The boys screamed in terror, begging for rescue as their sodden clothes dragged them relentlessly down. But Warren and Mortimer just callously stood and watched, waiting for their helpless victims to drown, smiling with satisfaction.

People passing by the area have reported hearing those

pitiful cries at the dead of night, echoing from beneath the bridge and constantly reminding everybody of that heinous deed.

68. The Thirsty Scholar Pub

At Wrexham's old Thirsty Scholar pub (now called Arnold's Bar), the owner had to call in a vicar to exorcise ghosts who had terrified staff and customers by throwing things at them.

In 2006, Rev Ron Evans carried out blessings at the Thirsty Scholar in Wrexham, which is believed to have once been used as a mortuary, Paranormal behaviour, included objects flying across rooms, incidents that were witnessed by both staff and customers.

The female owner, who ran the pub from May 2005 until it closed in 2006, said there had been a number of strange sightings: crisps being thrown, glasses breaking in your hand, ladles being thrown across the room, beer mats on the floor, doors opening and shutting of their own accord, and a generally cold atmosphere permeating the place.

The owner also claimed she could feel 'spirits' at around opening time, leaving people feeling scared. She also believed that there was more than one ghost haunting the place, one of which was a particularly nasty entity, as evidenced by its aggressive tendency towards throwing things and smashing glasses.

Stories about the pub's history suggest that it was once used as a mortuary, and in the cellar, there is thought to be an underground tunnel that leads to the former War Memorial Hospital, now nearby Yale College.

After the vicar's blessing, the supernatural activity seemed

Alan Toner

to calm down.

69. The House of Commons Ghost

We all know just how much history The House of Commons has got. Many a lively - and often quite heated - political debate has gone on in its chambers over the years. But did you know that the main epicentre of politics may have a resident ghost?

A strange case was reported in 1989 by a lift operator, who claimed to have had an actual encounter with a ghost. He says that he was picked up by this entity - all eleven stone of him - and hurled fifteen feet across a corridor. When he looked around for his mysterious assailant, he saw nobody. Not surprisingly, he was completely creeped out by this incident.

Staff also claim to have seen a shadowy bearded figure, clad in doublet and hose, walking through the corridors of power. A Labour MP thinks that this apparition might be that of James I, as do many other people. An eerie atmosphere always accompanies this apparition.

70. The Whistling Ghost

A LONG-dead stable lad who claimed to have been a victim of Jethart Justice is said to be haunting a pub on the Isle of Wight.

Legend says that in the 18th century the young man hanged himself in the stables adjoining the Castle Inn at Newport after a heady love affair.

Like the previous landlords, Stuart Luke and his wife Sarah have often been woken in the middle of the night by the mysterious sound of whistling. But the subsequent check for intruders in the pub always reveals the premises to be peaceful, although five pence pieces are left strewn about the place.

According to a local ghost walk guide and 17-year expert on paranormal investigations on the island, the whistling comes from the stable lad whistling at his horses.

A team of paranormal investigators and mediums spent a night in the pub earlier this year in an effort to make contact with any spirits haunting the ancient inn – the oldest on the Isle of Wight, dating from the mid-16th century. The medium, who claimed to have made contact with the dead stable lad during the investigation, told the group the long-dead groom wanted to let everyone know he had not committed suicide, but had been murdered by a woman and three men. He is said to have told her he was hoisted onto one of the stable beams where he had died of asphyxiation.

The lad allegedly owed the woman money, and when he could not pay his debts, she had him strung up. Then the medium told the team the spirit had used the words 'Jethart Justice' and 'lichwake'. Initially, these words meant little to the paranormal team, but later research on the internet revealed that "Jethart Justice" meant hanging someone first, then holding a trial afterwards. The term 'lichwake' refers to the wake, or watch, kept over a corpse before it is interred.

As Newport was more than 300 miles from Jedburgh, the intrepid investigators were unable to unearth any proof that the tragic stable boy had links to the Borders town, or even Scotland. In regard to the five pence pieces, investigators believe the coins are similar to those used in the 18th century – and the ghostly stable lad is still attempting to pay off his debt.

The Isle of Wight is now believed to be one of the most haunted places in the world, and the Castle Inn is a very popular attraction for paranormal buffs and ghost hunters.

71. Liz Taylor's Haunted House

In 1988, the actress Elizabeth Taylor was desperately trying to sell her house in Puerto Vallarta in Mexico because she believed it was being haunted by the ghost of her deceased ex-husband, Richard Burton. However, all the reports of the spooky goings-on at the palatial mansion scared off all potential buyers for nearly a year, despite Taylor dropping the original asking price from almost £1 million to £625,000.

Taylor and Burton bought the mansion as a romantic holiday home just after their second marriage, but after all the paranormal incidents she subsequently experienced in the residence, she soon came to shun the place. Maids who worked at the mansion claimed that the actress had at least four frightening encounters in the four years since Burton had died. One night, she woke up to find him lying in the bed beside her. She also saw his apparition sitting in his favourite rocking chair. On another occasion, she was forced to flee from the house crying, dressed only in her black lace nightie.

When Taylor sought the help of a spirit medium, there were also claims that she'd had the house exorcised. She is said to have told friends that she went through enough ups and downs with Burton while he was alive, without being put through more now that he was dead!

72. The Charity Shop Ghost

There is a certain little charity shop in Bedford, West Midlands, where there have been many reports of ghostly activity over the years.

The entities haunting the shop are said to be those of five people: three children and two men. The story goes that the shop was built on top of a graveyard, and many believe that the bodies of these spirits were disturbed when construction work started on the shopping centre.

The severity of the paranormal activity in the shop is such that it has dissuaded many people from visiting the place and, consequently, sales have dropped dramatically. The incidents which have occurred in the shop include items being moved around - and even thrown across the premises by unseen hands; a table in the back office being scratched during the night; mysterious dark shadows creeping around the rear of the shop, as if contemplating their next move with a view to disrupting business again. More worryingly, members of the shop's staff have complained about feeling dizzy for no reason, in addition to feelings of nausea.

The most amicable spirit in the shop is that of a man named George, who used to own a local shoe store. Staff believe he is the one responsible for moving the shop's items around because he was dissatisfied with the way they were being displayed. He conveyed the impression that he was just being helpful from beyond the grave!

Alan Toner

The spirits of the three children haunting the charity shop are called Geoff, Henrietta and Jessie. It is believed they may all have fallen victim to carbon monoxide poisoning from a faulty gas fire whilst living close to the shop. This could account for the members of staff feeling so ill - maybe they are suffering the harmful effects of carbon monoxide poisoning, as did the children when they died. The scratching on the table has been attributed to one child, who apparently just wanted something to draw on.

The fifth spirit, Fred, is thought to be the entity that is preventing people from buying anything by generating an uncomfortable, oppressive atmosphere in the shop. It is also believed that it is his shadowy figure that has been seen the most by staff. Fred is said to be a rather sad soul, due to his body being disturbed during the construction of the shopping centre, on which ground the charity shop now stands. Many believe that his corpse may have been moved to another site and was not given a religious burial. This may be the reason why he is so restless and unhappy and is still haunting the location.

73. The Pint-Pulling Spirit

In 1995, a series of spooky occurrences was reported by the landlady of the Bonnie Moor Hen pub in Stanhope, Weardale. These incidents usually took the form of the pump tap being pulled up and down by unseen hands. According to the landlady, this mysterious entity behind the bar pulled enough beer to fill a half-pint glass!

In time, both the landlady and her husband became accustomed to these paranormal incidents. However, there were some pretty scary moments that shook the couple. The pub was situated right next door to a graveyard, and whilst the couple just laughed off locals' stories of resident spirits, they did experience blood-curdling screams emitting from down in the cellar, and barrel taps being switched on and off by an unseen presence. The landlady, whilst admitting she has been disturbed by these incidents, said that to alleviate her fear, she just sings loudly all the time when she goes down into the cellar, repeatedly telling herself that the ghost - whoever's ghost it is - won't harm her.

74. The Face On The Floor

One of Spain's most famous ghost stories is the so-called Face On The Floor case.

The incident occurred in a tiny house in the village of Belmez de la Moraleda, near Cordoba. An old woman was busying herself in the kitchen preparing the evening meal when her grandchild suddenly let out a scream. The grandmother turned around from the oven and was shocked to see a tormented face staring at her from the faded pink tiles of the kitchen floor. Although she tried to wipe away the vision with a rag, the eyes just opened wider, conveying an even greater aspect of despair.

The woman sent for the owner of the house, who had the tiles taken up and replaced with concrete. But that wasn't the end of the spooky incidents, for just three weeks later, another face began to appear on the floor. This one was even more clearly defined than the first. And before long, other faces began to appear in different parts of the house.

When paranormal investigators were called in, their audio equipment detected sounds of whimpering, screams, and voices arguing with each other. Eventually, the whole kitchen floor was excavated . . . and the remains of several human corpses were found. The corpses had apparently been buried alive in 1823. Finally, when the surface was replaced, the eerie faces and sounds ceased as mysteriously as they had begun.

75. The Groping Ghost

In June 1979, a case was reported in The Daily Mirror about a rather frisky poltergeist that was harassing a teenager who lived in a reportedly haunted council house in Cannock, Staffs. The entity's lecherous advances finally caused the teenager to flee from her home.

Apparently, the sexy spirit looked like a poacher, and would grab the teenager's arm and touch her leg, conveying a clear impression that it had lascivious designs on her. It would also pin her down roughly to the bed. The teenager described the entity as having broad shoulders and black greasy hair, and clad in baggy trousers. The groping ghoul had been haunting the council house for twenty-six years, and had always had an eye for the ladies, according to the teenage girl's mother. Before her older daughter left home, the ghost would often pop out of the wardrobe to stand staring at them as they lay in bed. The entity eventually grew so brazen that the family decided they'd had enough of all this harassment, and moved out to stay with relatives whilst they sorted out what to do about the groping ghost in their home.

When they called upon the services of a local vicar to exorcise the place, so that they could move back into their home without any more supernatural trouble, their suspicions of the entity's intent were grimly confirmed when the clergyman described the house as being haunted by a

Alan Toner

"definite presence of evil".

76. The Haunted Lizzie Borden House

Everybody who is interested in famous murder cases is well familiar with the rhyme about the notorious axe killer Lizzie Borden:

Lizzie Borden took an axe
Gave her mother forty whacks
When she saw what she had done
She gave her father forty-one!

Borden was the acquitted suspect but notorious perpetrator of the horrific double murder of her father, Andrew Borden, and her stepmother, Abby, on August 4th, 1892. As a result of its rather grisly history, the former Borden residence, in Fall River, Massachusetts, has now become a major tourist attraction. Now the public can not only view the murder scene, but also spend a night in the actual house where the murders took place. The home is now called the "Lizzie Borden Bed and Breakfast" And among those tourists, there are always those who are particularly drawn by all the reported hauntings and ghostly sightings in the Borden home.

Various guests at the B&B have reported hearing voices of a woman softly weeping in the night. Some guests have seen shoes move across the floor, while others have had an older woman, in old-fashioned dress, tuck them in at night.

Lights mysteriously flicker, video equipment is suddenly turned on and off, and cameras work of their own accord. Also, the restless ghosts of Andrew and Abbey are said to wander the house where they were slaughtered.

77. Toasting The Ghosts

A historic pub - The Hanbury Arms in Pontypool, South Wales - is serving up a different kind of spirit: namely the spirits of a hangman and two children from the Victorian era.

Staff at the pub have all been reluctant to work alone for fear of seeing the ghosts of the little girl and boy, and the executioner, who is said to have once hanged criminals on the site.

There have been many reports of glasses being smashed when nobody is present and lights being switched on and off.

The owner of the pub has said that all these ghostly incidents have been so profound that you just cannot dismiss them, as there is definitely something quite paranormal going on in The Hanbury Arms.

78. The Mackie Haunting

One of the most terrifying hauntings ever recorded in the annals of paranormal research first took place in February 1695, at the Mackie Farmhouse in Scotland. This haunting was attributed to the work of a particularly violent poltergeist. Some even claimed it was the work of a demon.

Andrew Mackie, an honest, good-living and decent man, lived in the modest farmhouse with his wife and children. The property did have a reputation for being haunted, but initially the Mackies experienced nothing paranormal at all . . .until that fateful February in 1695.

The attack on the Mackies began with an assault of stones and other objects, viciously thrown by some malevolent, unseen force. The missiles struck and hit several family members. The family sought the aid of Alexander Telfair, the parish minister, who upon arrival experienced first-hand the strange phenomena. "Whatever the entity was," Telfair said, " it threw stones and other things at me, and beat me several times on the shoulders and sides with a great staff."

The hateful presence persisted in its malevolent attacks. The Mackies claimed that it attacked their children one night in their beds, delivering merciless spankings. Quite frequently, the entity would drag people all around the house by their clothes, an investigation reported. A blacksmith narrowly escaped death when a trough and ploughshare were hurled at him. Small buildings on the property spontaneously burst into flames and burned to the ground. During a family prayer meeting, chunks of flaming peat pelted them. A human shape, seemingly made out of cloth, appeared, groaning, "Hush... hush."

Considering the times in which these paranormal incidents occurred, when belief in the Devil was very much widespread, the Mackies were quick to attribute the phenomena to demons. On April 9, Andrew Mackie enlisted five ministers to exorcize the farmhouse of the hellish spirits. But the ministers found that the ritual proved anything but easy. Stones hailed down on them relentlessly. A few of the ministers, including Telfair, claimed that something had grabbed them by the legs or feet and lifted them into the air. The clergymen were not willing to concede victory to the entity, however, resolutely continuing with the ritual of exorcism for more than two weeks.

Then, on Friday, April 26, a voice from the invisible spectre declared to them, "Thou shalt be troubled 'till Tuesday." When Tuesday arrived, the witnesses watched in astonishment as a dark, cloud-like shape formed in the corner of the Mackies' barn. The cloud grew larger and blacker, until it nearly filled the entire building. Blobs of mud flew out of the cloud into the faces of the witnesses. Some were gripped by a powerful vice-like force. And then it vanished, just as it promised it would, and as mysteriously as it had come.

After months of hellish, terrifying torment, the poltergeist hauntings at The Mackie Farmhouse had finally come to an end.

79. The Ghost of Broomhill House

Broomhill House, situated in Larkhall, a small mining town close to Glasgow, is said to be haunted by the ghost called "The Black Lady".

The Black Lady's tale is quite a tragic one. She was an Indian woman called Sita Phurdeen, who arrived at Broomhill in 1902 when it's last resident, Captain Henry McNeil Hamilton, retired from the army. They met when the Captain was in service in South Africa during the second Boer war. It was reported that they were lovers. The Captain was already discontent in his marriage. Sita was brought to Broomhill as his mistress, though under the guise of a servant. But she wasn't there long.

Helen Perry recalled seeing Sita at 10pm one night, following the evening meal. The next day, Sita was gone. When he asked around, Mrs Perry was told that Sita had been unhappy and left. This seemed odd to Mrs Perry, as the last train from Larkhall was at 9pm. No one had seen Sita walk the considerable distance to the train station. Nor had the horses and carriage been out. Local rumour claimed that the Captain, regarded as an unpleasant man with a violent temper, murdered her. When he died prematurely in 1924, it was a low-key funeral; his family avoided Broomhill House afterwards. It was badly damaged by fire in

1943 and left to ruin.

The ruins of Broomhill House are said, by many psychics, to have an evil aura, which they attribute to black magic being practised there. Ghostly incidents were much reported. Many people reported seeing Sita's wraith flitting around the area. In 1954, one local girl, Jean, encountered her twice. The first occasion was at a gathering in the ruins. It had gone awry. Jean was leaving when she walked right into the Black Lady. For a moment they just stared at each other, before the ghost pointed to the ground between them. Jean didn't hang around after that, but she later returned alone to the same spot. The Black Lady reappeared and, once again, pointed to the ground. The she pointed behind Jean, who turned around . . . and was shocked to see thirteen ghosts sitting on the slope behind her!

In the 1960's, local ghost hunter, Tom Robertson, tried to exorcise the Black Lady in a live TV broadcast. In what appeared to be an act of revenge, Robertson says that she broke his back with a heavy lintel stone, and even killed one of the TV crew in a car crash shortly after the broadcast. Then, in 1990, he published photographs in the national press of what he claimed was the ghost amongst the Broomhill ruins.

In Scottish Ghost Stories, James Robertson (no relation) dismisses these strange incidents as just 'lurid' stories which do not correspond with the accounts of other witnesses.

Years ago, a woman broke her leg whilst visiting the ruins, and she was trapped there overnight, totally helpless and unable to move. She claimed that she was comforted during the night by a strange, dark lady, who suddenly vanished with the coming of dawn . . .

80. The Green Lady of Swanbourne

The ghost of a Green Lady is reported to haunt the village of Swanbourne, Buckinghamshire. The woman reputedly walks soundlessly up the main street toward the Grade II listed, 13th Century, Church of St Swithin, with her head bowed and her hands clasped, wearing a green dress. This is said to be the ghost Elizabeth Adams, who lived in Swanbourne during the 17th century.

Elizabeth was the wife of Thomas Adams, and they had four children. In 1626 Thomas was ambushed whilst travelling on the road and was killed during a robbery. He was then buried at the Church St Swithin, where Elizabeth would apparently visit his grave each evening.

Elizabeth raised her children in Swanbourne, and as they grew up and moved on, she is said to have lost the will to live after never fully recovering from her husband's unlawful killing. Eventually, she just passed away quietly.

Shortly after her death, the Green Lady started haunting the village, and those who have encountered her identified the ghost as being that of the widowed Elizabeth Adams.

81. The Ghost of Bonnie Prince Charlie

Over the years, there have been many reports of the ghost of Bonnie Prince Charlie being seen, most notably in a certain hotel in which he once stayed.

Bonnie Prince Charlie was Charles Edward Stuart and was also known as The Young Pretender. He was the leader of the 1745 Jacobite Uprising. He escaped from the Battle of Culloden and lived out his life first in France and then in Rome. He never returned to Scotland whilst alive, but in death his ghost has haunted his favourite Scottish hotel.

The Salutation Hotel in Perth began providing accommodation in 1699. In September 1745, Bonnie Prince Charlie marched from the Island of Eriskay across mainland Scotland. He used the Salutation Hotel in Perth as his headquarters. He may believe that his campaign to be King of Scotland is far from finished, because he has become the Salutation Hotel ghost. It is said that the Bonnie Prince Charlie ghost haunts the bedroom that he used.

82. Gwydir Castle

Gwydir Castle, in the Vale of Conwy in North Wales, has a long and colourful history. Not surprisingly, a building so replete in such history also has its fair share of ghost stories.

The first owner was Howell ap Coetmor, whose family members fought at the battles of Poitiers (1356), Shrewsbury (1402) and Agincourt (1415). It has also been the ancestral home of the Wynn baronets, who were descendants of the Kings and Princes of Gwynedd, and a significant Welsh family during the Tudor and Stuart periods. The Wynn's rebuilt the house in the 1490's. Gwydir Castle is now a privately owned country hotel, and it is purportedly one of the most haunted houses in Wales.

The ghosts reported to haunt Gwydir Castle are:

1. The Grey/White Lady is said to be the ghost of a servant girl who was murdered after becoming pregnant during a romance with one of the lords of the manor. She has been seen on the second floor in the north wing and along the corridor between the Hall of Meredith and the Great Chamber. The body of the murdered girl was allegedly hidden in a wall space beside a chimney breast (a priest hole). This apparition is said to be accompanied by the stench of decaying flesh. Some people have also felt themselves being tapped on the shoulder in this corridor, accompanied by the feeling of a big drop in temperature. It is not clear whether the murderer was the first or fifth Wynn

baronet.

2. The ghost of a monk has often been seen. This entity is said to have been trapped in a tunnel from a secret room.

3. The ghost of Sir John Wynn is said to haunt a spiral staircase that leads from the Solar Hall to the Great Chamber. There have been several accounts of this apparition throughout the years. He wears a tall black hat and a ruff, and has been seen walking through a wall where a door once stood.

4. The eerie sounds of crying children have been heard.

5. A phantom dog has frequently been seen.

6. A procession has been seen at night on the Great Terrace near Saint John's Arch. Gwydir Castle was last purchased in 1994 by Peter Welford and his wife Judy Corbett. They started a programme of restoration for the house, Judy Corbett has written a book of the recent history of the house entitled 'Castles in the Air'.

83. Old Tooele Hospital, Utah

Old Tooele Hospital in Utah was featured in the Stephen King movie The Stand. However, the hospital has experienced the kind of real-life paranormal incidents that could quite easily have come right out of a Stephen King novel.

The hospital was originally a home that was built by Samuel Lee for his family before it was sold. After being a poor house for the elderly in 1913, it then became a hospital. The hospital was closed down in 2000 and remained vacant until 2006, when it became an annual Halloween haunted hospital attraction. The owner was rather sceptical of the fact that the hospital could have some resident ghosts . . . that is, until he started to witness strange things for himself. These experiences decided him to call upon the services of a local paranormal group to investigate them.

The paranormal incidents witnessed in the hospital include strange mists, ghostly apparitions of a patient who was suffering from Alzheimer's Disease, and the spirits of nurses walking through the corridors and rooms of the building.

Ghost tours are held twice a month at the hospital, from January to July.

84. Royal Hope Hospital, Florida

The original Royal Hope Hospital in Florida stood on the ground of 3 Avilles Street from 1784 to 1821. The building that stands in its place now is not the original one. This hospital performed operations on the casualties from the Civil War and the Seminole War. When the town excavated the water lines, they discovered a large amount of bones believed to be Timucan Indian burial ground.

Many believe that the new building now standing there is still being haunted by the spirits of the original hospital. There have been reports of hospital beds being moved around and rolled across the floor, heavy sobbing, the sound of footsteps in the hall, the feeling of being scratched by unseen hands, and the appearance of orbs, which have been captured on camera.

85. Haunted Great Wall of China

The Great Wall of China has long been a popular tourist attraction. Built many years ago to deter any potential aggressors, like barbarians, invading China, it took centuries - and many, many workers' hands - to build the awesome wall. Eventually, the great structure was completed and it became the pride of China.

During the construction period of the wall, many workers perished on the spot. Due to the wall's immense height, countless workers accidentally fell off it and died. This is why the Great Wall of China can be described as one of the most haunted places in the world.

Some tourists visiting the Great Wall met with mysterious and sudden illnesses like nausea, aches and pains in the body, and bad headaches. Others report witnessing strange sightings, and hearing the sound of marching footsteps. Many locals are extremely reluctant to venture near the wall alone, especially at night, fearing that something horrid will happen to them if they do. The TV series Destination Truth sent an expedition to spend the night there investigating these paranormal incidents.

The Great Wall of China is not only an extremely popular sightseeing attraction, but is also a very good spot to do some serious ghost hunting!

86. Llancaiach Fawr Manor, Caerphilly

Ghosts, by virtue of their ethereal nature, tend to be rather elusive entities, but at Llancaiach Fawr Manor, near Caerphilly, they appear to be quite brazen. There have been many reported cases of them showing visitors around and pretending the English Civil War is still going on. The place has often been described as a "living museum", frozen in the year 1645, and the people in period costume are actors. However, any reassurance this gives is soon dampened, as the Tudor manor house has often said to be the most haunted in Wales.

As well as the ubiquitous spectral children, some of the most reported paranormal activity is the constant chatter of disembodied voices around the house. And there is one particular room which is said to frequently cause visitors to burst into tears.

Regular ghost tours are held at Llancaiach Fawr Manor on Thursday and Friday evenings, October-March.

87. The Ancient Windmill, Essex

The John Webbs Mill, or Lowes Mill, in Thaxted, Essex, was built in 1804 for John Webb, a local farmer and landowner. Repairs were reportedly made to a mill on this site from as early as 1377, and the current mill was constructed using material from local resources, with timber from two local farms, and the bricks were made at a nearby location in the Chelmer Valley. It was last used as a working Mill in 1910, before standing disused for over twenty years before it passed into the ownership of Thaxted Parish Council in the 1950s.

Staff responsible for the Mill's maintenance have reported hearing strange footsteps and banging coming from the upper floors when nobody is there. Eerie shadows are often seen within the building. Also, on one of the four floors, a strong feeling of being watched is a common occurrence.

A paranormal group investigating the building reported the presence of spirit children. Flickering lights, cold spots and whispering voices were also reported.

The Mill is a regular source of fascination for ghost hunters. Paranormal activity has also been captured on camera by some paranormal groups.

88. Haunted Auschwitz

The notorious Auschwitz death camp, in Oswiecim, Poland, was in operation from May 1940 until its liberation by Soviet forces in January 1945. It is thought that 2.1 to 2.5 million people were killed in the gas chambers during that dark time of human history, of whom 2 million were Jews and the remainder were Poles, Gypsies and Soviet POWs. However, the total number of deaths at Auschwitz and its sister camp Birkenau can never really be known.

Often described as one of the world's most haunted locations, Auschwitz has caused many people to experience multiple cold spots while wandering the fields, as well as a sense of dread and sadness overcoming them as they pass through the gates. Some even claim to feel the hands of spirits hold onto their own as they walk through what was once the children's centres or the gas chamber. People suddenly become intensely emotional and burst into tears, becoming totally inconsolable upon entering the camp, their sudden onrush of intense sadness still lingering even after they have left the camp.

It is claimed that birds never venture inside the camp, and on the rare occasions that they do, they never sing.

One visitor reported that someone, or something, tugged on her clothes, the sensation accompanied by a strange voice whispering to her. However, she could not make out anything but a couple of words: " please" and "leave".

Alan Toner

Over the years, there has been much photographic evidence depicting the presence of spirit manifestations in the form of misty apparitions, shadows, light anomalies and orbs.

To date, and probably out of respect for the millions of people who died there, no paranormal investigation has ever been permitted inside Auschwitz.

89. The Paranormal Playground

There is a certain playground in Huntsville, Alabama, where some people claim ghosts come out at night for a bit of playtime.

Maple Hill Cemetery is situated just outside the city, and is the oldest and largest graveyard in the area. Just behind the cemetery is a playground. To many people, this playground is also known as "Dead Children's Playground." Legend has it that after the sun goes down, strange things start to transpire there.

Over the years, there have been many reports of swings mysteriously moving by themselves, and stories of children's voices floating through the air have been posted on many Internet chat boards. There are many theories as to the exact causes of these occurrences. One rumour is that after a string of child abductions in the 1960's, many of the kidnapped children's bodies were found on the playground. One witness heard the tragic story that some kids fell off a slide, and that the spirits of these dead children never leave. These ghostly children are said to always come out at night.

Despite these spooky reports, nobody knows for sure if the playground really is haunted.

90. Hell's Gate

One of the scariest haunted places to visit on Earth is the so-called "Hell's Gate", situated at the base of Green Mountain in Huntsville, Alabama.

On Green Mountain, there is a huge mansion that has attracted the interest of locals for several years. At the foot of the mountain, about three quarters of a mile out, there is a heavy, black gate whose sole purpose is to protect the mysterious mansion from all visitors. The story goes that if anybody drives to the gate and turns to get out, a sinister phantom vehicle will suddenly appear from out of nowhere to frighten the visitor off. Usually, in normal circumstances, this would not seem so strange . . . except that this particular vehicle disappears into thin air!

Behind the area of Hell's Gate stands "Owens Cross Roads". At these crossroads, spooky chants have often been heard. There have also been reports of screams, sounds of running and walking, and various other unexplained phenomena.

91. Brede Place

Brede Place, situated in Brede Valley, West Sussex, is a 14th Century house with a rather horrible legend associated with it: it used to be the home of a cannibal, the hugely built Sir Goddard Oxenbridge, who had a rather gruesome propensity towards eating babies. He was eventually killed by the disgusted villagers, who sawed his enormous bloated body in half.

Stephen Crane, young author of 'The Red Badge of Courage', lived here for a while, and he wrote a play based on the story of the ghoulish Sir Goddard returning as a ghost. Some of his literary friends, including Henry James and H G Wells, performed it here in 1899.

In reality, though, the baby-eater does not haunt Brede Place. However, there are many other ghosts, earning it its place in the list of the most haunted places in Britain. These entities include a woman dressed in Elizabethan clothing, and a maid who was hanged in the grounds. The ghost of the headless Father John, a priest who may have died during the persecution of Catholics, is said to haunt the chapel. When Brede Place was used as a garrison for soldiers during World War 2, some officers reported seeing ghostly monks and furniture being moved about by unseen hands.

Brede Place is now a private home and not open to the public.

92. The Haunted Vicarage

Situated at the top of what is arguably the steepest city street in England – Chester's quaint St Mary's Hill – is the mysterious and haunted Old Rectory. In a corner of the churchyard of the former vicarage of nearby St Mary's Church are the unmarked graves of three local witches found guilty at Chester Assizes of black magic and conjury – and hung by the neck until dead.

A few people who have worked at the Old Rectory claim that there is a small room at the top of the house that is always icy cold. Its door often bangs shut when there's no one present, and there is never a breath of wind.

Nobody really knows what is exactly behind these strange occurrences. Could it be the ghosts of the three witches who were hung there?

Whatever the cause of this paranormal activity, it's not something that you really want to dwell on as you walk down the spooky, cobbled St Mary's Hill late at night.

93. The Old Hospital, Chester

Situated on the outskirts of Chester there stood, until recently, the old City Hospital on Hoole Lane. Many incidents of paranormal activity were experienced in the hospital by various people.

The hospital was originally a workhouse where the poor and destitute were split into male and female sections. Once segregated, they were made to live and work in harsh conditions. The workhouse later became a hospital, with all its usual suffering, illnesses and deaths.

Former patients, retired nurses and other staff report witnessing the misty shapes of human figures in the corridors. They also describe certain rooms as being icy cold, even in the middle of summer. Others report hearing the sound of beds being dragged across empty, locked wards on the floors above, or of catching the faint sob of a child in the dead of night.

Demolished in the 1990s, the site of the old hospital is now occupied by a housing estate. Do the spirits that haunted the old hospital continue to be restless in these modern dwellings? Time will tell.

94. Denbigh Mental Hospital, Wales

The North West Wales hospital in Denbigh, which now, sadly, stands derelict and abandoned, was built between 1844 and 1848. The Victorian Gothic-style asylum has been the subject of many a paranormal investigation due to its reputation for being a hotspot of paranormal activity, and in the autumn of 2008, the TV paranormal show Most Haunted Live spent a whole week there investigating the building.

The ground below the village of Denbigh was said to be the home of three witches, who were tried and executed. Before they were put to death, legend has it that they cast a curse over the land and everyone who lived on it.

As the old building was once a mental hospital, it is therefore not surprising that all the upset, pain and torture that a lot of the patients must have been subjected to has left some kind of lasting, indelible impression on the land. The ghostly sightings that have been reported there over the years are:

1. The apparitions of two old ladies, along with other ghostly figures, seen wandering through the Infirmary.
2. The sightings of a matron dressed in 1940s style uniform, plus a tall male lab assistant and two of the witches,

in the Morgue.

3. Strange figures spotted walking through the Isolation Ward.

4. Flying demonic entities, said to have been invoked by the witches who cursed the ground, on the upper floors. These creatures have also been seen by staff and inmates.

5. On the Treatment Ward (the main building), chilling screams of pain have been heard.

6. In the grounds, lab assistants have been seen, also a ghostly matron. The spirits of two murdered students have also been sighted here.

7. In the Nurses' Quarters, the apparitions of nursing staff have been seen, as have those of the witches.

In November 2008, the hospital was ravaged by a fire, just as it was being converted into apartments. Following the arson attack, some locals staged a march and protest outside Denbigh council chambers demanding that the hospital be restored. Last year it was one of a handful of sites mooted as the potential home of a North Wales prison and planning permission was granted by Denbighshire Council in 2006 to build homes and commercial buildings. Both those plans failed to materialise and permission has now lapsed on the residential scheme.

95. Preston Manor, Brighton

Preston Manor, a charming stately house on the outskirts of Brighton, has a long history of being a hotspot of paranormal activity - over 500 years of it, to be exact.

It is reported that a monastery used to occupy the site on which the manor now stands, and when the manor was built, it used the original monastery as its foundations. The colourful history of the manor - including the occupancy by a prominent Victorian family - would suggest paranormal activity from every era of its past.

Alongside the ghost of the famous Sister Agnes, there are also reports of the apparitions of a grey, black and white lady. There is also a rather lewd and cheeky ghost by the name of "Mad Jack" - the son of the manor's last owner Ellen Stanford - who has a propensity towards pinching ladies' bums, and messing around with cameras. In the Blue Room, spine-chilling sounds have been heard, and in the maid's quarters poltergeist activity has been witnessed, along with strange odours, and even ghostly pets. It is also reported that people have been locked in rooms, and doors have slammed shut of their own accord.

The TV show Most Haunted filmed at Preston Manor back in June 2006, when the crew experienced one of their most active nights of paranormal activity.

96. Wolfeton House

Wolfeton House, a grand manor house situated in Dorset, was the home of the Trenchard family for many years.

The building is said to be haunted by the wife of Sir Thomas Trenchard, who was a famous 17th Century judge. In what seemed to have been a weird kind of premonition, Sir Thomas claimed he saw the ghost of his wife while she was still alive, with blood oozing from a wound in her throat. Just a few hours later, his wife committed suicide by cutting her throat.

Another resident ghost at the house is that of a priest, an Irish Catholic clergyman by the name of Cornelius. The story goes that he was hanged, drawn and quartered at nearby Dorchester, and now reportedly haunts the staircase in the gatehouse at Wolfeton Hall. The sound of his footsteps is often heard on the stairs leading to the room where he used to stay.

There is also a third ghost reported to haunt the manor: the spirit of Sir Thomas himself. Witnesses claim to have sighted him driving a phantom coach and four horses up the main staircase of the house.

97. Treasurer's House, York

The atmospheric Treasurer's House, in York, is reported to be haunted by a variety of spirits.

One of the Aislabie family, who once owned the house, is said to have haunted the rooms for around 300 years. Sir George Aislabie was killed in a duel over one of his guests, and his ghost has been haunting the place ever since.

The most eerie ghostly sighting happened in the 1950s, when a plumber was installing pipes in the cellar. He was suddenly distracted from his work by the sound of a trumpet being blown, and as the noise drew nearer, a large horse came through the wall, astride which was a Roman soldier, closely followed by an entire army on foot.

When excavations were carried out in the city, it was discovered that the road level in Roman times was of a much lower height than it is today. This could explain why the ghostly soldiers were only visible from their thighs upwards.

98. The Hag of Pine Street

The so-called "Hag of Pine Street" was, in fact, an elderly woman that lived on Pine Street, Northwest Philadelphia, between 6th and 7th. She very much disliked noisy kids and young lovers. Whenever she saw them, she'd stick her face against the window and shake a broom at them, rattling it off the glass. She would also yell and swipe her cane at young people in the streets of Society Hill.

Not surprisingly nobody really missed the harridan when she finally died. However, her spirit proved to be very reluctant to pass over to The Other Side, as a series of strange incidents soon followed her demise. Her apparition was reportedly seen at the window, making eerie groans and screams at the passers-by.

Not surprisingly, in the light of these spooky incidents, the house remained vacant for quite a few years. Finally, house owner Betsy Bassett had had enough. She sent for a voodoo priest, who finally persuaded the pestiferous hag to pass on to eternal peace.

99. Brass Lantern, Vermont

The Brass Lantern Inn is located in the picturesque town of Stowe, Vermont. All around the Inn's exterior can be seen colourful clapboard facades and hand-painted wood signs, pastoral scenes and snow-capped hills. The Inn also has its resident ghosts.

Several guests have reported overhearing "people" arriving late to their room, talking and laughing excitedly, and loudly enough to be heard. They always talk about the good time they just had, as if they've just attended a party or dance. And the strangest thing is, no other guests happen to be registered in the room where the voices were coming from.

All of the accounts of this paranormal activity relate to the same room, always late at night, and with similar descriptions to those given by the other guests. And always, there were no guests across the hall. The real guests were the only ones occupying a room on that stairwell.

100. Thornewood Castle, Washington

The huge and imposing Thornewood Castle - also known as "the house that love built" - in Lakewood, Washington, is a secluded bed & breakfast, but is not open to the general public. A reservation is always needed to enter their premises. This in itself lends a somewhat mysterious and eerie feel to the castle. To add to the atmosphere of possible paranormal activity, they even filmed Stephen King's creepy miniseries, Rose Red, at this 500-year-old English Tudor/Gothic mansion.

But is the castle really haunted? According to some reports, the place does indeed have the odd resident ghost or two.

Some people believe one of the ghosts is the founder, Chester Thorne. Both guests and staff have reported seeing his ghost over the years. He seems to indicate his presence to the material world - especially if he disapproves of something being done - by unscrewing light bulbs in his former room.

Other ghosts said to be haunting the castle include Chester's wife, Anna. Her apparition has been seen sitting in the window seat of her former room, which overlooks the garden. Some have also seen her reflection in the mirror of her room. The Thorne's son-in-law, who shot himself in the gun closet, is said to be still roaming the castle.

According to the owners of Thornewood Castle, they believe their ghosts intend no evil or negative energy. They say that there have been accounts of guests who have contact with angels or visits from their dead relatives. They consider themselves as a kind of vortex for angelic energy.

Their own website has an extensive page about their haunted status, including guest accounts and photos, paranormal investigation reports and press releases.

101. The Ghostly Nurse

At St. Thomas's Hospital in 1943, a workman called Charles Bide had a strange experience whilst retrieving some furniture for his boss from a part of the hospital that had been damaged in the previous night's air raid.

As Charles, all alone at the top floor, was searching around for the furniture, he began to notice that the temperature in the room was dropping considerably. Simultaneously, he happened to glance in a mirror that was still intact and hanging on the wall. In its glass he saw, standing quite close behind him, a woman dressed in a nurse's uniform. The uniform was by no means modern, but looked to be in a style from the Victorian era. The nurse looked completely distraught, as if she were utterly fed up with life and even contemplating suicide. Charles just stood there, open mouthed and transfixed, without even turning to face the vision. Finally, he managed to tear his gaze away from the weird apparition and flee from the building.

When Charles relayed his vision of the ghostly nurse to a doctor, he was just told to keep the sighting to himself, for the pressures on the hospital at that time were quite considerable, and so the last thing they wanted was reports of strange apparitions, especially of ghostly nurses.

The ghostly nurse has been seen by many more people over the years, although unlike Bide, none of them has had the misfortune to encounter her whilst on their own, and in a building that was so cold, empty and in such a dilapidated state.

102. The Girl of Bluebell Hill

The following case has been well documented over the years. It has much relevance to the stories of phantom hitchhikers that have been reported by various people throughout the world.

On the 13th July 1974, in the early hours of the morning, a man by the name of Maurice Goodenough was driving home to Chatham when he was suddenly confronted by the sight of a small figure that looked like a little girl, in front of his car. The figure wore a white blouse, skirt and white ankle socks, and appeared to be ten years old. Startled by the sudden appearance of this figure, Mr Goodenough slammed down on the brakes, but he could not avoid hitting her as the car struck her with tremendous force.

Bringing the car to a skidding halt, Mr Goodenough jumped out and ran back to the slumped figure. He found her, heavily bruised and bleeding, at the side of the road. However, she didn't look quite as injured as he had initially feared. He then took a blanket from his car and gently wrapped her in it before going to summon help.

When he returned to the scene of the accident accompanied by police officers from nearby Rochester, he was stunned to see that injured girl had vanished, and that only the blanket in which he'd wrapped her was left. The police used a tracker dog in the hope of picking up the scent, but it couldn't sense anything. They then thought that maybe another passing motorist had picked the girl up and taken her to one of the local hospitals. However, if that really was the case, there were no matching records of any such hospital admission that evening.

As sometimes happens with cases like this, the police became suspicious of Mr Goodenough, and so inspected his car. However, they found no signs of damage whatsoever. So had the whole thing been nothing more than the result of a weary mind playing tricks on Mr Goodenough as he travelled along the deserted road so late at night? Who knows?

One thing that is certain, though: there have been many other reports, very similar to Mr Goodenough's encounter, of late night motorists encountering ghostly young women on that particular stretch of road by Bluebell Hill.

103. Mrs Molloy

In the early 19th Century, a lady in Perth, Scotland, sought the services of a local priest, Father McKay, to help her with a ghost that had been haunting her for some time. The lady was called Anne Simpson, and even though she was not a Catholic, she certainly had every reason to contact the clergyman.

The spirit that had been appearing to Anne every night was that of a woman whom she had known from the local army barracks. The woman was called Mrs Molloy, and she had worked in the laundry of the barracks. The ghost of Mrs Molloy was unrelenting in her pestering of Anne, and said that it owed money - three shillings and ten pence - and wanted Anne to tell the priest to set the matter straight once and for all.

Father McKay proved to be very understanding when Anne went to him, and listened carefully to her story. He then told her would see what he could do to help.

Firstly, he made enquiries at the barracks, and discovered that there had indeed been an employee there called Mrs Molloy. However, she had passed away some time before. When the priest asked if she had owed any money to anyone in the barracks, he was told that she hadn't. The priest then had to extend his enquiries further, and he visited local business owners. At a grocer's shop, he asked about Mrs Molloy, and was told that when she died, she was in debt to the grocer. And the amount of the debt was three shillings ten pence exactly.

Father McKay, out of the goodness of his heart, settled the debt and left the shop. A few days later, when he saw Anne Simpson, he asked whether she'd had any more visitations from Mrs Molloy's ghost. He was very happy to hear that the ghost seemed to have desisted from its hauntings, suggesting that now that the outstanding debt had been paid on her behalf, her spirit was now finally at peace.

104. The Beasts of Tuamgraney

Around Halloween time, in Tuamgraney, County Clare, Ireland, there have been many reports of ferocious animal ghosts being encountered in the woods there. These entities have been called "The Beasts of Tuamgraney".

Due to its eerie reputation for these ghostly beasts, many locals avoid the area, especially during Halloween. However, one young man – possibly fearless or just a hardened sceptic – went for a stroll around there one day in late October. It was a peaceful autumn day, and there didn't appear to be anything odd or malevolent lurking around. However, the man was suddenly hit by an inexplicable, overwhelming sense of unease, coupled with a great sense of sadness. He stopped for a moment, and contemplated turning back, but then shrugged off the feeling and attributed it to just his imagination playing tricks on him. He continued on, this time more cautiously, but was still unable to completely shake off the feeling of fear and foreboding that continued to plague him. There seemed to be more and more trees, and more densely packed than he remembered.

Then, just ahead of him in the overgrown path, he saw that the wood was bathed in a subdued, strange kind of light. This immediately evoked recollections in his mind of how spots like this were used in previous times for various arcane rites and rituals, many of which are said to have even involved summoning the devil himself. His unease grew.

As he made his way slowly along, he saw movement in the bushes ahead. It was a black dog, although its size was hard to fully discern in the darkened woodland.

Red-hot malevolence glowed from its glaring eyes. His first thought was that it was a stray, but his heart started pounding vigorously in his chest, the creature's sudden appearance only precipitating his fear and anxiety.

Then he jumped with shock as something leaped into his path. But it was only a hare, a big, black hare, with glaring red eyes like the dog. As it stared at him, he felt another ripple of unease run through his body. Then the hare bounded away into the bushes . . . to be replaced by a cat, whose fur was the colour of straw. It stood right in front of him in the path, back arched, teeth bared, eyes glaring. Finally, it too disappeared into the shadows.

He felt the urge to turn and flee, but then the ground beneath his feet started to rise upwards, so he decided it would be easier to press on rather than to retreat.

However, there was more to come.

The direction in which he was going led into a clearing. The sky was almost as dark as the forest cover had been, although he saw that the clearing was occupied. Two animals seemed to be engaged in some sort of struggle there: a deer hind and a black ram with wild eyes and enormous curled horns. The deer fell onto its side, wounded and exhausted, and the man thought he saw a look of appeal in its eyes. He immediately ran forward, brandishing his stick, and tried to beat off the ram. But as he deftly brought down the stick, he was stunned to find that his blow connected with just thin air. However, when the ram turned on him, he felt a vicious buffet as the ram's huge horned head butted him. Reeling from the impact, and winded, he fell to the ground and lost consciousness for a moment. When he came to, everywhere was deserted, and much to his surprise, there were only a few trees instead of thick woodland surrounding the clearing. Sides still aching appreciably from the impact of the ram's horns, he rose to his feet and slowly made his way home.

When he told of his frightening experiences back in those woods, an uncle confirmed that many other people had encountered the beasts of the phantom around the same time of the year.

105. The Haunted Willard Library

Willard Library is the oldest public library building in the state of Indiana. More than 110 years old, the library, situated in a beautiful Victorian Gothic building in Evansville, is nestled near the downtown area of this southwestern Indiana city of 130,000 people, providing a sharp contrast with the modern high-rises and six-lane freeways.

Ghost cams were set up all over the library following reports that the building is haunted by a spirit known as "The Lady in Grey". Thousands of people come to the library every year in the hope of witnessing some paranormal activity. The site is a virtual ghost-hunting Mecca.

According to reports from visitors, some of the most frequent encounters with the legendary Lady in Grey ghost have occurred in the children's reading room in the basement of Willard Library.

Willard Library has been investigated by several organizations, including MESA (multi-energy sensor array), TAPS (the TV ghost hunting team), and other paranormal groups seeking evidence of ghosts.

The first reported incident of the ghost of Willard Library occurred sixty years ago, and it involved a library employee who plodded through the freezing snow for his night shift. Since then, many other employees and visitors have reported seeing this apparition, each giving an eerily similar description. These eyewitness accounts include policemen who spotted two ghosts in an upstairs window of the library when responding to a security alarm at the building.

Other odd occurrences which have been reported in the library are: water being turned on and off, the smell of perfume, cold spots, strange and unexplained noises, books and furniture being moved around of their own accord, and feelings of being touched on the head and body by unseen hands.

106. The Wyrick House

The Wyrick House is situated in Ellerslie, Georgia, and is reported to be home to a few resident ghosts. The case of the haunted Wyrick House originally ran on the October 21, 1994 episode of Unsolved Mysteries. It was also featured in the paranormal TV series, A Haunting, and made into a movie called "A Haunting In Georgia."

The main focus of attention for the spirits haunting the historic Wyrick House was Heidi Wyrick, a gifted psychic and the daughter of Andrew and Lisa Wyrick.

It all began in February 1989, when the Wyrick family moved to Ellerslie. At the time, Heidi was just 8 years old. She started seeing the friendly apparition of an elderly man named Mr Gordy, who played with her on the property. Initially, knowing all too well how some children could have such vivid imaginations, Lisa thought this apparition was just an invisible friend. However, Heidi eventually encountered another spirit named "Con" who appeared at the front door in a t-shirt covered with blood.

When she told her mother, Lisa thought someone was trying to kidnap her daughter. Consequently, Andrew conducted a search of the entire neighbourhood for someone matching the description, but to no avail. Eventually, Lisa happened to mention Con and Mr Gordy to her sister, who had just bought the house next door.

It was later discovered that a man named James S. Gordy

had previously lived in the house. It had once belonged to Catherine Ledford's family, and when Lisa got in touch with her, Catherine verified that James had died in 1974.

James Gordy owned a real estate company in Columbus, and for many years he was a Sunday school superintendent at Ellison Methodist Church. Although she had no photographs of him, she confirmed Heidi's description that he had grey hair and wore a suit, tie, and shiny black shoes. Heidi began looking through them and picked out Catherine's Uncle Lon "Con" Batchelor. He had died in 1957 of cancer, but he had lost his hand before he was twenty-years-old in a cotton gin in Ellerslie just as she had seen him.

For the next four years, Heidi continued to encounter the benevolent spirits of the two long-dead men. In 1993, Lisa became pregnant, and an evil spirit began to make its presence known to her. This entity scared Heidi very much, and whenever she saw it in the hallway, she would instantly become hysterical.

Although Lisa and Andrew did discuss the option of moving out of the house, they feared the possibility of Heidi seeing spirits in another location. Her baby sister, Jordan, was born on February 3, 1994. Two weeks later, Lisa noticed deep scratches down Heidi's face. Andrew just assumed she had inadvertently scratched herself during the night. However, just two nights later, he too woke up with a searing pain caused by three claw marks going around his side. It was believed that the perpetrator of the scratches was the same dark entity that Heidi saw.

The famous parapsychologist, Dr. William Roll, has investigated the Wyrick House at their request. He had Heidi identify Mr Gordy's picture from a photo line-up.

She was able to correctly identify him. He consequently became convinced that the girl was having genuine paranormal experiences. However, he did wonder why all these things were happening to this little girl in particular.

The paranormal activity that the Wyrick family encountered continued to an intolerable level, until the family's minister, Brother Stephen Shelly anointed them all at the congregation to help protect them from what he believed was a demonic force.

After this, Lisa and Alex seemed reassured and strengthened by the support they received, and were more able to cope with their situation. Also, there were fewer manifestations in the house, although they didn't stop completely. At the end of the account on "A Haunting", Heidi admitted to having some continuing experiences that she would probably never reveal.

Heidi is now grown up and has left the Wyrick House. She says that while she has not seen Mr Gordy's ghost for years, she still sees the mysterious dark figure, as well as numerous other spirits. The sightings are so regular now that she just takes them for granted.

107. Eastern Airlines Flight 401

Perhaps the most famous case of paranormal phenomena in the aviation industry is that of the "Ghosts of Flight 401". Although it happened way back in the early 1970's, the case still fascinates and intrigues people to this day.

On December 29th, 1972, an Eastern Airlines Tri-Star jetliner, Flight 401, crashed into the Florida everglades. The pilot, Bob Loft, and the flight engineer, Don Repo, both perished in the plane crash, along with all the other 101 people on board. There were just 75 survivors. The cause of the crash was attributed to the entire flight crew becoming too preoccupied with a burnt-out landing gear indicator light, thus failing to notice that the autopilot had inadvertently been disconnected. Consequently, while the flight crew was distracted with the indicator problem, the aircraft gradually lost altitude and crashed.

Shortly after the disaster, the ghosts of both Loft and Repo were reported to have been seen on many occasions by various crew members on other Eastern Tri-Stars, particularly on those planes which had been fitted with parts salvaged from the Flight 401 wreckage. The spirits of Loft and Repo were described as being extremely vivid and real, and were not only reported by people who had known Loft and Repo, but also by people who hadn't known them but recognised them from their photos. Not surprisingly, the strange stories of the ghostly airmen of Flight of 401 soon spread like wildfire through the airline community. The case was even highlighted in a 1974 US Flight Safety Foundation newsletter.

In 1976, the writer John G. Fuller wrote a bestselling book about the case: The Ghost of Flight 401. The crash was also documented in Rob and Sarah Elder's 1977 book Crash. In 1978, two television movies based on the crash were shown: Crash of Flight 401, aired in October, was based on the Elders' book, and dramatized the crash, rescue efforts and NTSB investigation; while The Ghost of Flight 401, screened earlier in February, was based on Fuller's book and concentrates more on the ghost sightings in the aftermath than on the actual crash itself.

Many of the stories of the ghosts are extremely credible, and come from people in highly important positions, such as pilots, flight officers, and even a vice president of Eastern Airlines, who allegedly spoke with a captain he assumed was in charge of the flight, before recognizing him as the deceased Loft. Other sightings are convincing because they have quite a few witnesses. A flight's captain and two flight attendants claim to have seen and spoken to Loft prior to take-off, before watching him mysteriously vanish - an experience that disturbed them so much that they cancelled the flight.

Out of concern, one female passenger enquired to a flight attendant about the quiet, unmoving man in Eastern Airlines uniform seated beside her. He subsequently disappeared in full view of both of them and several other passengers, leaving the woman in a state of shocked disbelief. When she was later shown a sheet of photos depicting Eastern flight engineers, she immediately identified Repo as the officer she had seen.

Another, similarly strange, incident occurred when one of the L-1011 passenger planes that had been equipped with salvaged parts was due for take-off. The flight engineer was in the middle of carrying out the routine pre-flight inspection when Repo suddenly appeared to him and told him not to worry about the pre-flight, as he, Repo, had already done it.

Repo and Loft are apparently not content to just appear on these airplanes, but they also adopt a more active approach. For instance, a flight attendant claims she saw the spirit of a uniformed Repo fixing a galley oven. He was also seen in the compartment below the cockpit by a flight engineer, who had accessed it in order to investigate a knocking he'd heard coming from there.

Another flight attendant, Faye Merryweather, claims she saw Repo's face looking out at her from an oven in the galley of Tri-Star 318. Naturally startled, she fetched two colleagues, one of whom was the flight engineer who had been a friend of Repo's, and recognized him immediately. The trio heard Repo warn them to be on their guard about a possible fire on this plane. Sure enough, the plane later had serious trouble with its engine, and so the last leg of its flight was cancelled. What made it all the more weird was the fact that the galley of Tri-Star 328 had been salvaged from the wreckage of flight 401.

The sightings were all reported to the Flight Safety Foundation, which took them seriously and deemed them very significant. Later, records of the Federal Aviation Agency recorded the fire, which broke out on that same aircraft.

A vice president of Eastern Airlines also had a ghostly

experience when he boarded a Miami-bound TriStar at JFK airport and spoke to a uniformed captain sitting in First Class. Immediately, he recognized the captain as Loft. The apparition then vanished.

There was another ghostly incident involving a captain. Repo appeared to him, telling him that there would never be another crash, as "we" would not let it happen.

A female passenger found herself sitting next to an Eastern Airlines flight officer who looked pale and ill, but would not speak. When she summoned the stewardess, the man disappeared. This was also witnessed by several people. The woman was later shown photographs of Eastern Airlines engineers and she identified the man as Repo.

Unfortunately, further research into the paranormal incidents was severely hindered by the airline company, which obstinately refused to give their support to the paranormal investigators, despite all the witness accounts of the ghostly activity.

108. The Supermarket Ghost

A store owner in South Australia claims he has captured a ghost on videotape hurling packets of fruit snacks around his supermarket.

Brompton IGA store owner, Norm Hurst, told Adelaide Now that previous store owners had informed him that the market had a resident ghost. He is now certainly giving credence to their claims, after security camera video apparently caught something weird occurring in the market. One night, upon closing time, Hurst reportedly shut up the market with everything in order. But just before midnight, security video cameras apparently caught a Fruit Roll-Up package being hurled to the middle of an aisle by unseen hands.

One of the cameras shows the packet of Roll-Ups just arriving on the ground. It has not just slid off; it has been thrown out of the pasta. But the strange thing is, the Roll-Ups are kept 12 meters away.

Although the video of the supermarket ghost has received over 1.3 million hits on YouTube, there are some who are not convinced that is a genuine case of a haunting, dismissing it as just a hoax. Even so, a number of supernatural detectives are reportedly looking into the situation. One theory being bandied about is that the ghost causing havoc in the supermarket has a potential connection with the death of a boxer, who was gunned down in front of the store in 1998.

109. The Ghostly Chicken

One of London's most unusual spectres is said to haunt Pond Square. In fact, you could call this case that of a "Poultrygeist". If you can't guess yet just what that facetious term refers to, then read on.

Sir Francis Bacon, (1561-1626) was an eminent politician, writer and philosopher who was also a keen scientist. He was also one of the first people to subscribe to the theory that refrigeration might be used to preserve meat. One icy winter's morning in January 1626, whilst accompanied by his friend Dr Winterbourne, Bacon decided to put his theory to the test. He bought a chicken from an elderly lady on Highgate Hill. First he slaughtered it, then plucked it, and then stuffed its carcass with snow.

Unfortunately, by some strange quirk of fate that seemed to give him his comeuppance for his slaughter of the fowl, Sir Francis Bacon caught a severe cold as a result of his experiment. He was rushed to nearby Arundel House where he was placed in a damp bed. Shortly afterwards, on 9th April 1626, he died of acute pneumonia.

Ever since Bacon's death, there have been frequent reports of a ghostly white bird, resembling a plucked chicken, that materialises from out of nowhere to rush all around the square in frenzied circles, flapping its wings as it goes.

In 1943, Terence Long was walking along Pond Square

late at night when he heard the sound of horses' hooves and the low rumble of carriage wheels. Suddenly, a loud raucous shriek cut through the silence, and the ghostly, half-bald figure of a chicken appeared before him. The fowl proceeded to race frantically around, before vanishing into thin air.

Another incident of the "ghostly chicken" occurred in the 1960's, when a motorist whose car had broken down encountered the same apparition. Also, in the 1970's, a courting couple had their lovemaking rudely interrupted when the phantom fowl dropped suddenly from above and landed right next to them, squawking its head off as it went.

In recent years, though, sightings of the ghostly chicken appear to have abated.

110. Nan Tuck's Ghost

In Britain, there is a certain quiet country lane, one mile from Buxted that is reported to be haunted by a ghost called Nan Tuck.

Ms Tuck – also known as "the Witch of Tuck's Wood" - was from Rotherfield and was said to have poisoned her husband in 1810. It didn't take long for the authorities to discover the murder, and over the next few days Tuck avoided arrest by clambering over hedges and hiding in hayricks. Approaching the lane, she sought refuge in a nearby church, mindful of the old legend that if one could reach a church and touch the altar, a fugitive might evade human punishment. Spurred on by her rising courage, Tuck ran several miles down the lane towards Buxted Parish Church. However, she was too late. The local authorities were closing in on her. Utterly exhausted, Tuck ran into the woods.

Her capture became inevitable from that moment. However, she had mysteriously disappeared completely into the woodland, and was never seen again.

Nan Tuck's ghost is reported to have appeared to several people in the parish of Buxted. According to local legend, she met with a mysterious death in the woodlands. In that particular location, a circular patch of land is unfertile and no vegetation has been known to grow there.

111. The Ghostly Major

At the Naval and Military Club in Piccadilly, London, it seems that a former member has been making his presence known again more than half a century after being killed by a German bomb.

Major William Henry Braddell - who was christened the nickname "Perky" - is said to haunt the Egremont Room. A porter reported seeing the apparition, in the early hours of the morning, and it was wearing an ankle-length First World War trench coat. The porter watched the figure glide slowly from a corner before vanishing completely. The floodlights outside the club, which switch off automatically at midnight, came on as the ghost appeared at 3.07 a.m. Then they went off as the spirit faded into the wall.

The porter who witnessed this apparition, a Mr Trevor Newton, was described by staff as a very sensible and down-to-earth man, who had never heard of Major Braddell. Ever since his eerie experience, Mr Newton has been less than enthusiastic about entering the Egremont Room.

Peter Brabbs, a former club steward, instantly identified the spectre when Newton described it to him, for he had known the Major well, and instantly made the connection when the trench coat was mentioned. This was the Major's favourite form of attire, and he was actually wearing this coat when he was in the club on the 19th May 1941 when the German bomb it. Returning to the room after making a phone call, the Major was shocked to find his two fellow drinkers dead. Just a week later, the Major himself was killed by a bomb in Kensington.

Although there has been considerable interest in the case from paranormal investigators, there are no plans to actually exorcize the Major's ghost. Peter Brabbs says that he doesn't think the ghostly Major has returned from the grave to just scare people silly, but has probably come back because he was happy and content there. And it seems that the Major is not without friends either, for according to Brabbs, there are a few other ghosts said to be haunting the place. One of these spirits is said to be that of a man who went hysterical after visiting the club. This ghost always makes his presence known by the "icy blast" he sends through the rooms.

112. The Ghost of Marc Baus

The following incident was experienced by a man called John Allen, while he was cycling through France in August 1951.

After setting out on his cycle tour from Calais, he was just outside Anger in Brittany when he had a puncture. As he had come with no spare inner tube, he had to spend some time in the pelting rain trying to repair his tyre. Unfortunately, his efforts were to no avail, and so he had to start pushing his bike in the hope of reaching a village before darkness fell.

Two hours later, walking along the deserted road, he finally came upon a house in the distance and approached it, seeking either assistance or shelter. When he finally drew nearer to the building, he found that it was an abandoned and dilapidated farmhouse. The ground floor windows were all boarded up, but for some reason the door had been left unlocked. The building was redolent with the stench of dampness and decay, the furniture discoloured with mould.

Shivering with cold and feeling very tired, John thought he'd light a fire in the old fireplace. He managed to find some dry wood and placed it in the grate. Then he went out to the entrance hall to get some paraffin from the saddlebags on his bike, which he'd left there. Then something jolted him into a state of fear and unease: he saw a wet trail showing up against the dust on the hall floor. As he followed the trail into the living room, he saw that it came to an end on an old settee, on which lay a few pieces of rotting material – material that looked like the remains of a pair of pyjamas. As he picked them up, he was hit by an intense force of nausea and disgust, making him sway unsteadily on his feet.

At first, he thought that a mixture of weariness and hunger had affected him, and although he found the farmhouse rather unpalatable and unwelcoming, he decided to spend the night there, then move on in the morning. So he lit the fire . . . but it was immediately extinguished by a sudden gust of wind.

Then a sudden noise startled him. It sounded like something wet falling on the hall floor outside. When he went out to investigate, though, he found nothing there.

When he returned to trying to relight the fire, he heard the noise again, and when he looked into the hallway, he was gripped by an icy fear. The floor was now totally soaked in water, which moved towards him, ran through the doorway and reached the old pyjamas. More weirdly, the pyjamas began to assume the shape of a man as water ran from them.

This was now too much for John. Gripped by intense panic and fear, he ran from the house. Finally reaching a bar, his distress was immediately evident to the owner, and he poured him a glass of cognac. The drink seemed to help John regain some of his composure, and he began to relate his terrifying experience to the owner. As he spoke, he came to notice that nobody in the bar seemed either disturbed or surprised. After he had finished telling his story, and still feeling very tired, he rented a room. He was told not to lose any sleep worrying about leaving his belongings back at the house, as he was assured they would be safe.

Over breakfast the next morning, John discovered the

awful secret of the farmhouse. During World War II, the building had been the home of a collaborator, an artist called Marc Baus, who had betrayed many Resistance fighters. When he was finally arrested and tried in 1946, Baus was found guilty but was sentenced to just two years.

When Baus returned home after serving his two-year sentence, his house was attacked one night by a mob of people. The next day, fearful for his life, Baus disappeared. He was found dead two years later, wearing his pyjamas, in a shallow pond just behind the farmhouse. His body was taken into the house and laid out on the settee – the very spot where John Allen saw its ghost.

113. The Black Volga

During the 1960s and 1970s, there were many reports made of a ghostly black car appearing in various places right across the Soviet Union. This ghostly car struck fear into the hearts of anybody who saw it, and the story of "The Black Volga" became legendary.

The Black Volga was a limousine that featured white alloys and curtains that would often appear as if from nowhere. Also, it often featured devilish horns in the place of its rear view mirrors. It generated quite a notorious reputation for abducting children, who were then murdered for their organs, and was said to be responsible for the deaths of all that approached it, whether immediately or within 24 hours.

Another version of the The Black Volga legend tells us that vampires, mysterious priests, Satanists, body snatchers — and even Satan himself — drove the black Volga car.

Although the legend has never been proven or debunked, it's an interesting fact that Volga limousines were the most expensive cars available to Russians at the time. There is the possibility that perhaps the Black Volga represented something far more disturbing than a ghostly presence. Maybe instead it was the personification of all the fear, brutality and oppression that was administered by the seemingly omnipotent Soviet regime.

114. The Haunted Vicarage Site

A reportedly "haunted" site close to Liverpool's oldest church, All Saints, is at the centre of a planning permission battle.

The Diocese of Liverpool wants to build three houses in the garden of the vicarage at All Saints Church in Childwall, near the so-called "Bloody Acre", which was supposed never to be built on due to the fact that the area has a curse on it. However, the council is intending to refuse permission for the houses to be built, even though the church needs to build them to help funding for its refurbishment and new church hall.

Nobody really knows why this patch of land is called "Bloody Acre", for no major battle ever took place there. However, strange tales do abound of the various "entities" that are said to haunt the area, among them corpse candles, ghosts and black goblins of the acre who occasionally cross over into our physical world and cause mayhem. There is also a sinister black entity called the "Angel of Death", which is said to rise up from the acre when a world war is in the offing.

While "Bloody Acre" is something of an enigma for local historians, it is a source of utter fascination and pleasure for paranormal groups.

115. The Ghostly Lioness

In a certain zoo in Cincinnati, USA, there have been many reports over the years of a phantom lioness. It is alleged that visitors who stroll around isolated areas of the zoo alone may suddenly find themselves being stalked by the ghostly big cat. They may hear the ominous sounds of heavy footsteps and low growls. However, when they turn around, they find nothing at all behind them. Moreover, rumour has is it if you speed up your pace to try to get away from your unseen follower, the footsteps will too.

In addition to the ghostly sounds, a pair of glowing green eyes are said to shine from wooded areas of the zoo.

The book, *Haunted Cincinnati and Southwest Ohio*, by Jeff and Michael Morris, features this eerie tale of a phantom lioness that stalks her prey among the pathways of the Cincinnati Zoo and Botanical Gardens.

Nobody really knows which of the zoo's many lionesses this phantom could pertain to, or even why she should be haunting there in the first place, as there is no record of any lions ever being involved in any fatal tragedies. Thus many believe that she is simply a spiritual guardian of the zoo.

While some people say that the only time the lioness comes out is at night, others claim she pays scant attention to whatever time of day it happens to be, just so long as you are walking alone. Since the zoo is often quite busy during the day, it's difficult to find a place during normal business hours where you're completely alone, which is probably why the phantom lioness prefers to appear nocturnally.

116. The Coney Island Ghosts

Coney Island is situated on the Atlantic Ocean in South West Brooklyn, New York. It was once a hugely popular seaside resort and amusement park, attracting millions of people from all over the globe every year. However, the area's many attractions began to decline in popularity after World War II (a fact said to be attributable to the rise of private car ownership which gave New Yorkers more attractive, less crowded holidaying options) and consequently were neglected.

Another factor which may have contributed to the area's decline was the problem of the 1950's New York street gangs, whose crimes spilled onto Coney Island's once carefree streets, further dissuading people from visiting its attractions. In recent years, however, the area has experienced something of a major revamp, with the erection of hotels, the New York Aquarium, and the MCU Park Stadium, as well as the launch of a sparkling new amusement park among a couple of smaller ones. Also, the Brooklyn Cyclones minor league baseball team have set up their headquarters there.

According to local legend, there is a certain roller coaster ride at Coney Island with a tower, which is said to be haunted by the spirit of L.A. Thompson. Thompson became famous for building many roller coasters in his time, but not this particular one, so the reason why he chose it to haunt is unknown.

Moonlite Gardens, situated in the Coney Island amusement park, is reported to be haunted by a ghostly man and woman who look out from first-floor windows in the music pavilion. Also, strange mists settle over the park on clear nights. There have also been reports of Indian chanting in the picnic area.

117. The Lustful Ghost of Liverpool

In a certain house in Liverpool, a woman is being plagued by what she can only describe as a "demon ghost".

From the outside, this house looks just like any other normal, semi-detached residence on a quiet street. But inside, the house harbours dark secrets, and that includes constant incidents of paranormal activity. In fact, the house has spooked the woman's family and friends so much that they are now too scared to set foot inside.

The woman claims she has been haunted by a ghost of possible demonic origin, and is often woken in the night after the entity attempts to get into bed with her - in the style of an incubus or succubus – forcing her to flee and spend the night in her neighbour's caravan.

The woman's daughter has now moved out after being scared out of her wits by the ghost, who has smashed vases, thrown mirrors off the walls and whispered threats to those who inhabit its home.

And as if all that isn't enough, the entity has also acted in a very sexual way, stroking, groping and grabbing the woman with such over-zealous force that is has even left marks of this harassment on her skin.

Despite being terrified by all this paranormal activity occurring constantly in her home, the woman refuses to be driven out by this pestiferous entity. She says that when she first felt the phantom touching her, she totally freaked out. She regarded it as the "weirdest feeling" she'd ever experienced, and it left her with marks and bruises.

She has also seen strange shadows flitting around her bedroom at night, and she says that just the thought of these happening while she's asleep terrifies her. She is convinced that there is an incubus-like demon hiding in her bedroom, with a view to trying to seduce her and making her feel utterly powerless. She does not know what this demon looks like, or who it is.

In desperation, the woman decided to call upon the services of the Liverpool Catholic Cathedral. A priest visited her house and said mass there. He also performed an exorcism ritual and ordered the demon to depart and leave the woman in peace. But this seemed to only aggravate the demon all the more - as sometimes happens in exorcism cases – and a statue of Bhudda was flung across the room, terrifying the woman.

There have also been masses said for the woman in church, and she is grateful that people pray for her, and that so many are concerned for her welfare in her constant fight against the entity inhabiting her home.

She is worried that in addition to haunting her home, the ghost also seems to harbour lustful designs on her. She has often felt it stroking her hair and shoulders while she's watching television, and when she's in bed, she feels its invisible body pressing tightly against her own. It also flutters against her breasts, as if trying to make love to her.

She says that some people have suggested that she and the entity were partners in a previous life, but the woman doubts this very much. She has no idea who it is, and just wants it to leave her alone.

She first moved into her home in the summer of 2010. She described the area as a "friendly street", and said that the house was lovely, containing three bedrooms and a garden. Having just been through a very stressful time after her divorce, she regarded the house as a fresh start. She found the neighbours to be very hospitable, and thought it was going to be the ideal place for her to settle down in. How wrong she was.

After just seven days in the new house, weird things started to happen. A large vase in her back bedroom inexplicably fell off a shelf and smashed into pieces. Then a succession of strange noises frightened her in the dead of night. She heard doors banging and bumps, but initially she just assumed it was the wind or the usual structural sounds of a house settling down for the night. However, as time went on, she began to realise that there might be a more sinister, more paranormal explanation behind these strange occurrences.

The ghostly activity has now become so frequent that the woman is convinced that there is a demon inhabiting her home. One evening, she and her friend found two pairs of scissors arranged in the shape of a cross on the floor. She had no idea where the scissors had come from, and ran from house screaming, as did her friend.

On another occasion, she heard footsteps running down her stairs, then felt something grabbing her from behind. She says that the sensation was very uncomfortable and painful. Other times, though, the contact is more gentle, but still quite scary.

The woman first saw the apparition in 2012, when her sister paid a visit to her home to borrow a dress for a wedding she was attending. The woman took photos to see which dress her sister preferred. When they looked at the images, they were horrified, for on the bed was an image of a black demon! What puzzled them was that when the photo was taken, there was nothing on the bed at all.

From that moment, there have been countless sightings of the entity, and the woman has become so frightened that neighbours have had to come rushing in during the night. She says that she always tries to take pictures, but the spirit often refuses to make another appearance. Also, she finds herself shaking so much that the snaps come out all grainy and barely discernible. Everybody in the neighbourhood knows about the ghost, and local people make the sign of the cross whenever they walk past the woman's house.

When the woman decided to research the history of the house for some clues as to the true identity of her resident ghost, she discovered that the area was once a popular place with witches. She also found that a previous resident had the house blessed, but could not find out why.

The woman says she is still as determined as ever not to let the demon drive her from her home. However, her family have been less brave. Her daughter has now moved out, and her mother rarely visits and refuses to stay in the house any longer than she has to.

One night, the woman's sister came to stay, and at one o'clock in the morning she heard a strange, commanding voice from the TV screen screaming for her to "Get out!" Weirdly, the TV set was actually switched off at the time. Not surprisingly, the sister fled in terror from the house, and has never returned.

The woman has continued to summon the help of various other people with a view to driving the demon from her house forever: priests, paranormal investigators and mediums. Unfortunately, none of them have been successful.

More recently, the hauntings took another sinister twist, when the demon grabbed the woman in bed. She describes the incident as feeling something "heavy" leaning on her legs in the bed. It slowly worked its way up, and made a "fluttering" motion against her breasts. The woman was so frightened by this that she ran out into the street in her nightie.

The next morning, she was shocked to find bruises on her legs, and immediately went to her GP for his opinion on how they might have been caused. The doctor said it looked like the marks had been caused by some kind of injury, although the woman assured him that she hadn't accidentally knocked herself against anything.

Although the demonic ghost has driven away her family and friends, the woman still insists that she will not leave her home, and remains strong in the face of the entity's incessant persecution. She says that she is scared, but also very defiant and angry. She doesn't see why she should leave. All she wants is for the ghost to leave her alone. Whether or not it eventually will remains to be seen.

One can only wish the woman well in her brave stand against the demonic, over-amorous spectre.

118. Walt Disney Magic Kingdom Ghost

The Walt Disney Magic Kingdom Park opened in 1971 and is one of the most visited parks in the world. It is built over a warren of tunnels. Located on the Magic Kingdom grounds are Main Street, Adventure Land, Frontier Land, Liberty Square, Fantasy Land, Tomorrow Land and Mickey's Toontown Fair. This park was a major part of Walt Disney's grand vision, but unfortunately he never lived to see it being completed.

The Pirates of the Caribbean ride is the area that is supposed to be haunted. Every morning when the workers come in, they have to remember to say good morning to the ghost, or the ride does not work that day. When they try to run the ride without acknowledging the apparition, it will invariably break down.

The ghost is called George, who died while welding together the Pirates of the Caribbean in the late 1970's. There are varying stories about exactly how he met his death there, none of which have been proved beyond doubt. Various cast members claim to have seen a ghostly figure wandering around on the attraction through the monitors, but never in real life.

Aside from the ghost of George, there are allegedly a few more phantoms said to haunt various parts of Disneyland.

Alan Toner

For example, there is a spirit known as "Disco Debbie" in Space Mountain, a little boy in The Haunted Mansion, and Dolly, who met her death on the Matterhorn Bobsleds.

Other haunted locations include Tom Sawyer's Island, The Christmas Shop and the stock room of Star Trader. But the most famous spirit said to haunt Disneyland is that of the great Walt Disney himself. The two areas where Disney's ghost has been seen are in his apartment, located above the Main Street Firehouse. This is where Walt would work or spend time with his family. The other location is the former Disney Gallery, located above the Pirates of The Caribbean ride. This was originally intended to be a suite for Walt, but he died before it was complete.

119. The Korean Ghost

We've all seen photos and films of that iconic Korean ghost, like the female apparition in the horror movie The Ring. The entity usually comes in the form of a young girl with long, straight, raven-black hair framing her porcelain-white face, and has a horrifying propensity towards suddenly popping up from nowhere to terrify - and sometimes even kill - the living. But did you know that this female entity is based on a real girl, known as Arang, who is the subject of a true ghost story from the mid-1500s in the town of Miryang near Busan?

The governor of Miryang had a daughter by the name of Yun Jeongok (her nickname was Arang), a young virgin teen who was cared for by a nanny. One day, a man who was hopelessly besotted with the girl persuaded the nanny to bring the girl out on a full moon night to a place where he could approach her. On arriving at the spot, the man suddenly jumped on the girl and tried to rape her. As Arang bravely fought back against the man, she was tragically killed during the attempted rape. The man then buried her body in a bamboo forest.

After discovering that his daughter was missing, the father tried to find her, but to no avail. Simultaneously, a rumour began to circulate that she had left town with a young man, which was considered a shameful act back then. So upset and grief-stricken was her father that he resigned his position as governor and left the area.

Shortly afterwards, her father was replaced. But the man who replaced him was murdered, as were all the other men who followed him. Eventually, a young man took the position, and he had a strong interest in solving the series of deaths. One night, Arang appeared to him, and when he asked her what had happened, she told him exactly how she'd died and where her body was located. After listening to her, he promised to give her a proper burial and to set up a shrine in her memory (that shrine is still in Miryang today). The girl also said she would appear in the form of a butterfly sometime during the daytime and fly around the head of her killer. After her body was found, the young man kept his promise to give the girl proper funeral rites, and her murderer was identified and punished.

The Arangsa shrine stands on the site of the old Arangjak (the original site), and every year a ceremony is held to commemorate Arang's fight to preserve her virginity against a rapist.

This Korean ghost is called "virgin ghost" or "cheonyeo gwishin", and is synonymous with almost any restless spirit in modern times.

120. Ghosts at The OK Corral

One of the most popular stories of the old Wild West is the Gunfight at the OK Corral. This epic showdown that took place on October 26th 1881 in Tombstone, Arizona, between outlaw cowboys and lawmen has been immortalised in both movies and books. The most well known movie is the 1957 blockbuster, Gunfight at the OK Corral, which starred Kirk Douglas as Doc Holliday and Burt Lancaster as Wyatt Earp. Although the shootout was depicted in the movie as a heavily-armed affair fought at medium range, the real-life event itself lasted only about 30 seconds, and was fought at close range with only a few firearms.

In the small town of Tombstone, Arizona, the spirits of Doc Holliday and the Earps are said to be active even to this day, as the infamous shootout appears to have left quite a bit of residual energy behind. Also, there have been many paranormal investigations in the town - including visits from TV ghost show teams - after countless reports of these supernatural occurrences.

A number of people have reported seeing the figure of someone who resembled Billy Clampett walk across the corral. Others have seen spirits who look like the Earp brothers, although none of them actually died there. This is more commonly known as a "residual haunting" or place memory, which is an image caught on time and repeats itself over and over again, like an incessantly playing movie tape.

Alan Toner

At the Birdcage Theatre in Tombstone, a bullet-ridden Old West saloon that has stood there since 1881 and was once a brothel, a jealous woman murdered another who was flirting with her man by using a stiletto to cut out the offending woman's heart. The victim is among the reported 31 spirits that haunt the place, which isn't surprising, considering that at least 26 deaths have been reported in the building. The former saloon is now a museum, and staff members there have reported seeing apparitions. Also, many people have heard the ghostly strains of music and merry laughter, both inside and outside.

In addition to the haunted buildings, more ghosts are said to walk even the streets of Tombstone itself, which again isn't surprising when you remember that many incidents of violence took place there. Residents and tourists alike have seen a former madam, reportedly hanged in her nightgown, and a man dressed in old western gear leaning against a post.

121. The Haunted School House

In the small town of Prosperity, Missouri, just outside Joplin, there stands a certain a two-storey brick schoolhouse that is said to be rife with paranormal activity.

The schoolhouse was built for the children of the local miners. Classes were held there from 1907 until 1962, when the district was consolidated and the school closed.

The school was home to 1,200 students, but when it closed down there were only 32 children attending it. The building remained unused for 30 years until it was restored in the 90's as a bed-and-breakfast establishment. The hard wooden floors still display scuff marks and stains, which bear testament to the many generations of children who used to play there. Also, the old chalk trays still circle the rooms where slate blackboards use to hang.

When Richard and Janet Roberts took ownership of the building, they were not told that the place was haunted by the previous owners. However, they were really quite pleased when they found out, having stayed at the haunted Crescent Hotel in Arkansas, the Myrtles Plantation in Louisiana, and Cloudcroft Lodge in New Mexico looking for ghosts. And there have been so many unexplained incidents witnessed by various guests that the couple have started writing them all down. They have also had a few paranormal groups at the hotel, and none of them have come away feeling that their vigils were a fruitless exercise. Even Jason Hawes, the star of TV's Ghost Hunters programme, has spent a night at the building.

Among the various incidents of paranormal activity experienced at the hotel are the ghostly sounds of metal on metal, as if somebody was doing some kind of plumbing job. However, only plastic pipes have been used there. Also, strange shadowy forms have been seen by both the owners and the investigators. Ghostly footsteps walking through the building have also been heard at night, despite the fact that no guests are present. This ghostly nocturnal walker has even been known, according to a family member of a former custodian, to turn off lights and lock doors.

122. Moss Beach Distillery

The Moss Beach Distillery is situated in Moss Beach, California. During the Prohibition of the 1920's, it became one of the most popular meeting spots on the West Coast. It was also known as "Frank's Place". Among its clientele were many silent movie stars, who were probably attracted by its illegal booze. When Prohibition ended, the premises continued to be a popular restaurant, and it still is to this day.

The Distillery's most famous ghost is "The Blue Lady", an entity which has been investigated by such famous ghost hunters as Loyd Auerbachand, and TV paranormal shows like Unsolved Mysteries.

The story behind The Blue Lady goes back to the 1930's, when a beautiful young woman, possibly named Cayte, fell in love with a piano player of devious character and they started an affair, despite the fact that she was already married. The woman was tragically killed by an unknown assailant on the local beach, and it is believed that her spirit, all dressed in blue, still haunts the place in constant search of her lover.

In addition to sightings of The Blue Lady, other paranormal activity reported by various guests and restaurant staff include a levitating cheque book, mysterious phone calls, glassware moved around by unseen hands, doors that strangely lock from the inside, and anomalous magnetic field

Alan Toner

and temperature fluctuations.

123. The Haunted Antique Emporium

Bygone Times is an Aladdin's Cave of antiques, collectibles and memorabilia. Situated in Grove Mill, an old mill in Ecclestone, near Chorley, it houses four distinct warehouses of fine furniture and curios. It is an antique market with a unique shopping experience, offering something to interest and inspire every generation, with an antique fair everyday. But there is something else that the Emporium offers, and that is many fascinating stories of paranormal activity.

The long, colourful history of the Grove Mill seems to have had considerable effect on the buildings that stand on the site, for certain ghosts from those bygone times still linger. Much paranormal activity has been experienced there over the years, and word has travelled fast about the site being haunted.

One spirit that has often been seen is that of a monk, who allegedly haunts the mill. He is said to be from medieval times, and has some connection with the nearby Park Hall, which was once a monastery. He now, however, seems to prefer wandering about the area of Bygone Times.

Another phantom haunting the site is said to be the spirit of a young woman named Abigail, who was murdered during the early 16th Century.

The ghostly sound of horses galloping has frequently

been heard near Syd Brook. Also, the spine-chilling voices of deceased people have been experienced. An apparition clad in red Cavalier-style garb has also been seen wandering around what used to be the shop floor of Grove Mill. These phenomena have been attributed to the time when the site was an army base during the English Civil War.

The Grove Mill site once experienced a huge explosion caused by soldiers mixing gunpowder for army supplies. Two men are believed to have lost their lives in this explosion, and it is believed that their earthbound spirits are the ones that are still haunting the site.

The presence of a young stable boy, Jacob, has also been sensed here. He is reported to have lived during the 18th Century, and was a murder victim of his employer, an evil blacksmith. The ghost of the blacksmith's dog has also been experienced, as people have reported feeling something brushing against their legs in Bygone Times – which is probably the canine running excitedly around them.

As weaving mills were a regular place of work for young children as well as adults, it is not surprising that there have been many reports of children's ghosts still resident at the Grove Mill site. Visitors to the site have described how they have sensed these ghostly kids in Bygone Times, and how they have even seen their apparitions in the cobbled alleyway at the old mill. The ghosts of two young friends – Martha Wrennell and Mary Ann Baybutt – have also been sighted.

One of the strangest – and even comical – entities reported to haunt Bygone Times is that of a clown in a woollen hat. His ghost has been sighted in different parts of the building, and has been blamed for prodding people in the back to cheekily let them know he is around.

Another strange incident occurred when a man emptying

a slot machine in the penny arcade at Bygone Times saw one of the pennies mysteriously disappear into the ground. And another workman, this time a painter, saw a figure dressed in a smart suit walking towards him one night while he was painting part of the old mill.

On realising that the suited figure was not a living, physical being, the painter fled from the building and never returned to complete his job.

It is said that more than fifty ghosts haunt the site of Bygone Times.

124. The House of the Dead

By a lonely country path in a village situated near Pangbourne, an old house stands which is reported to contain the spirits of the dead. The house is around 500 years old. It was originally three separate cottages, and these were later converted into one house.

The strange experiences of a family who lived in the house from the mid-1950s to the 1970s were clear evidence that the place was a paranormal hotspot.

One of the first strange things that the family experienced involved the mother and daughter. They had been decorating an upstairs bedroom and were just taking a break when they were suddenly startled by a loud crash, which sounded as if the paint pots had been knocked over. When the two women dashed upstairs to see what had caused the noise, they were surprised to find that everything was exactly how they had left it. There was nothing at all out of place.

On the house's wooden staircase, many paranormal occurrences were experienced, including wooden floorboards creaking as if somebody was walking upstairs, but nobody was there. Also, the family dogs would suddenly start barking for seemingly no reason. This suggested that the pets were possibly seeing something that was invisible to human eyes – spirits, perhaps?

Oliver Cromwell was supposed to have stayed at the property after a battle near the house during the Civil War.

He is said to have kept his horses in what became the family's dining room, which became redolent with the odour of horses and stables when the weather was hot.

Another strange happening involved the family's gravel drive. They would often hear the crunch of gravel outside, as if vehicles were driving over it. However, when they went out to have a look, they saw no evidence of any such vehicle or person.

Another weird incident occurred one dark winter's night. The mother saw lights approaching the house from the main road. Her initial thought was that it was just her husband returning home. However, as the vehicle drew closer, she saw that it was not car headlights, but the lanterns of a horse-drawn carriage. Also, much to her disbelief, she saw that the carriage was not being pulled by horses. By the time she'd moved to another window for a better view, the carriage had totally vanished into thin air.

Quite often, the family would hear a knock on the door at midday or midnight, but when they went to see who it was, there was never anybody there. The family later found out that the previous owners of the house experienced the same strange thing.

125. The Stag and Hounds, Bristol

Bristol has a very haunted pub called The Stag and Hounds. Over the years, many strange occurrences have been witnessed there by different people. A building has stood on the site of the pub since the 15th Century, but the structure of the building that stands today is mainly from the 18th Century.

The Stag and Hounds has quite an interesting history. The site on which the pub now stands was formerly an open-air court - known as a Piepowders Court - set up by the Normans to deal with people who had committed offences while they were in the area attending a market or fair. Later on, the court moved into what is now the upstairs function room of the Stag and Hounds.

People have seen sinister dark shadows wandering around the corridors and corners of the pub. The apparition of a male, dressed in scruffy modern attire, has been seen on an upstairs landing. Another male apparition, wearing a trilby hat and dressed in clothes dating back to the early 1900s, has been sighted wandering around. This ghost also walks through the cellar wall, and this area is said to have a very depressing, gloomy atmosphere about it. Residents of the property next door have also seen a strange figure vanishing through walls in their own building.

Also, large orbs and similar light anomalies have been sighted inside the pub, especially around the main bar area. Some people have even complained about experiencing a heavy and energy-sapping feeling throughout their whole bodies when they've been standing in the bar, and on a few occasions glasses have been flung off tables onto the bar floor of their own accord.

Even the toilets have seen paranormal activity, as the doors of the cubicles have been seen opening and closing weirdly when nobody is around to use them. In addition, strange and inexplicable knocking sounds have been heard on the stairs of the cellar.

126. Jack The Ripper Ghosts

We are all well familiar with the story of the notorious Victorian serial killer Jack The Ripper, who was responsible for the horrific murder and mutilation of five prostitutes in the Whitechapel area of East London in 1888. But did you know that the history of Jack The Ripper has spawned many real-life paranormal experiences?

Records tell us that there have been many reported sightings of the Ripper's victims pretty much ever since they met their unfortunate ends. For instance, within a few years of Polly Nichols' murder on Bucks Row (now Durward Street), people reported seeing her body lying on the ground as it was discovered, surrounded by an unearthly glow. Apparently, it can still be seen there occasionally.

The Ten Bells Pub, on Commercial Street, is the drinking hole that is most associated with the Ripper. Its posh interior, with its grand tiled wall, has scarcely changed since the early hours of November 9th 1888, when Mary Kelly, Jack the Ripper's last victim, left the pub. Kelly's horrifically mutilated body was found next morning in Millers Court of Dorset Street, on the opposite side of the road from the Ten Bells. For several months after her murder, some people claimed they saw the ghost of Mary Kelly dressed in black and looking sadly out of the window of her room.

In the 1970's and 1980's, the pub was renamed the Jack

the Ripper, until, thanks to a landlord who was tastefully selling dark red "Ripper Tipple's", the brewery resumed its original name in 1989.

In the late 1990's resident staff, whose bedrooms were situated on the upper floors of the building, reported terrifying encounters with a ghostly old man dressed in Victorian clothing. They would often be awoken in the middle of the night by an uneasy feeling, and when they turned over in bed, they would be confronted by his ghostly form lying beside them. As they cried out in shock, the figure would disappear. Staff with no previous knowledge of his ghost would often report seeing him, and their descriptions would always match. Nobody knew exactly who this man was, and those who lived on the premises eventually just accepted him as the "oldest resident".

When a new landlord took over the pub and decided to clear out the cellar, he found an old metal box hidden away in a corner. When he opened it up, he discovered it contained the personal belongings of a man named George Roberts. The items dated from the early 1900's, and among them was a brown leather wallet. Inside the wallet was a press cutting of the same period, reporting that he had been axed to death in a Swansea Cinema. Subsequent research revealed that a man named George Roberts was indeed the proprietor of the pub in the late 19th and early 20th centuries. Consequently, the landlord concluded that it was his ghost whom staff had been encountering.

In 2001, a tenant who lived on the premises would often hear footsteps followed by a faint peal of laughter outside his door, even though there was nobody else on the premises. Whenever he went to investigate, he would invariably find the corridor outside empty. When he went down into the bar to investigate further, he would often be pushed roughly on the back by an unseen hand.

One time, a psychic was summoned to the pub to investigate the premises. When she reached the top floor, she paused outside one of the rooms and was reluctant to venture any further. Gripped by unease, she said that she could sense that something terrible had happened in the room, and was sure that it involved the brutal death of a baby in the 19th century.

A few years late, Lindsay Siviter, a top expert on Jack the Ripper, was being shown around the pub and was allowed onto the roof space. It was there that she spotted some material embedded in the floor behind the water tank. When she pulled at it, she found it was a sack tied at the top. She opened it up and found it contained a mouldy set of Victorian baby clothes that appeared to have been slashed with a knife. Significantly, the tank happened to be directly over the room that the psychic had refused to enter.

It is said that if you stand on Westminster Bride on New Year's Eve, and look eastwards as midnight approaches, there's a chance you could see the ghost of one of London's most notorious criminals. As Big Ben chimes in the New Year, a shadowy figure will suddenly materialise on the parapet and desperately leap headlong into the icy waters of the Thames below. It is said that this is the hour when, in 1888, Jack the Ripper committed suicide by plunging into the river from this spot, and that every year since, his spirit has been condemned to repeat his descent into notoriety over and over again.

And if you can't visit the area during the festive season, on misty autumn mornings you might just see a ghostly barge, which is reported to drift towards the bridge, pass beneath it, but disappear before reaching the other side.

Mitre Square is now surrounded on three sides by modern office blocks and bordered on its south side by the Sir John Cass Foundation School. All that remains of the Victorian square now is its cobblestones, across which people walk on their way to work. It was in the southwest corner of Mitre Square that the horribly mutilated body of Catherine Eddowes – Jack The Ripper's fourth victim – was discovered at 1.45am on the 30th September 1888. It is said that on the anniversary of the killing, people have occasionally glimpsed Catherine's spectral figure lying on the spot where she was murdered.

Berner Street is reportedly haunted by the phantom of poor Elizabeth Stride, who was found dead in a yard on the night of 30th September 1888. Spooked passers-by reported that late at night, they heard the unfortunate woman's screams and struggling as she was attacked, although when they peered into the darkness, they saw nothing.

The Truman Brewery, now a conglomeration of buildings, was built on the site of number 29 Hanbury Street. It was in the back yard of the Brewery that the body of Annie Chapman, the Ripper's second victim, was found at around 6 a.m. on 8th September 1888. When the brewery was operating, its customers and staff would often sense a strange chill drifting through the boardroom at 6 a.m. on the anniversary of the murder. Also, Annie Chapman's ghost was occasionally seen standing by the wall of the storeroom that occupied the spot where she died.

If you are fascinated by the Jack The Ripper case, and all the supernatural events surrounding it, you can explore all the murder sites and get a real feel for the
    complete story of the infamous Victorian killer by going

Alan Toner

on London's popular Jack The Ripper Tour, which explores all the old alleyways and thoroughfares where the murders took place in 1888.

127. Haunted Hollywood Movie Sets

Over the years, there have been certain Hollywood movie sets, especially horror movie ones, which have been plagued by real life paranormal activity. Here are just a few creepy tales from the archives.

Next to The Exorcist (1973), The Omen (1976) is ranked as one of the most terrifying movies ever dealing with the subject of the demonic possession of a child, this time a young boy, Damien Thorn, in the form of the Antichrist. In fact, The Omen has gone down in cinema history as being one of the most cursed movies ever.

The Omen tells the story of Robert Thorn (Gregory Peck) and his wife Katherine (Lee Remick), who tragically lost their son shortly after his birth in Rome. Robert secretly adopts a baby, whose mother allegedly died after giving birth. The couple raises the child as their own, naming him Damien. But it's not too long before a series of weird and often disturbing events begin to occur in Damien's presence, including the scene where his nanny commits suicide on his fifth birthday. But perhaps the creepiest and most disturbing scene in the whole picture is the one where Damien's sinister nanny (Billie Whitelaw) creeps into Lee Remick's hospital room at night and forces her into plunging to her death through the window.

Alan Toner

The string of strange events that plagued the set of The Omen is as follows:

Two months before filming of The Omen began, Gregory Peck's son shot himself in the head. Peck also narrowly escaped a plane crash when he cancelled his flight reservation. When the plane crashed, all passengers on board were killed.

The hotel in which Executive Producer Mace Neufeld and his wife were staying was bombed by the IRA, as was a restaurant where the executives and actors, including Peck, were expected for dinner on November 12th.

Scriptwriter David Seltzer's plane was hit by lightning as it traversed across the Atlantic.

Just a few weeks later, it was executive producer Mace Neufeld's turn to fly to Los Angeles, and experience the same electrifying experience during his flight. Neufeld described his ordeal as the "roughest five minutes" he'd ever had when flying.

An animal handler helped the cast and crew shoot the baboon scene in the zoo. A lion attacked him two weeks later and ate him alive.

John Moore, director of the 2006 remake, reportedly spent a whole day filming the scene where Robert Thorn would discover the ominous birthmark of his adopted satanic-son. However, the footage resulting from the hard day's work was lost when 13,500 feet of film was mysteriously destroyed in the processing lab. Moore said that the lab guys were very upset over the loss, and were unable to find any logical explanation.

The Omen jinx even seemed to follow the people who'd worked on it. The stuntman Alf Joint went to work on A Bridge Too Far, but was badly injured and hospitalised when a stunt went wrong. He only had to jump from a roof on to an airbag, an average day's work for someone like him. But this time, something odd happened. He appeared to fall suddenly and awkwardly. When he woke up in hospital, he told friends he felt like he had been pushed.

The late Pete Postlethwaite, who played Father Brennan in the 2006 remake, fell victim to the curse when his brother reportedly died after drawing an ominous combination during a card game. The combination was three sixes, and we all know what those three numbers signify!

But perhaps the creepiest of all strange coincidences was this: John Richardson, who designed the set for the 1976 movie, created a particularly gruesome scene where a photographer (David Warner) gets his head sliced off by an out-of-control lorry carrying a sheet of glass. While in Holland in August 1976, Richardson and his assistant, Liz Moore, suffered a similarly grisly fate. They were involved in a head-on-collision, in which Moore was cut in half. The horrific accident happened on Friday the 13th, near a road sign displaying the words: "Ommen, 66.6 km."

The strange stories surrounding The Omen have now been collected for a Channel 4 documentary, The Curse Of The Omen.

The sets of the Poltergeist trilogy of movies were also said to be cursed. Four actors died over the six-year period that it took to film and release them. The little blonde child star of the series, Heather O'Rourke, died of cardiac and septic shock just four months before the release of "Poltergeist III." Actor Will Sampson, also a Native American shaman, reportedly blessed the set before dying just a year later of kidney failure. Some people attributed the curse to the fact that real human bones had been used as props in the first movie, particularly in the notorious pool scene. The reason they used real corpses was because they were cheaper than the plastic ones. Craig Reardon, a special effects artist who worked on Poltergeist, said that it was cheaper to purchase real skeletons than plastic ones, as the plastic ones were too laborious to make. Not only did they use real corpses in the first film, but they also used them in the sequel.

The deaths of two of the young actresses who played sisters in Poltergeist are the events that especially make people think the movies were cursed. On November 4th 1982, six months after the filming of Poltergeist, Dominique Dunn was strangled to death by her estranged boyfriend, John Sweeney, at her Hollywood apartment. Then, in 1988, the young girl who starred in the Poltergeist trilogy, Heather O'Rourke, died while filming Poltergeist 3. The cause of her death was a septic infection resulting from a bowel blockage. The ending of Poltergeist 3 had to be filmed with a body double of O'Rourke.

JoBeth Williams, who played Heather O'Rourke's mother Diane, said that during filming she would always return home from the set every day to find the pictures hanging on her walls crooked. She would straighten them, only to find them crooked again when she returned home the next day.

Other strange stories surrounding the making of Poltergeist are claims of production delays, actresses being haunted, and even an exorcism being required.

Roman Polanski's 1968 horror movie Rosemary's Baby, which told the story of an expectant Manhattan housewife falling victim to a satanic cult next door, was believed to be cursed right from its conception. The film's composer died of a brain clot just one year after making the film, the same way a character in the film dies. Then producer William Castle suffered kidney failure soon after the film was made, and swore the movie was cursed.

Mia Farrow (who played Rosemary) was served with divorce papers by her then husband Frank Sinatra's lawyer. A year after its release, Polanski's pregnant wife Sharon Tate was gruesomely murdered in their home by followers of Charles Manson. In December of 1980, ex-Beatle John Lennon was shot dead by Mark Chapman outside the Dakota, the building where he lived, and where Rosemary's Baby had been filmed.

The Crow (1994) is a movie spin-off of the comic book of the same name. When The Crow was being filmed, strange stories were bandied about that the set was cursed. A carpenter was severely burned after the crane in which he was riding struck high-power lines. Then a sculptor who had worked on the set drove his car through the studio's plaster shop, causing much damage. Also, another crewmember slipped and drove a screwdriver right through his hand. Then a lorry full of equipment mysteriously went on fire.

The Crow was directed by Alex Proyas and starred Brandon Lee. Lee was accidentally killed during filming when his character, Eric Draven, walks into his apartment and witnesses the brutal rape of his fiancée by thugs. The bullet, unseated from a dummy round, was lodged in the barrel of the handgun. The bullet was not noticed and the gun was loaded with a blank cartridge. When the blank was fired, the bullet hit Lee in the abdomen. The original footage showing Lee's actual death was never developed, and was destroyed immediately. It remains a mystery to this day exactly who was responsible for the live rounds in Massee's gun.

Alan Toner

As the home of all the classic Hollywood horrors like Frankenstein and the Wolf Man, it's no surprise that Universal Studios has its fare share of real-life spooky stories. For instance, on Stage 28 - the lot created exclusively for the filming of 'The Phantom of the Opera' - security guards and production staff have reported seeing a ghost dressed in a black cloak. This spirit is said to be that of Lon Chaney - the Phantom himself!

The Exorcism of Emily Rose (2005) was a part-courtroom, part supernatural drama involving the possession and tragic death of a young girl, Emily Rose. Jennifer Carpenter, the actress who played Emily, thinks she was followed home after a day spent filming the eerie real life story. She says her stereo kept turning itself on in the middle of the night. This really disturbed her, as it started playing Pearl Jam's 'Alive' — but just the 'I'm still alive' part.

128. Bidston Hill, The Wirral

As the author of this book, I have to say that probably the nearest haunted location to where I live is Bidston Hill. Famous for its windmill (built in 1800) and observatory, the area has long had a reputation for paranormal activity. It is also known to be a favourite meeting place for various witches and occultists.

Bidston Hill sits on top of a warren of tunnels. Some suggest that these tunnels are used to connect the houses of witches together and that the cellar of Bidston Hall acts at the nexus.

A number of ghosts have been seen around Bidston Hill. For instance, the misty spectre of a man, said to be that of a miller who was murdered in the early 19th Century, has been seen near the windmill many times over the years. Also, the eerie phantom of Richard Tilly, who was an 18th Century Satanist, lecher and murderer, has been seen rising from its grave, like a hellish zombie, late at night. If the reports are to be believed, it seems that Tilly's lust has even extended from beyond the grave, as his ghost has allegedly assaulted young girls who have been walking through the hill late at night.

Bidston Hall was formerly a Masonic lodge, and visitors to its bedrooms – especially women – have complained about being "touched up" by unseen hands. Also, other guests wake up only to discover that they cannot move, feeling an oppressive weight on their chest or an invisible force holding them down. This feeling is very similar to the so-called "Night Terrors" phenomenon – or "Old Hag Syndrome" - which thousands of people have reported experiencing throughout history.

The Bidston Hall cellars are also reported to be hotspots of paranormal activity. Mediums believe that a number of deaths have occurred in the lodge.

In addition to its paranormal links, Bidston Hill is also popular with UFO researchers, as strange crafts and lights have been spotted in the skies there over the years. In fact, as recently as July 2012, a 25-year-old engineer, Mike Dunne, photographed a dark disc-shaped object that appeared over Bidston Hill and hovered over nearby houses before disappearing. Many other people saw this UFO as well.

129. Abraham Lincoln's Phantom Train

The ghost of the actual funeral train in which Abraham Lincoln (a keen paranormal buff himself) made his final trip is said to run through 180 cities every April.

People claim that whenever this ghostly steam engine appears, watches and clocks immediately stop. The crossing guards at the Miami Street junction also drop mysteriously when there is nothing on the tracks.

Although Lincoln himself is not actually seen on the train (save for a coffin covered by an American flag), his ghostly remains are guarded by the spirits of faithful soldiers clad in Union uniforms.

The Lincoln Ghost Train is said to emerge from a cloud of dense, black fog, towing its dark cars. Its arrival makes the air noticeably heavier and colder to everybody present. Its progress seems to mirror the 2,700-kilometre (1,650-mile) funeral procession of the actual funeral train, except that it never arrives at its historical destination of Springfield, Illinois.

Various paranormal groups and ghost hunters flock to the area every April in the hope of spotting the famous Lincoln Ghost Train.

130. Coronation Street Ghosts

Coronation Street has been on our TV screens now since the 9th December 1960. Arguably Britain's most loved soap opera, on the 17th September 2010 the programme became the world's longest-running TV soap opera. We all know Coronation Street for its depiction of a typical down-to-earth community, plus its light-hearted humour and memorable characters.

Over the years, there have been many iconic actors and actresses who have walked the cobbled streets of Weatherfield and drank in the Rovers Return, many of whom are sadly no longer with us. However, some of these deceased stars are still keeping their spirits very much alive on the Granada set, as reports of paranormal activity have been made by both the staff and the cast.

The late, great Pat Phoenix played Elsie Tanner, who was one of the original core characters on Coronation Street and appeared in the very first episode. She is still regarded as one of Coronation Street's most loved and remembered characters. Her life was just as colourful and vibrant off screen as it was on, indeed a soap opera in itself. Pat made her final appearance in January 1984, when Elsie decided to emigrate to Portugal. Pat had made the decision to quit the series in 1983 to pursue other projects. However, three years after leaving the Street, Pat died from cancer on 17th September 1986.

Some cast and crew members claim to have sensed and seen the ghost of Pat Phoenix, while others say they've been spooked by an apparition with long dark hair and wearing a long coat. They even blame this apparition for the string of bad luck that has plagued the set. Others claim to have seen Pat's ghost during the 1990 celebrations for the show's 30th anniversary. Even the show's original creator, Tony Warren, claims to have seen the ghost of Pat Phoenix wandering around the studio, and is convinced that the Corrie set is haunted. He says he would smell the strong fragrance of her perfume and that one of his dogs, who would always go bananas when Pat came to the house, suddenly started to behave as if Pat was actually present again. Although Warren describes his experience as "very odd", he says Pat is welcome at his place anytime, dead or alive.

Another iconic character of the Street was Ena Sharples, played by the late Violet Carson. She played Ena from 9th December 1960 to 2nd April 1980. She died in a Blackpool nursing home three years later. At Blackpool Waxworks, in Blackpool, Lancashire, there is a mock up of the soap opera called `Coronation Street. It is said that if you look into the window of the dummy front of a pub called 'Rovers Return`, you can clearly see a surprised face of a lady who looks very much like the late actress Violet Carson.

It is rumoured that the set of Coronation Street was built on the site of a former cemetery where around 22,000 people were buried, and many believe this adds credence to the sightings. However, some local experts believe that the set isn't built on the site of the old cemetery, but across the road from it.

The stories of Coronation Street's ghosts attracted the attention of the Most Haunted team, and they invited a small

Alan Toner

number of cast and production staff to join their investigation to discover the truth about the alleged hauntings.

131. The Haunted RAF Station

At the Montrose Air Station Heritage Centre in Scotland, there have been reports that a 70-year-old radio has been playing sounds from the Word War II era, including vintage broadcasts from Winston Churchill and the music of the Glen Miller orchestra. And the strange thing is, the Pye valve wireless at the Station has no power and is not connected to any electricity supply!

And it's not only the radio that has been the target of paranormal activity, for the aerodrome has been a hotspot for many other strange sightings and sounds for nearly a hundred years, with reports of phantom figures, creepy footsteps and door handles turning of their own accord. However, the mysterious wireless broadcasts have baffled even the most sceptical staff at the station, as they search for a logical explanation.

The apparently haunted radio set is kept in a recreation of a 1940s room. The strange broadcasts of Churchill and the Miller band come on at random, and their duration is usually up to half an hour. Experts who examined the radio removed the back, but found only spiders and cobwebs.

The most famous case involving ghostly activity at the Station was the apparition of Lieutenant Desmond Arthur of the Royal Flying Corps, who was killed when his biplane crashed. He is said to have haunted the area until honour was satisfied in 1917, when a government inquiry concluded

Alan Toner

that he had not been killed by his own carelessness, but because his plane wasn't repaired adequately.

The air station was established in 1913 by the Royal Flying Corps as Britain's first operational military airfield.

132. Haunted Yorkshire

The city of York has cultivated something of a reputation for being one of Britain's most haunted cities. Ghost tours, lectures, walks, special "ghost evenings" and paranormal weekend breaks have all become established and popular events in York. Also, over the years, there have been many books and DVDs produced appertaining to the ghosts and spirits of the city.

Now the rest of Yorkshire is starting to equal its main city in exploiting the supernatural, and ghost tourism is becoming an annual activity throughout the whole of Yorkshire.

One of the most publicised cases of a Yorkshire haunting is that of Kiplin Hall at Scorton, near Richmond. In February 2007, the 17th-Century property held ghost tours hosted by curator Dawn Webster and volunteer Mavis Palfreman. These tours proved so popular that they have now become a regular event. The ghostly activity reported at Kiplin Hall includes footsteps and the sound of sobbing in a drawing room, the apparition of a woman dressed in Victorian-style clothing on a staircase, and an airman from the 1940s in the kitchen. There has also been strange olfactory activity reported in the hall, for visitors and volunteers have smelled pipe smoke in an old kitchen, and the whiff of cologne has been sensed in another drawing room. Also, images of orbs have appeared in photos.

Another reportedly haunted building in Yorkshire that is popular with paranormal investigators and buffs is Temple Newsam House, Leeds. An entity called the "White Lady", said to be the ghost of Lady Jane Dudley who hanged herself after losing her lover to Mary Queen of Scots, has been seen a few times. Also, another phantom called "the Hissing Monk" is reported to haunt the building. Both these entities have been represented at ghost tours by various members of staff dressing up to look like them. Temple Newsam House has earned the reputation as being "the most haunted house in Yorkshire", and some people believe this title arose from its inclusion in a list of "Halloween Hotspots" that appeared in the Independent on Sunday.

Halifax Parish Church is another Yorkshire paranormal hotspot, and a popular place for ghost tours and paranormal buffs. The spirit of a headless priest reputedly haunts the church. Apparently, this phantom prefers to make an appearance when he thinks nobody is around.

At the Ring 'O Bells public house in Bradford, West Yorkshire, there is a basement in which a gravestone, with an inscription relating to the Priestly family, is hidden. Quite frequently, the spirit of an old man has been seen sitting near the fireplace. Also, there have been reports of various objects being thrown around by unseen hands, and light switches being flicked on and off of their own accord. In addition, one person claimed they saw the ghostly figure of an old woman dressed in old-fashioned clothing walking by, exuding an odour of lavender.

At the former police building in Prescott Street, Halifax, many police officers experienced strange activity when the building was in use, including whistling, doors opening and closing when nobody was around, cold spots, and ringing bells that were connected to empty cells.

At Shibden Hall, one of the jewels in Halifax's heritage crown and amongst Calderdale's best-known tourist attractions, the ghost of Anne Lister – who tried to take her life there by slitting her wrists – is often seen walking the hall after dark. Also, there have been reports of a headless coachman driving a yellow coach around the grounds. In addition, during the summer months, some people claim they have seen the ghost of a little girl who tragically drowned in a nearby pond.

The Malt Shovel pub in Oswaldkirk is reportedly haunted by the spirit of a five-year-old boy. The proprietor claims she encountered this ghost within a week of moving in. She says that one day she was walking down the stairs when she suddenly felt a strange presence behind her. Looking sharply around, she briefly saw a light shining before it vanished. She describes this light as being like a torch. An exorcism was supposed to have been performed there in the 1990s by a local clergyman. The ghost was reported to haunt the stairs and landing. Also, chairs and tables were supposed to have been thrown about the place, and objects flung through the air. Some people attribute all this paranormal activity to the fact that the body of a man called Thomas Bamber was kept for weeks upstairs by his mother before burial was finally permitted.

At the Cross Keys Inn, Saddleworth, a woman called Donna Harcourt reported seeing the figure of a little girl in her bedroom. The girl wore clothing that looked to be from the 1960s or 1970s. Around 5.30 a.m., Donna heard somebody knocking on her bedroom door, as if intent on waking her up. The knocking was then followed by a strange dragging noise coming from the passageway. Donna's daughter, Katie, also heard the dragging noise, as well as the sound of horses' hooves. Also, a reporter was spooked by a voice whispering in his ear: "Come here."

At the Old Vicarage Bookshop on Zetland Street, Wakefield, petrified staff reported seeing a plague-ridden man standing in doorways and on the stairs. Other paranormal activity reported at the bookshop included gas fires lighting themselves, and water completely flooding the basement. The paranormal occurrences first started after construction work uncovered a 17th-century gravestone in the basement of the store.

Even the Yorkshire press hasn't escaped the paranormal activity. The offices of the Barnsley Chronicle, which were built partly on the site of an old morgue, are said to be haunted by the spirit of a woman dressed in white and an eerie figure which seems to be made up of black smoke.

Nunnington Hall in South Yorkshire, which was once featured on Most Haunted, is said to be haunted by the phantom of Lady Nunnington. Witnesses have heard the sound of her dress dragging up and down the staircase, but when they have gone to investigate, the sound suddenly stops. Also, doors mysteriously open and slam shut in the middle of the night of their own accord, and sounds of sobbing have been heard, again in the dead of night. In addition, the eerie sounds of children whispering have been heard coming from the attic. In the ground floor rooms, the sounds of a party have been heard, but upon investigation, there isn't a reveller in sight and the sounds abruptly stop. Again, children's voices have been heard, and books have been seen being hurled across the room by unseen hands.

Finally, in the city of York itself, the Golden Fleece, which was also the subject of a Most Haunted investigation, is said to be York's most haunted pub. The ghost of Lady Alice Peckett, who was the wife of the mayor of York, has been seen by various people, along with up to fourteen other phantoms, including Roman soldiers and a man known as "One-Eyed Jack", who is frequently seen wearing a 17th-century red coat and carrying a pistol.

133. Haunted Railway Stations

Railway stations are, of course, places through which many thousands of people pass every day and night. They are also places where, from time to time, many tragic accidents have occurred over the years. It is therefore not surprising that there are quite a few railway stations where both passengers and staff have witnessed all kinds of paranormal activity - possibly the earthbound ghosts of different people who have lost their lives there over time.

Here are just a few of the railway stations where supernatural activity has been reported.

At the Begunkodor Train Station, India, the spirit of a white sari-wearing lady is thought to be the ghost of a woman run over by a train years ago. This phantom has been seen dancing on the platform or wandering along the tracks. Her appearance so spooked the railway workers that they abandoned the station. However, Begunkodor reopened in 2009, and railway officials denied that the closure could be attributed to the ghost.

The Waterfront Station, in Gastown, Vancouver, Canada, is an extremely busy railway station. It was built in 1915, and is said to be one of the most haunted buildings in the city. Reminiscent of a scene in The Shining, a security guard on his rounds one night saw a woman dressed in 1920's style attire, dancing to music from that decade. As he walked up to her, the woman vanished and the music stopped. Another guard encountered the glowing white ghost of an old lady who reached out to him as he approached her. Terrified, the guard fled the room. Still another guard experienced what can only be described as poltergeist activity, when a number of desks moved themselves around to bar his way out of a room. Not surprisingly, he too fled in terror from the building. Also, ghostly footsteps, phantom figures walking the rails and other paranormal activity have been experienced at the station.

In Bishan MRT Station, Singapore, various stories of hauntings began circulating right from its opening in 1987. One such strange incident occurred when a woman leaving the train one day in the early 1990s fainted. When she came round, she reported to bystanders that she had been "groped" by unseen hands on leaving the train. Also, maintenance workers have seen coffin bearers walking the tracks, headless figures have been encountered and phantom passengers have been spotted, all in or around the station. And as if all that isn't enough, people have reported hearing footsteps on the roofs of moving trains.

Glen Eden Railway Station is situated in West Auckland, New Zealand. Built to service Waikumete Cemetery, it transported the dead and those accompanying them to the local graveyard every Sunday. In 2001, a new café opened in the station building as part of a restoration, and the workers there have had a few visits from a ghostly figure, whose identity they suspect may be that of one Alec MacFarlane, who was a railway worker there in the twenties. MacFarlane was killed at 3pm on January 11, 1924 when a mailbag hook from a passing train struck him in the forehead. The witnesses of this ghost describe a man with a grey beard and a trench coat. Another worker encountered a man in a top hat who vanished before her eyes. There have also been reports of a ghostly face peering out of a window.

In the North Road Station, Darlington, there stands The Head of Steam Museum, a grand, historic building at the epicentre of the town's rail service. There is a ghost story attached to the premises that has become very famous in Darlington. It concerns an employee at the station called Thomas Winter, who committed suicide in February 1845. Suffering from depression due to a complaint made about him by an irate passenger, he shot himself in one of the gents' toilets. A few years later, James Durham, a watchman at the station, entered a cellar, which doubled as a "bait room" and a coalhouse. The instant he entered the room, he saw a stranger coming out of the coalhouse. The man, he noted, was dressed in a smart coat with metal buttons and sported a "Scotch cap". He had a large black Labrador dog with him. Without warning, the man launched an attack on Durham. The watchman fought back and threw a punch at the mysterious assailant. Durham was amazed to see that his fist went right through the man, as if he wasn't there, and collided with the wall, hurting his knuckles in the process. The stranger then clicked his tongue at the dog for it to follow him, and both man and beast walked back into the coalhouse. Durham immediately followed, only to find that both the stranger and his dog had disappeared. It was common belief that Durham had encountered the ghost of Thomas Munro Winter. This was the very same room where Winter's body had been taken and wrapped in a shroud. Since then, there have been a couple of other reported sightings of the ghost of Thomas Munro Winter.`

134. An Irish Haunting

Said to be Ireland's most haunted house, Loftus Hall is a 22-bedroom period mansion situated on Hook Peninsula in County Wexford. The isolated residence is set on 60 acres, overlooking a lonely stretch of the South East coast. Built over the remains of Redmond Hall and home of the Redmond family since around 1350, in 1666 it became the home of the Loftus family and was renamed Loftus Hall. Since it was abandoned over three decades ago, the grand building has only had structural repairs.

Loftus Hall is said to be haunted by not only the ghost of a young woman, but also by the devil himself. The building opened its doors to the public, for the first time in 30 years, in 2012, and now regular ghost tours are held there. These tours are based on the story of Anne Tottenham and a visitor to the house in the 18th century whose body, during a game of cards, went 'through the roof', leaving a hole in the ceiling which is visible to this day, and left young Anne in a state of fright.

A tourist caught on his camera a spectral female figure walking in the grounds of Loftus Hall. But it wasn't until he started flicking through his camera images whilst driving home that he noticed this figure. It is believed that the figure is the spirit of little Anne Tottenham, who became ill after an unpleasant encounter with a demonic entity. She was put into a room called the Tapestry Room to rest, and it's in this room that she stayed completely silent until she died in 1775. In addition to the image of the little girl, the tourist also captured the spooky image of an old lady looking through the window next to the front door. This ghostly photo of the little girl and the old woman went viral on the Internet.

Over the years, a number of servants have reported seeing a strange, shadowy figure roaming through the hall, causing disturbances.

135. The Ghost of TV's Superman

George Reeves played the iconic hero Superman in the 1950's TV series Adventures of Superman. His death in 1959 from a gunshot sparked much controversy, as the official verdict was suicide, but many believe Reeves was murdered or the victim of an accidental shooting. His story was dramatised in the 2006 movie Hollywoodland. Police attributed his suicide to the fact that he became depressed over his inability to get an acting job playing anything other than the Man of Steel.

The restless spirit of George Reeves is reported to haunt the Beverley Hills home where he was found dead. The stories of paranormal occurrences at the residence first started in 1969, a decade after Reeves' death. However, his lover, Toni Mannix—who inherited the place from Reeves and had struggled to keep it rented for years—refused to even broach the subject. The renters revealed that one night, while entertaining guests in the living room, they heard noises emanating from Reeves' bedroom. When they went into the bedroom to investigate, they were surprised to see it was a complete mess (it was usually kept neat and tidy). Linens had been torn off the bed, and clothes had been strewn all around. After tidying up the room and returning downstairs, they found that all the drinks on the coffee tables had been moved to the kitchen. On another occasion, the couple's German shepherd started barking like mad at the bedroom door, before suddenly cowering and slinking away, as if it had been scared by something unseen to the human eye. When the tenants peeked inside the bedroom, they discovered that the bed had mysteriously been moved across the room.

The tenants' toleration of all this paranormal activity finally wore out one summer morning, at 3.00 a.m., when the apparent ghost of Reeves, dressed in his TV Superman costume, appeared in the living room. Without any more hesitation, the tenants immediately packed their bags and moved out.

The singer Don McLean ("American Pie") recorded a song called "Superman's Ghost," about the problems Reeves had with being typecast in the Superman role.

136. Annabelle, The Possessed Doll

You are all probably familiar with the prequel to the movie The Conjuring, Annabelle (2014), which tells the story of a possessed doll. But did you know that there is actually some truth in the weird story of Annabelle?

It all started back in 1970, when a lady who was doing some shopping in a thrift store spotted a rather cute Raggedy-Ann doll. She decided to buy the doll for her daughter, a college student, who fell in love with the doll so much that she put it in her apartment. However, it wasn't long before she and her roommate started to experience strange things, things that seemed to centre around the doll.

For example, the doll would move around by itself, and was frequently found lying in another room, even though nobody had actually been near it. Also, they found small scraps of parchment paper, which they didn't even own, with kids' handwriting scrawled on them. They even found the doll standing incredibly on its rag doll legs one day.

Terrified by all this paranormal activity, the girls decided to seek the help of a psychic medium. The medium told them that the doll was possessed by the spirit of a young girl who had died in the apartment building. "Annabelle" relayed a message that she liked the college girls, and wanted to stay with them, so they told her that she could. However, granting the spirit's wish sparked off increased supernatural activity in their apartment. One of these incidents involved a male friend getting attacked by the doll one night and sustaining vicious scratch marks all over his body.

Nearly out their minds with sheer terror, the girls contacted famous psychic investigators Ed and Lorraine Warren, who'd investigated the notorious Amityville Horror case. The husband-and-wife team soon found that the doll was not possessed by the spirit of a child at all, but by a demonic entity who had lied about its identity in order to get close to the girls, with a view to perhaps possessing one or both of them. Thus the girls decided that the best thing to do would be to give Annabelle to the Warrens, who encased it in a glass display cabinet in their Occult Museum in Connecticut. The sign on the glass reads, "Warning: Positively Do Not Open." Wise advice indeed, given the sheer terror that the possessed doll brought to its original owners!

137. LaLaurie Mansion, New Orleans

Built in 1832, the LaLaurie Mansion in New Orleans - a building notorious for having once been the home of the prominent socialite and evil serial killer Marie Delphine LaLaurie - is said to be haunted by the ghosts of several of Madame LaLaurie's ill-treated slaves. This story arises from a fire that gutted the building in 1834, when neighbours helping to save furniture from the flames reportedly discovered tortured slaves chained up in the attic.

The fire had started in the kitchen, and when police entered the building, they found an elderly woman, the cook, chained to the stove from the ankle. Upon hearing all about the vicious, horrific treatment that Madame LaLaurie had meted out to these unfortunate captives, and once the fire was out, an enraged mob converged on the house and virtually destroyed it.

The current season of American Horror Story, Coven, features Kathy Bates in the role of the evil Madame LaLaurie.

LaLaurie methodically brutalised her slaves to keep them firmly under her control.

The mansion, which was rebuilt to resemble the original, was once owned by actor Nicholas Cage from 2007 until 2009.

Alan Toner

Any knowledge of what happened to LaLaurie after the fire is pretty vague. However, the writer Harriet Martineau claimed that LaLaurie fled New Orleans during the mob violence, taking a coach to the waterfront and travelling by schooner from there to Mobile, Alabama and then on to Paris. She is said to have died in Paris in a boar-hunting accident.

Not surprisingly, of all the haunted houses in America's most haunted city, the LaLaurie Mansion has surely witnessed the most gruesome history.

In regard to the supernatural activity that has occurred there, many people have reported seeing the ghost of a young slave girl fleeing across the LaLaurie roof. Agonized screams emanating from the empty house were often heard, and those who stayed there after it became occupied left after only a few days. At the turn of the century, a poor Italian immigrant who lived in the house reported seeing a black man in chains. The entity attacked him on the stairwell before vanishing into thin air. The next morning, most of the other residents abandoned the building.

The LaLaurie house has been a saloon and a girl's school, a music conservatory, an apartment building and a furniture store. The bar, also known as "The Haunted Saloon," opened in the 20th century. The owner documented the strange experiences of his customers. When it was a furniture store, the owner's merchandise was often found covered in a mysterious foul-smelling fluid. After staying up to catch the suspected vandals, the owner found the liquid had somehow re-appeared in plain sight, although no one had actually entered. Consequently, the business closed down.

People passing by the building on tour have experienced

fainting or feelings of intense nausea. Also, spine chilling disembodied screams and strange wailing sounds have been heard coming from the house. In addition, orbs have been spotted floating around the roof.

Today, the house has been restored and is a private home. Despite its horrific and turbulent history, the owner says he has experienced no paranormal activity since his residence there.

138. Haunted Roads

We all know that there are many haunted houses and crumbling old castles all over the world, but what about our roads? Although perhaps nowhere near as rife with ghosts as the aforementioned buildings, there are still quite a few roads that have had more than their fair share of paranormal activity over the years. A late-night drive down a lonely country road is occasionally all it takes to encounter supernatural activity of the most terrifying kind.

On Hawkins Hall Lane, Hertfordshire, the ghost of an old lady dressed in black has often been seen walking with a hunch. Then, according to the reports of eyewitnesses, as you walk closer to her, you realise to your horror that she has no head! The spirit is believed to be that of an old woman whose husband died unexpectedly. In a desperate attempt to be reunited with her husband, the old woman tragically hung herself.

Blue Bell Hill, Kent, has the most famous road-ghost story of all to come out of the UK. It has been reported in various national newspapers over the years, has attracted many curious paranormal investigators, and there have been many recurring experiences. Motorists driving along the road late at night have witnessed a woman suddenly running out in front of their cars. The woman frequently locks eyes with them, before being hit and vanishing into thin air. No evidence of a collision has ever been found, nor has there ever been a victim found. The ghost is thought to be that of a woman who died in a tragic car accident in the area in 1965. In addition to the ghostly woman, there have also been reported experiences of a female hitchhiker haunting Bluebell Hill. Motorists pull over to give her a lift, only for her to disappear from the back seat shortly after setting off.

The A75 Kinmont Straight, in South West Scotland, has been the scene of numerous hauntings for many years. In fact, there have been so many incidents of paranormal activity there that the road has incurred the name 'the Ghost Road' It's actually said to be Scotland's most haunted road, and has received hundreds of reports of strange sightings. For instance, in 1957, a truck driver saw a couple step right in front of his truck. Immediately panicking, he thought he'd hit them. However, when the driver stopped to investigate, the couple had mysteriously vanished.

In America, Dead man's Curve (once the subject of a pop song by Jan and Dean) is a dangerous turning intersection in Clermont County. Shaped like a gigantic horseshoe, the road was part of the Ohio Turnpike built in 1831. Over the years, many people have met their deaths there. For example, on October 19, 1969, five teenagers were killed there when their 1968 Impala was hit at breakneck speed by a 1969 Roadrunner. Only one survivor emerged from the horrific crash: a guy named Rick. Ever since, a "faceless hitchhiker is said to haunt the intersection. Rick himself has seen this ghost five times. It is described as the "pitch-black silhouette" of a man. Not surprisingly, Dead Man's Curve is said to be the most haunted place in Ohio.

On the Stocksbridge By-Pass, England, ghostly children have been seeing playing late at night under the bridge. Also, the apparition of a monk, who just stands and looks out, has been spotted. This ghostly monk has even been known to suddenly appear beside people in their cars. Other witnesses have reported hearing the sounds of children singing in the vicinity when there are none around.

The M6 Motorway is not only the longest road in the UK, but it is also its most haunted. Motorists travelling down this road have experienced a variety of strange phenomena, including Roman soldiers marching, a distressed woman trying to hitch a ride, and a lorry going the wrong way down the road. Motorists have also reported eyes peering out from bushes in Platt Lane, Leigh, Manchester - the scene of a mining disaster years before.

On the A229 from Sussex to Kent, England, a motorist encountered a girl in white with "beautiful eyes". The figure stepped in front of his car and disappeared under the front wheels. Gripped by anxiety, Sharpe stopped the car, fearing that he had killed her. However, on leaving the car, he found nothing there. Over the years, the local police have investigated many reports of people crashing into pedestrians, particularly a woman in white, only to lose track of the body. The ghostly lady is said to be that of Judith Langham, who was tragically killed in a collision on her wedding day, still wearing her dress.

139. The Real Blair Witch Ghost

The Blair Witch Project, which spawned the current found-footage craze, was the 1999 blockbuster paranormal movie which told the story of a group of young film makers terrorised (and disappearing, one after the other) by some unknown entity whilst exploring a local legend about a witch in the woods. In the village of Bradley, Lincolnshire, there is a local story that has a remarkable parallel to the eerie spectre in The Blair Witch Project. The story is known as "The Black Lady of Bradley Woods".

For many years, parents have terrified their kids with tales of "The Black Lady", warning them that if they were not in bed by a certain time, "the Black Lady will get you."

People who claim to have seen this spectre in the woods describe it as about 5ft 6in tall, and dressed in a black cloak and hood that obscures her hair. The only thing discernible of her body is a pale, sad face that suggests she has been crying.

A recent sighting of "The Black Lady" concerns two young women who had visited the adjoining Dixon Woods. Both keen photographers, the women had been taking photos in the woods. When they returned home, one of the women noticed strange figures in some of the snaps. She claims these images looked like faces, and although she says she doesn't believe in ghosts, she is at a complete loss as to exactly what these images could be. There was nobody else in the woods apart from the two women. A local parapsychologist, having carefully examined the photos, is of the opinion that the women could be blessed with psychic abilities, being able to see things that most people can't.

It is said that if you venture into the woods on Christmas Eve and shout out "Black Lady, Black Lady, I've stolen your baby!" three times, the Lady will appear to you to take back her child.

140. The Chester Hospital Ghost

Over the years, there have been many reports of a ghost haunting the Countess of Chester Hospital in Chester, England. The ghost is said to be that of a woman in a white veil, and many members of staff and patients have reported seeing this spectre in various areas of the hospital.

The hospital stands on the site of the old Cheshire County Lunatic Asylum, built in 1829. The asylum was later replaced by the hospital, which was opened by Princess Diana in 1984 and renamed the Countess of Chester Hospital. The hospital takes its name from one of Diana's former titles: Countess of Chester.

The most recent case involving a sighting of this ghost was reported by a man who took a photo of his grandfather in the hospital, in the hope that it would be an image he could treasure after the pensioner was told by doctors that his bladder cancer was terminal. However, when the man got back home and examined the photo, he was stunned to see an eerie figure of a woman dressed in a veil and apparently standing right behind his grandfather. When he showed staff at the Countess of Chester Hospital the photograph, they told him that it looked to be the image of the 'long haired blonde girl', who, they claim, a lot of patients see standing at the end of their beds.

Alan Toner

And the strange thing about all of this is, the ghostly figure may have had some impact on the grandfather's condition, as he has since been released from hospital and claims to be sleeping better than before, despite the previous grim diagnosis. He also believes that the ghostly apparition is "watching over him."

141. The Legend of Robert The Doll

There is no doubt that dolls have been a great source of amusement for both children and adults since time immemorial. However, occasionally, there can be a rather dark side to them as well a light side. This suggestion might instantly evoke perturbing images in your mind of Chucky, the demonic doll from the Child's Play movies. But perhaps the most famous true story of an American haunted doll is that of Robert The Doll.

Robert was a lifelike doll which stood 3 feet tall, had buttons for eyes, human hair, and was filled with straw. Dolls that resembled children were rather common around this time, but this one proved to be rather unusual. Robert belonged to Key West painter and author Robert Eugene Otto, and it had been given to him by a Bahamian maid who was in the Otto family's employ. Robert named the doll after himself, and often dressed it in his clothes. Robert the doll became his regular companion, and he took it with him everywhere he went. In 1906, the maid who'd given the doll to Robert cursed the toy after Robert's parents fired her when they discovered she'd been secretly practising black magic. Following the maid's bitter departure, a series of weird happenings began to occur in the Otto household.

Young Robert loved talking to his namesake, and servants

swore blind that the doll actually talked back. They also claimed that the toy had the ability to change expressions at will, and move about the house unaided by any human hand. Even the neighbours witnessed the doll move from window to window when the family was away. Also, members of the Otto household heard insane bursts of laughter coming from the toy.

Robert the Doll unnerved plenty of people during the day, but at night he focused most of his attention on young Robert Otto. The boy would often wake in the middle of the night, screaming in terror, as the heavy furniture in his room crashed to the floor, apparently of its own accord. When his parents demanded to know what had happened, Otto always attributed the disturbance to Robert the Doll.

Robert Otto died in 1974, and his eerie doll now sits on display at the Fort East Martello Museum in Key West, still clad in his white sailor suit and clutching his stuffed lion. It is said that the doll will curse anyone who takes a photo without permission, which Robert grants by slightly tilting his head. Anybody who forgets this can always beg for forgiveness, which is exactly what camera crew from the Travel Channel did after their camera mysteriously malfunctioned!

It is cases like this that might suggest, especially to hardened sceptics, the anxiety disorder known as Pediophobia, which is the fear of dolls, a relatively common kind of phobia. It is a disorder pertaining to a wide range of dolls, from old-fashioned china dolls and porcelain dolls, to dolls that can talk and move. However, in the case of Robert the Doll, it is quite obvious that there is something much more going on here than just a simple irrational fear of dolls . . .

142. The Mysterious Moving Coffins

In the cemetery of the Christ Church Parish Church in Oistins, Barbados, there stands a structure called the Chase Burial Vault. The Caribbean paradise of Barbados is especially noted for all the stories bandied about there over the years about "mysterious moving coffins," and this case is certainly a good example of these strange occurrences. The story has become one of the most enduring and enigmatic mysteries on the island.

The vault was built half sunken into the ground, and is constructed out of compacted blocks of the coral that comprises much of the island's foundations, as well as concrete. The vault is entered by descending stone steps and is sealed by a huge slab of blue marble that reportedly required around seven men to move. According to local reports, each time the heavily sealed vault was opened in the early 19th century to inter a family member, all of the lead coffins had mysteriously moved around. The actual details of the story are unconfirmed, and consequently sceptics do regard the whole thing as rather dubious. Nevertheless, there are still many people who actually give credence to the story, and firmly believe that paranormal forces are very much at work at Chase Burial Vault.

The tale appears to have stemmed from anecdotes

Alan Toner

related by Thomas H. Orderson, Rector of Christ Church during the 1800s, and subsequently retold in James Edward Alexander's 1833 Transatlantic Sketches.

143. The Manila Film Centre

The Manila Film Centre, located at the southwest end of the Cultural Centre of the Philippines complex in Pasay City, Philippines, is the site of a construction accident which occurred there in the early 1980s. When construction of the centre was stepped up for a film festival, the ceiling scaffolding collapsed, killing several workmen. Rather than halt construction to rescue survivors and retrieve the bodies of the dead workmen, Imelda Marcos, the First Lady and the main financier of the project, allegedly ordered cement to be poured into the orchestra, entombing the fallen workmen, some of whom were even buried alive.

Many incidents of paranormal activity have been reported on the site, including strange sounds, eerie voices and poltergeist activity. Also, bleeding walls and arms sticking out from under doors have been witnessed. These supernatural occurrences have been attributed to the angry ghosts of the construction workers who lost their lives in the building.

Naturally, with a tragedy of such appalling proportions, there are bound to be restless souls still lingering around the building. Some of these ghosts have even been spooking guests of nearby buildings. In one such case, a stranger approached a passer-by, who gave him a calling card and asked him to telephone his family and tell them that he was well, and that he would be leaving soon. When the passer-by made the call, a stunned voice explained that her husband was dead - his body was among those encased in the film centre!

In the late 1990s, a group called the Spirit Questors paid regular visits to the film centre, with a view to contacting and appeasing the souls of the workmen.

Although some of these spirits have apparently moved on, a few are said to remain.

144. The Haunted Wal Mart

At the Wal-Mart store in Panorama City, CA, the ghost of a woman apparently killed in an elevator accident has been witnessed. According to reports, this female phantom appears on the third floor, and items of stock tumble to the ground when there's no one around. Many people have also reported experiencing eerie feelings in the elevators and upper floors, including sensations of coldness. One evening, a department manager heard someone call his name and felt a tap on his shoulder. However, when he turned around, he was stunned to see that there was nobody there.

Later research into this ghost, however, discovered that it wasn't actually a woman who was killed in an elevator accident there, but a 15-year-old boy named Durrell Beazer. In 1985, Beazer and two pals got trapped in the elevator and escaped by crawling out through the top. Unfortunately, the elevator then suddenly moved and crushed Durrell with its weights. The accident happened at The Broadway department store, which is now Wal-Mart.

At another Wal Mart store in 776 S. Route 59 Naperville, IL, staff have experienced several types of supernatural activity. For example, warehouse workers have reported cold spots and intense feelings of unease, while store employees have often seen securely placed items falling off shelves of their own accord. Though the Wal-Mart is now open 24-hours, before the policy change, several night staff encountered, on various occasions, a woman in white wandering through the aisles after closing. When they would attempt to escort this mysterious customer from the store, the woman would disappear into thin air.

145. Island of the Dolls

On Lake Teshuilo in Xochimilco, near Mexico City, there is a certain island called La Isla de la Munecas which, due to the strange happenings that have occurred there over the years, has been dubbed "The Island of the Dolls". For decades it has been home to hundreds of dilapidated - and rather sinister looking - dolls. In fact, aside from the eerie atmosphere evoked by all the dolls, the island is actually said to be the creepiest place in Mexico.

In the 1950's, a man named Julian Santan Barrera moved to the island, totally unaware of the strange history surrounding the location. According to local legend, three young girls were playing near the water in the 1920's, when one of the girls fell in it and drowned. Local people believed that ever since her death, the young girl's ghost has been unable to leave the island. Consequently, the island soon generated quite a reputation for being a paranormal hotspot, and locals refused to venture anywhere near it at night for fear of experiencing any supernatural activity.

Julian claimed that as soon as he moved on the island, a little girl began holding conversations with him from beyond the grave. The girl told Julian every detail of her tragic death, and that she was now trapped on the island. Spooked by this ghostly visitation, he then began to sell off fruit and vegetables that he had grown on the island so that he could buy old dolls for her to play with, in the hope that she would then leave him in peace. He gathered them from dump heaps and hung them all around the island like eerie Christmas decorations. For over half a century, he amassed more than 1,500 of these creepy-looking dolls. The oldest doll is still there, hanging in a shed by the entrance. From a distance, it looks very much like the decaying corpse of a young child.

Julian later told his nephew that it was becoming harder to satisfy the girl's craving for these dolls. He was even worried that she wanted him to join her in her watery grave. On the same day he had this discussion, his nephew was returning to the island when he found his uncle lying face down in the canal. His body was in the exact same spot where the little girl had apparently drowned seventy years ago.

To this day, tourists to the island often report of the doll's eyes following them everywhere they go. Others have also claimed that the mutilated dolls whisper in their ear, especially at night. Julian's ghost is also said to haunt the island, as well as the young girl's.

146. Ghosts of the Kremlin

The Kremlin in Moscow, Russia, is a building steeped in all sorts of history and mystery. And alongside all those much-told legends and myths, there are also some pretty creepy stories of paranormal activity. The Kremlin, according to hundreds of witnesses, is most certainly haunted.

The most famous ghost stories of the Kremlin concern three leaders: Tsar Ivan the Terrible, who reigned Russia in the 16th century; Vladimir Lenin, who led the 1917 Bolshevik Revolution; and the notorious Soviet dictator Joseph Stalin. It is said that Ivan's shadow can occasionally be seen and his footsteps heard in Kremlin's Ivan the Great Bell Tower. There have also been reports of his spirit visiting the last tsar, Nikolay II and his wife, on the night before Nikolay's coronation. Many regarded this as an omen that the Romanov royal dynasty would fall.

Lenin is also thought to be a frequent visitor to the Kremlin. His ghost was allegedly first seen by a security chief in October 1923, even though he was still alive at that time and would not die for another three months yet. The official was puzzled as to why Lenin came with no guards accompanying him, but then was informed on the phone that in fact Vladimir Ilich was in Gorky at that time. Subsequently, other witnesses claimed they saw Lenin in the Kremlin that night, but certain discrepancies in their stories have only perpetuated the mystery. Lenin was in very bad health at the time, and couldn't walk without the aid of a stick. However, those who claimed they saw him in the Kremlin that night said he had no stick, and was in fact walking quite effortlessly and rapidly. Was Lenin's spirit somehow separated from his body months before the time of his death?

But it is Joseph Stalin who is said to be the most frequently seen apparition in the Kremlin. Some believe his phantom wants to establish order and stability in the country, and so usually appears when Russia is suffering a major crisis. Legend has it that one of the usual signs that Stalin is haunting the Kremlin is when the room suddenly becomes very cold. Staff in the Kremlin, and even politicians, have noted the appearance of their former leader with a great sense of unease. When Stalin was alive, he had a few painters shot for not portraying him as accurately as he wished. Perhaps that's why no one has dared take a blurry photograph of his ghost!

147. Spooky Celebrity Ghosts

It is always a very tragic moment when we hear news of another celebrity who has just passed away, especially if that celebrity happens to be one that we have loved for so many years. But have they really left us for good? Here are just a few true-life cases which seem to suggest that the spirits of our deceased idols may still be wandering the earth.

The spirit of 'I Love Lucy star' Lucille Ball is said to still haunt the house where she once lived. Residents have reported windows being mysteriously broken, furniture being moved around and items disappearing and reappearing. They have also experienced sounds of a party going on up in the attic, punctuated by raised voices, as if revellers are talking over the loud music. Also, Lucy's spirit is said to frequent the Hart Building at the Paramount Studio where the 'I Love Lucy' show was produced. Night watchmen have reported experiencing her ghost haunting the upper floors, exuding a profound scent of an old perfume redolent with the smell of flowers.

The legendary horror movie actor Lon Chaney Sr. passed away in 1930, but his ghost is said to be still active right to this day. People have seen his apparition at Sound Stage 28, which was where The Phantom of the Opera was filmed. It is said that Chaney's spirit likes to make appearances wearing a cape on the stage, and it also appears to be responsible for the lights going on and off by themselves, as well as doors that open and close of their own accord. Montgomery Clift was a hugely popular star from the '40s and '50s. He is perhaps best known for his role in the film 'A Place in the Sun.' Like Marilyn Monroe, he also haunts the Roosevelt Hotel in California, having spent three months there, learning his lines for his next movie project. His ghost reportedly haunts Room 928, and even though the room is unoccupied, strange noises can still be heard coming from it. Also, the phone is frequently found off the hook, and the room always feels chilly. Some visitors have reported that they've even experienced Clift's presence too, one guest claiming that she felt a ghostly hand touch her shoulder.

Thelma Todd was a popular 1930s actress who starred alongside the Marx Brothers and Buster Keaton. She eventually became an entrepreneur and opened up her own restaurant, Thelma Todd's Sidewalk Cafe, where her ghost is often sighted today. The starlet passed away in 1935 from carbon monoxide poisoning, but her ghost has often been seen in the building that used to be her beloved restaurant, descending the stairs.

Ozzie Nelson was best known for his singing skills. He also starred in the television show 'The Adventures of Ozzie and Harriet.' Ozzie's ghost is still being seen long after his death. Owners of Ozzie's former residence report that the faucets are turned on and off by invisible hands, doors open and close on their own, and the lights switch on and off. One owner even claims that Ozzie's spirit was teasing and flirting with her, for one night she felt the bed covers being moved slowly down her body, and felt light kisses being planted on her neck.

Roger Daltrey, lead singer with The Who, claims to have spoken with the band's deceased drummer Keith Moon, who tragically died of a drugs overdose in 1978.

Daltrey says he's spoken to Keith's spirit on a number of occasions, and has even sought the services of a female psychic, who has no background knowledge of either Daltrey himself or Moon.

Jane Fonda, daughter of late movie star Henry Fonda (who died in 1982), claims her father's spirit visits her regularly. She says she welcomes the great interest he seems to take in her work.

Lee Ryan, lead singer of the pop group Blue, has a keen interest in the supernatural, and claims that he has been visited by the spirit of dead rock legend Janis Joplin, who apparently gave him some useful advice. She told him to improve his vocal ability by working on his lower range. She also advised him not to take drugs, for that is how she herself died. Ryan firmly believes that the star is still watching over him. Initially, he didn't really know who Janis Joplin was, then he found that she was this massive rock star.

The late pop star Michael Jackson claimed that he could communicate with the spirit of dead pianist and vocalist Liberace, and even had a secret room in his house for the purpose. Apparently, Jackson claimed that Liberace gave him permission to re-record his song 'I'll Be Seeing You'. The singer felt that Liberace was very close to him, and regarded the deceased pianist as his "guardian angel".

Elvis Presley, the King of Rock 'n' Roll, who tragically died in August 1977, is said to still Gracelands. He has also appeared to stagehands in his famous white sequinned outfit at the Vegas Hilton, where he performed frequently back in the 1970s. The King has also made a ghostly appearance at the old RCA recording studios from the 1950s, the site where he recorded his first big hit 'Heartbreak Hotel.' It's not a recording studio anymore, but is still used as a TV studio for music projects. Many workers have reported witnessing strange occurrences every time somebody mentions Elvis, such as unexplained noises on the sound system and the lights mysteriously being switched off.

148. The Surrey Ghost Crash

In December 2011, a very strange incident occurred on the A3 Motorway between Portsmouth and London. The incident has gone down in Surrey folklore as "The Surrey Ghost Crash".

It all started on a dark December Sunday night in 2002, when a member of the public reported seeing a car lose control, with its headlights blazing, and swerve off the A3 around 100 metres before the emergency slip road at Burpham. When the police were called to the scene to search for the wreckage, they were initially unable to find any indications of a crash. It was as if the vehicle had just vanished into thin air. But then an officer stumbled upon a gnarled and rusted maroon Vauxhall Astra lying nose down in a ditch, just 20 yards from the road, windshield spider-webbed, driver's door smashed in, and covered in undergrowth. Furthermore, lying not far from the car, was a badly decomposed body.

After forensic examination, police identified the body from dental records as that of a 21-year-old man, Christopher Chandler, who was last seen in London on the 16th of July. He'd been on the run from the Metropolitan Police since July 16 that year. He was wanted for robbery. The police therefore concluded that the car had crashed five months prior to its discovery.

Not surprisingly, the findings generated much hysteria

and speculation from the public, as it was suggested in the national press that the sighting of the car swerving off the road the night before could only have been a ghostly replay of the fatal crash earlier in the year. However, this view was certainly not shared by Surrey Police, as they insisted that the incident had only ever been treated as a normal road accident, and the fact that the car was obscured by leaves and branches probably prevented it from being reported sooner.

So is it really possible that what those worried motorists saw that night was a ghostly re-enactment of the crash that claimed that young man's life? Who knows?

149. Music Hall Ghosts

Built in 1878, Music Hall is one of Cincinnati's most treasured buildings, and was designated a National Historic Landmark in 1975. It is Cincinnati's top classical music hall, and serves as the home to many popular local orchestras. It is also well familiar to paranormal buffs as one of Cincinnati's most haunted sites, with many stories of paranormal activity dating from the early 1800s.

Various people who have worked at the hall have described experiencing strange occurrences. One music conductor, now deceased, once stated that whilst working late at night in the hall, he'd experienced "people" upstairs. He described these apparitions as "friendly", and even invited any disbelievers to pay a visit to the hall in the early hours of the morning to see these "people" for themselves.

Another incident involved a certain exhibitor, who saw the figure of a tall, young and fair lady standing before his booth. The lady was clad in an old-fashioned dress, and wore her long hair flowing loose and unrestrained by any hat. When he approached the white figure, it became diaphanous, faint, and finally vanished into thin air, leaving behind it an unnatural chill that bit into the man's bones.

On President's Day 2003, a box office assistant working alone at Music Hall experienced several unusual events in the form of strange noises. He heard music stands in the lobby falling over, but found the stands still upright when he checked. The button to alert him that a customer was at his window rang a few times, but no one was there. He heard what sounded like the crystal chandelier in the lobby crashing to the floor and shattering. When he investigated, the chandelier was still hanging from the ceiling. He heard the glass doors in the lobby opening and closing all day long, even though there was nobody else in the building apart from himself. When he walked down to the restroom near the Critic's Club to see if anybody was there, he heard what sounded like a party going on inside the Critic's Club, with glasses tinkling, muffled voices, laughter, and the sound of a string quartet. But the strange thing was, the Critic's Club was locked and the lights were all switched off. When he knocked on and shook the door, the sound instantly stopped.

Another box office worker also reported having his call button pressed by an unseen visitor. Later on, he felt a tug on his clothing, and when he turned around, he was confronted by the apparition of a boy dressed in nineteenth century clothing. A night watchman described hearing footsteps following him on a nearby hardwood floor, even though was walking on carpet and not making any sound. A member of the maintenance crew claims he heard a piano playing a few times, only to find the hall empty. He also saw closed doors suddenly open, and witnessed a floor buffer turning itself on-and-off in the ballroom. Other staff at Music Hall have heard strange footsteps, doors slamming, and music playing, even though there is not another living soul in the building.

Other paranormal occurrences include phantoms dressed in vintage clothing in the ballroom late at night, an extra, unknown "cast member" appearing during an operatic production, mysterious figures appearing among the audience, the untraceable sound of a music box playing near an elevator, and a small boy asking about a man in the audience of Springer Auditorium when only himself and his father were present.

Many attribute all this supernatural activity to the fact that throughout its history, excavations in and around Music Hall have uncovered ancient human bones. In fact, a map from 1830 shows that the south part of the structure was built over a Potter's Field. It is believed to be these souls and spirits that haunt the rooms of Music Hall.

Music Hall was selected as one of The Travel Channel's Most Terrifying Places in America.

150. The Ghostly Witches

We all know just how much witches have always had a very close association with all things spooky and paranormal. With their stereotypical image of black pointed hat, haggard face, boiling pot and broomstick, they are just the perfect personification of Halloween. But of course, in reality, there is much more to witches than just that much-repeated, almost cartoon-like aspect, and that includes actual ghostly apparitions of witches.

A couple of years ago, in St. Osyth, Essex, there was a case reported in the local newspapers about a 37-year-old woman who lived in a cottage which, she claimed, was plagued by ghostly witches. She had only been living in the cottage for a few weeks when the paranormal activity first started. The ghosts apparently haunting her home would creep up behind her and hit her in the back, pull her hair, and try to push visitors down the stairs. They would also move objects around, rattled doorknobs and turned on taps. More disturbingly, they also made spots of blood appear in the hall.

The woman finally reached the end of her tether when she gave birth. When her son Jesse was born, she saw a male apparition standing over his cot. After three years of putting up with all this paranormal activity, she decided that she just couldn't live like this anymore, and so she fled her dream home - a home that had now become a living nightmare -

taking her baby son with her.

She later discovered that there were 12 ghosts there in total, and that the cottage - known as 'The Cage' - had once been a medieval jail. Thirteen women from the village, accused of witchcraft, had been imprisoned there whilst awaiting trial, among them Ursula Kemp, who was The Cage's most famous inmate. She was reportedly the most powerful and notorious of all the women, making her living as a midwife and a healer. She was executed before the others in 1582.

The woman still has the £147,000 mortgage for her haunted cottage hanging over her head, but she has taken drastic steps to address that by opening up her former home to ghost tours.

The most well known haunting involving a witch in the United States is The Bell Witch incident. In fact, it is the only known case of a ghost legally being responsible for the death of a person: the patriarch of the Bell family, John Bell Sr.

The Bell Witch Haunting is a poltergeist legend from Southern United States folklore, involving the Bell family of Adams, Tennessee. The story inspired the films An American Haunting (2006) and The Bell Witch Haunting (2004). The first manifestation of the haunting occurred in 1817, when John William Bell, Sr. encountered a strange animal, with the head of a rabbit and the body of a dog, in a cornfield on his huge farm in Robertson County, on the Red River, near Adams, Tennessee.

Bell shot at it several times with his rifle, but the creature escaped unharmed, and John went on home, not thinking any more about it. However, there followed a series of strange beating and gnawing noises manifesting outside and eventually inside the Bell residence. Betsy Bell, the family's younger daughter claimed to have been assaulted by some strange, unseen force. The witch entity seemed to derive particular sadistic delight in targeting John Bell himself for her incessant tormenting. She venomously and repeatedly cursed "Old Jack Bell," and warned him that she would eventually kill him, beat him and cause his tongue to swell so that he could hardly breathe, talk or swallow. When he died in 1820, a bottle of mysterious liquid was found near his bed, in the place of his medicine, which the witch claimed she had poisoned him with. The entity even made an appearance at Bell's funeral, laughing demonically and singing a song about a "bottle of brandy". It is said that her singing didn't stop until the very last person left the graveyard. The entity's presence became virtually non-existent after Bell's death, as if its purpose had finally been fulfilled.

Over the years, there has been much speculation and uncertainty as to the witch's true identity. Some believe it was someone who had been cheated by Bell, while others think it was a male slave whom Bell had murdered.

The eerie, disturbing events on the Bell Farm are still being talked about to this day, and some people even believe that the spirit returned in 1935, the year when the witch claimed it would come back to take up its place again on the property. Strange, unexplained things are said to still occur in the area, such as the faint sounds of people talking and children playing. There have also been sightings of "dancing candle lights" in the dark fields late at night.

The most famous account of the Bell Witch Haunting is recorded in what has come to be called the Red Book, the 1894 An Authenticated History of the Bell Witch of

Tennessee by Martin Van Buren Ingram, which cites the earlier Richard William Bell's Diary: Our Family Trouble. Richard Williams Bell lists several witnesses, including General (later President) Andrew Jackson. Signs at the entrance to the Bell Witch Cave promote ghost tourism in Adams, Tennessee, and the site continues to attract many tourists and paranormal groups every year.

In Native American legend, there is an entity called the Skadegamutc, or ghost witch. This is said to be an undead monster of the Wabanaki tribes, and was allegedly spawned following the death of a wicked magician who refuses to stay dead, but returns to life at night to kill, eat, and cast curses on any humans who are unfortunate enough to encounter it. The only way to destroy this kind of ghost-witch is by fire.

The most famous witch trials ever recorded in the UK are the Pendle Witch trials of 1612. The twelve accused witches all lived in the surrounding Pendle Hill area and were charged with the murders of ten people by means of witchcraft. Also known as the Lancaster Witch Trials, the Pendle trials saw eight of the witches being tried at Lancaster Castle with the Salmesbury witches and others. Another witch was tried at York and a twelfth witch died in prison before her trial. Around 500 witches were executed in total between the early 15th and early 18th centuries. The significance of the Pendle witches is evident here, in that it accounts for more than 2% of that total. Of the eleven people that were tried - nine women and two men - ten were found guilty and executed by hanging, and one was found not guilty.

The twelfth witch died in prison.

The Pendle Hill witches are said to still haunt the buildings and the villages. Visitors have reported feeling anger when visiting the grounds. Local people are also too scared to discuss the events that went on during the witch trial.

To this day, Pendle Hill continues to be linked with witchcraft and the paranormal. Hundreds of visitors climb it every Halloween, much to the disapproval, though, of the local authorities. The area is also very popular with ghost hunters and paranormal groups after Most Haunted visited it for a live investigation on Halloween 2004. Show host Yvette Fielding said it was the scariest episode they had ever made. The team reported being hurt by a mysterious presence. Some even said that they experienced the sensation of being strangled by unseen hands.

151. The Solicitors' Office Ghost

As the author of this True Ghost Stories series, I have had many ghost stories related to me over the years, many of which I have been able to use for both my books and for my website www.trueghoststories.co.uk

Among these stories is a particular favourite of mine, which was told to me by my mother, who first heard it from a young lady with whom she worked at a Wirral confectioners shop back in the early 90s. I think you'll agree that when you read this story, it's quite a creepy one. Here it is.

The young girl in question, before starting the job at the confectioners, commenced employment at a Birkenhead solicitor's office. On her first day there, she had to pop upstairs to fetch some important files for her colleagues. As the room containing the files was situated right at the very top of the building, the girl had to climb quite a few flights of stairs to get there.

Once inside the room, she began to rummage around for the files. Suddenly she heard the sounds of voices, interspersed with bouts of laughter and brisk footsteps, in the next room. Her first thought was that a couple of her colleagues had followed her up. Retrieving the files, she left the room and popped her head around the door of the adjoining one, expecting to see her colleagues in there. But she was surprised to see that the room was empty.

When she went back downstairs, she asked her colleagues if any of them had followed her up to the top of the building. They looked at one another and told her no, none of them had been up there at all. They then had to confess to her that the office had a resident ghost, and that the sounds she'd heard coming from the adjoining room had probably been made by that same entity.

Naturally, the girl was shocked to hear this, and so much so that she actually gave her notice in the same day. When she told her husband that she'd left the job after only one day, he looked at her in utter disbelief, and demanded to know why. When she told him of her ghostly experience, he said that it was ridiculous to give a good job up like that just because she'd experienced something strange. However, she was quite determined that she would never set foot in the office ever again.

The area where this incident happened does contain quite a few old buildings dating back to the Victorian era, and so it's hardly surprising that there may be the odd ghost or two still haunting certain premises here.

152. The Uninvited Wedding Guest

One of the most favourite ghost photos of all time on the Internet is the one called The Uninvited Wedding Guest. It was taken in October 1972 by a professional photographer, who was commissioned to snap pictures of guests arriving at the wedding reception of friends whose son had just got married in Paisley.

On the photo are four people – two women flanked by two men – and crouching behind the man in the bow tie and tuxedo, on the right of the photo, appears to be a mysterious figure wearing open-toed sandals. The photographer was at a complete loss as to a logical explanation for the appearance of this figure, for as far as he was aware, there was nobody standing behind the man when he took the photo, and nobody was there when everybody moved away from the spot. Furthermore, the photographer said that it would have been impossible for anybody to crouch behind without the person being aware of their presence, and without their body being visible to the person's left.

The Uninvited Wedding Guest ghost photo can be viewed at: http://www.paranormal360.co.uk/real-ghost-pictures-the-uninvited-wedding-guest/

153. The AllHallows Ghost, Bedford

In the central shopping area of Bedford, there is a spot called Allhallows, which runs from Midland Road in the south, to St Loyes Street in the north. The spot used to be called All Hallows Lane, but the Church of All Hallows was demolished in the seventeenth century.

In 1979 a number of shoppers walking by the Midland Bank (now HSBC) in Allhallows witnessed the appearance of a friar dressed in garb from the Middle Ages.

He wore a hooded gown and sandals, and was spotted casually walking down the street. Witnesses claimed that his attention seemed to be mainly focused on his rosary beads. Apparently, he was walking from the direction of Greyfriars, which was named after the Grey Friars Franciscans, who had a friary there from the late 1200s.

A similar ghostly apparition has been seen in the vicinity of the Greyfriars pub, and it is widely believed that this is the same ghost.

154. The Ghosts of the Pens

As well as being one of the most scenic and historical places to visit in Scotland, and home to the country's oldest university, St Andrews also happens to be one of the most haunted.

One of the most famous ghost stories of St Andrews is that of the Ghosts of the Pends. Situated at the very end of South Street, The Pends (also known as The Pends Gatehouse) is a quaint old street, which was once a vaulted entrance into the monastery. Even though it no longer has a roof, it is still quite a remarkable place to visit for tourists and the like.

In the early 1950s, Russell Kirk, a visiting American academic and the 'grandfather' of American conservatism, described how, whilst strolling up the Pends Road one moonless autumn evening, he sensed the presence of a "shadowy" figure walking alongside him on the opposite side of the road. The figure had an indiscernible face and an unidentifiable gender, and it followed him into the darkened gatehouse. Kirk moved away from the darkness and into the brighter area cast by the street lamps of South Street. He then waited for the mysterious walker to emerge from the gatehouse, but nobody did. And what made it all the more strange was that there was no other exit!

Kirk then realised that although his own feet had been crunching through gravel, the footsteps of his mysterious companion had made no sound at all. Of course, one explanation might have been that despite the lack of moonlight and street lights in the Pends, Kirk had somehow cast an amorphous shadow and, as a result, had mistaken it for the figure of another human. However, Kirk remained firmly convinced that he'd had a real-life encounter with the paranormal.

The novelist Fay Weldon apparently also encountered this same phantom one evening, during her student days, whilst visiting the harbour, which is accessible via the Pends Road. As she walked out to the very end of the jetty, something made her look behind her, and she saw the figure of a man dressed in a black cloak and broad-brimmed black hat. The strange figure then started to follow the student, and she hastened her pace, as did her follower. And then, when she looked behind her again, the figure had mysteriously vanished.

After making local enquiries, Feldon discovered that this apparition was known as 'the preacher', and that the harbour area was his regular haunt. On some occasions, he would manifest himself as a fully formed figure, but on other occasions he would appear as nothing more than a vague shadow, indicated by his distinctive broad-brimmed hat.

And it's not just shadowy, phantom pedestrians you need to watch out for should you venture to stroll through the Pens late at night, for a spectral coach - allegedly that of Archbishop Sharp, a harsh and hated churchman who had sided with Charles II after the Civil War - has also been seen on moonless nights gliding silently down South Street and the Pends, drawn by four large black horses. The Archbishop was murdered whilst travelling to St Andrews in 1679.

155. The Knickerbocker Hotel

Now known as the Hollywood Knickerbocker Apartments, the former Knickerbocker Hotel, located at 1714 Ivar Avenue in Los Angeles, California, has had more than its fair share of resident ghosts over the years. Designed by architect E.M. Frasier in Spanish Colonial Revival style, the historic hotel opened in June 1929. It became a popular place for moguls and celebrities from the region's film industry, playing a major role in Tinseltown history for decades. It is also a place where some of Hollywood's most famous dramatic incidents and scandals have occurred.

On November 15, 1962, a woman named Irene, who designed outfits for the stars, jumped to her death from a hotel window. She had made costumes for over 100 Hollywood movies, including "Easter Parade". She had become very worried over financial problems and, apparently, the death of Gary Cooper.

Another great tragedy that occurred at the hotel was that of Frances Farmer, who ended up in a screen-actors' psychiatric hospital after falling victim to alcohol addiction and various other personal and emotional problems. Whilst being treated in the hospital, Farmer went through different forms of ill treatment, including electroshock treatments and ice-water baths, all of which would eventually strip her of both her sanity and her talent. Finally, she was given a lobotomy, and although eventually released from hospital, she was never quite the same woman again. Tragically, the once-beautiful star died at the age of 57, penniless, isolated and broken.

Silent screen heartthrob Rudolph Valentino frequented the hotel bar, and apparently liked to indulge in the odd spot of tango dancing here. Valentino's ghost is said to still drop by here occasionally.

The famous magician Harry Houdini, despite the fact that he had always debunked spiritualists and mediums, made a deal with his wife that if he died before she did, he would do his utmost to contact her from the beyond. Consequently, on Halloween of 1926 (the first anniversary of his death), Houdini's wife, Bess, held a séance on the roof of the Knickerbocker hotel. When Houdini failed to communicate from the afterlife, she continued holding annual séances at the hotel for over a decade. But despite this determination to contact her husband, not once did he make a ghostly appearance.

Legendary screen goddess Marilyn Monroe honeymooned at the hotel with husband Joe Dimaggio in January 1954. Along with Rudolph Valentino's spirit, her ghost is said to appear occasionally in the hotel bar. Munroe's ghost has also been seen in the women's restroom. The hotel's bar is actually considered to be the hotel's most haunted spot.

Other, lesser-known spirits occasionally manifest themselves too. Various staff members have witnessed instances of lights turning on and off of their own accord, and things being moved about by unseen hands.

156. The Banff Springs Hotel, Canada

Built over 125 years ago by Canadian Pacific Railway as a stop off point for train passengers, the Banff Springs Hotel in Alberta, Canada, is said to be one of the most haunted buildings in the country.

Among the spirits seen at the hotel is that of a bride, who fell down the staircase and broke her neck after being struck with shock when her dress caught fire. The ghostly bride has been spotted both in the ballroom, dancing, and on the staircase. Some witnesses even claim to have seen the flames from the back of her dress.

The main ghost story of the hotel is the one concerning a family that was murdered in Room 873. Although the door to this room has long since been bricked up, the slaughtered family are still seen to this day, usually in the hallway just outside the room.

Another ghost that is frequently reported in the hotel is that of the former bellman. He was employed there during the 60s and 70s, and his phantom is still active. He especially has a propensity to assisting guests up to their rooms, still attired in the same uniform he always wore back in the 60s. He opens locked doors and switches on lights. But if you should try to strike up a conversation with him, or even give him a tip, he just vanishes into thin air.

157. Poveglia Island, Italy

The tiny island of Poveglia is situated between Venice and Lido, in the Venice Lagoon. During the Bubonic Plague outbreak in the 14th century, the island became a quarantine colony, and a large number of Venetians were sent here to die. Their disease-ravaged corpses were burned on large funeral pyres. The same thing happened in 1630, when Venice was hit by the Black Death.

Although there were some unconfirmed reports that the site was being used as a lunatic asylum, many people believed that this just wasn't true. However, disturbing stories of ill treatment and unorthodox experiments in the building continued to be bandied about.

In 1930 a doctor is thought to have taken his own life by jumping to his death from a bell tower. Poveglia Hospital was used as a geriatric centre until 1975, when it was closed down.

Today, the island has something of a dark and foreboding atmosphere about it, and many local people are reluctant to set foot on it for fear of incurring a curse. Also, fisherman are equally wary of venturing anywhere near the island, afraid that they might happen to drag up rotting human remains from beneath the sea.

Ghostly voices and screams from long dead patients and victims of disease are frequently heard on the island and in its buildings, and many of these eerie sounds have been captured on EVP equipment. Mysterious shadowy forms have also been spotted here and there. More disturbingly, there have even been cases of people being possessed by some evil, violent force. Visitors to the island have often complained of experiencing an oppressive sense of evil, causing them to leave the place in a disposition of extreme unease and fear.

158. The Black Lady of Bradley Woods

The story of The Black Lady of Bradley Woods has been told again and again over many generations. A lot of parents used to relate the story to their children to scare them, so that their kids would be sure to be safely tucked up in bed in case "The Black Lady" got them.

Some sources claim that The Black Lady was originally a nun, who would appear all dressed in black in nearby Nunsthorpe (which is now part of Grimsby), where there once stood a convent until the Reformation. However, this does not explain why the Black Lady should have moved from Nunsthorpe to Bradley, two miles away. Furthermore, although the lady is reported to be dressed in black, few witnesses have described her appearance as being similar to that of a nun.

There is also another theory that the Black Lady may be a spinster, who once lived the life of a recluse in her isolated cottage in the woods. This sort of lifestyle, especially when it involved lonely old women who would become angry when their privacy was invaded by children and the like, could often lead to suspicions of witchcraft, thus exaggerating the legend of the Black Lady.

The story of the Black Lady of Bradley Woods apparently stems from an incident that occurred hundreds of years ago, involving the wife of a woodcutter. Whilst her husband was away fighting in the wars that were ravaging the country at that time, the woman fell victim to a group of soldiers who broke into her cottage one day and demanded money. When she refused, the soldiers viciously beat and raped her, after which they snatched her baby and rode off with it.

The poor woman then spent most of her days wandering through the woods in desperate search of her baby, calling out for it again and again, but to no avail. And to add further weight to her misery, her husband never returned home. Sadly, now bereft of her family, the woman died of a broken heart.

To this day, the woman can still be seen in Bradley Woods, wandering between the trees and calling out repeatedly for her missing baby. If you want to have a chance of seeing The Black Lady of Bradley Woods, then your best bet is to go to the area on Christmas Eve and repeatedly call out, "Black lady, black lady, I've stolen your baby" three times. Legend has it that the woman's embittered phantom will suddenly appear and approach anybody who has the nerve to do this.

Be warned.

159. The Ghost of Elgar

Sir Edward William Elgar was an English composer whose works have entered the British and International classical concert repertoire. Elgar's influence on British culture was so profound that the Bank of England honoured him by featuring his image on the £20 note.

Elgar lived with his wife Alice in a house called Brinkwells, situated near the village of Fittleworth in West Sussex. He composed his last four major works here. In 1920 his wife died of lung cancer, which completely devastated him to the extent that he never really got over the loss.

Elgar died on 23rd February 1934, aged 76. He was buried beside his wife at St. Wulstan's Catholic Church in Little Malvern. Elgar himself did not actually die in Fittleworth, but many local residents believe that his ghost still haunts the area. Some claim to have seen a smartly dressed man with a moustache, wandering through the woods at dusk. On occasions, the apparition just stands still, staring fixedly out across the Sussex Downs. Invariably, the phantom then vanishes after a few seconds.

160. The Ghost of Ozzie Nelson

Ozzie Nelson was an American actor, bandleader and singer who was most famous for his role in the TV series The Adventures of Ozzie And Harriet, in which his wife was the co-star.

Nelson died of liver cancer on the 3rd June 1975. However, there are some people who believe the star's ghost still haunts his former home. Faucets are mysteriously turned on and off by unseen hands. Doors open and close of their own accord. Lights are switched on and off for seemingly no reason at all.

The spirit of Ozzie also appears to have a rather mischievous streak about him. One night, the female owner of the house, whilst in bed, felt the blankets being pulled gently away, and then light kisses by an invisible presence were planted on her neck.

161. The Vogue Theatre, Hollywood

The Vogue Theatre in Hollywood was built in 1941 and has long been a popular venue for all kinds of productions, from concerts to plays. The theatre is reported to have at least seven resident ghosts.

One particular phantom, commonly known as "Fritz", worked as a projectionist at the theatre. He actually died in the projection booth, and his spirit has been seen by a number of people in the theatre.

Among the other ghosts said to haunt the theatre are a maintenance engineer and a schoolteacher and her students, who lost their lives almost a century ago when Prospect Elementary School (which once stood on the site) was burned down.

Another spirit that has frequently been seen around the theatre is that of a narrow-faced man dressed in a long cream-coloured dinner jacket. This apparition has been witnessed in the basement's narrow corridor, just beneath the stage. And in 1995, a performer was doing a tap dance onstage when suddenly he spotted the ghost of the well-dressed man, standing just under the Exit sign. When the apparition vanished, this shocked the performer so much that he immediately fled the stage. And just the next day, the ghost was seen again, this time by a technician, who described the apparition as being in his mid-thirties, clean shaven, with short black hair.

Is this dapper man the ghost of an old performer, an attendee, or perhaps a former worker? Nobody really knows for sure.

162. Sax Rohmer's Ghostly Experience

British author Sax Rohmer is most famous for being the creator of the Fu Manchu novels, the evil Chinaman who wanted to conquer the world, and whose stories inspired many movie versions starring such top horror actors as Boris Karloff and Christopher Lee in the title role.

Rohmer, along with his wife, once stayed in a hotel in Haiti, which apparently had a resident ghost. Both of them saw the figure of a native girl slowly walking towards them, carrying a fan in her hand. The girl sat down in a cane chair, fanning herself and staring fixedly at the Rohmers. When the Rohmers started to speak to her, she just got up and, without uttering a single word, walked into the hotel. Puzzled at the mysterious girl's behaviour, Rohmer decided to follow her.

But when he stepped into the hotel, the girl was nowhere to be seen, and when he asked the desk clerk if he'd seen her, the worker just frowned puzzledly and said he'd seen nobody.

Rohmer never got to find out exactly who the girl was.

163. The Lady in the White Cloak

In 1987, around the area of Samlesbury Hall in Lancashire, there were many reports from drivers about the sighting of a mysterious lady dressed in a white cloak.

Other people claimed to have seen this apparition too.

One story of the Lady in the White Cloak involves a man called Alex Dunderdale. On the 16th November 1987, Dunderdale, accompanied by his wife, was driving along the A677 by Samlesbury Hall when he was shocked to see a white-cloaked woman suddenly appear in the path of their car. Although he quickly slammed on the brakes, the car didn't just hit her, but apparently ran right over her body. Then it skid to a halt.

Still in a state of severe shock, Dunderdale immediately jumped out of the car and searched all over the road for the woman's body. But she was nowhere to be found. Although his wife hadn't actually seen the woman in white for herself, she had felt the car jolt as it ran over her body.

Other witnesses have seen the white-cloaked lady standing by the side of the road, but when they have stopped to offer her a lift, she just vanishes. She has also been spotted, appearing and disappearing, by people walking down the road, late at night, who have missed the last bus.

164. The Haunted Co-op Store

In October 2015, there were reports from staff working at a Co-op store in Whaley Bridge about some terrifying paranormal activity. And so spooked out were the workers by their experiences in the building that management decided to close the store early on Halloween, so that the staff would not be further frightened by this apparent entity as they worked down the supermarket's aisles. This decision was probably prompted by one member of staff, who asked to have Halloween off after being so scared out of their wits by the strange things they'd experienced there.

Staff often complained to the manager about an oppressive and unsettling atmosphere. Some also witnessed strange occurrences, such as weird noises and a sensation of being watched and followed.

Although the store itself doesn't seem any different to other supermarkets on the outside, the basement over which it is built appears to harbour some very unnatural presences. According to staff, doors rattle in their frames, items of stock are tampered with and moved around by invisible hands, and lights flicker on and off of their own accord.

165. The Willard Library Ghosts

Two entities are said to haunt the 130-years-old Willard Library in Evansville, Indiana: an All-Grey Lady and a Dark Mass. In fact, the ghostly activity has become so well known that the library has now installed ghost cams.

In 1937, in the early hours of the morning, the janitor who was on duty at the Willard Library was making his rounds in the basement when he was startled by the sudden appearance of a lady wearing a grey veil. A strange grey light seemed to emanate from all around her body, illuminating her in the dark. Shocked, the janitor dropped his light, and when he bent to pick it up, he saw that lady's shoes were also grey. As he raised himself upright again, the apparition vanished into thin air. Not surprisingly, the janitor resigned from his job shortly afterwards.

This was documented as the first official sighting of the Grey Lady of Willard Library.

Over the years, the ghostly grey lady has been seen on numerous occasions, and by people from all walks of life. But the ones who have seen the ghost most frequently are the library staff. The most unnerving encounters have occurred in the elevator, whose confined space obviously makes it difficult to run away, so that the people inside it have to wait until the doors open before they can escape their spooky, nightmare ride.

So just who is this mysterious Grey Lady? Well, there are a few theories as to her identity. She could be the ghost of somebody who just loved going to the library in life, and has become the resident ghost there. Or she could be the spirit of a woman who once drowned. But the most popular theory is that she could be the ghost of the library's founder, Willard Carpenter.

The other entity that haunts the library is said to be a 'dark mass' or a 'shadow person'. A couple of photographs have been taken in the building that seem to show a dark mass, sometimes in the shape of a human form and other times apparently without any form at all.

Both entities have been seen at all hours of the day. However, the Grey Lady apparently becomes more active when major renovations are taking place in the library.

166. The Satanic Goat Ghost

Early in 2016, there was a newspaper report about a heavily pregnant woman who claimed to have seen numerous ghostly apparitions in her home, been pushed over by invisible hands, smacked on her bottom, and even seen blood stains appear on her floor. But most frighteningly of all, she claims she was even terrorised by a satanic ghost!

The lady in question had all her strange experiences in what is known as 'Britain's most haunted house', namely a cottage called The Cage, which is situated in St. Osyth, Essex.

When she first moved into her new home back in 2004, the lady was unaware that it was haunted. The cottage was once a medieval prison and was the centre of one of England's most famous witch-hunts where eight women died after being accused of sorcery in the 16th Century.

After living in the haunted cottage for eleven years, the woman finally decided she'd had enough and put the place up for auction after a picture was taken that appeared to show the face of a satanic goat. Some even believe that this is actually the face of the devil himself, and that some malevolent, unearthly force haunts the cottage.

Small wonder that the lady has now given up the cottage, for who would want to live in a place that harboured not just ghosts, but also the presence of the devil himself?

167. The Ghosts of Gettysburg

The bloodiest and most significant armed clash of the American Civil War was, undoubtedly, the Battle of Gettysburg. The battle took place during the period 1-3 July 1863, in and around the town of Gettysburg, and it was the battle that left the highest amount of casualties on both the Union and Confederate sides. It has often been described as the war's turning point.

Not surprisingly, a battle of such bloody and epic proportions, and with such a high death toll, is bound to leave some kind of supernatural imprint on the area. If ever there was a hotspot for spirits of slaughtered soldiers to make their presences known on occasion, Gettysburg was it. Many ghost hunters firmly believe that the battlefield and surrounding town are haunted. Indeed, the various buildings in the area - from bed-and-breakfast hotels to museums - have seen more than their fair share of paranormal activity.

Different people have seen Civil War soldiers dressed in their army uniforms, apparently still at war in a conflict that ended many years ago. Quite a few of these phantom soldiers have been spotted on horseback.

Are these phantom troops residual hauntings, playing over and over again like a broken record? Well, considering just how many human lives were lost in this epic battle, that could very well be the case.

168. Leamington Spa Railway Station

Over the years, there have been many reports of haunted railway stations in the UK. Perhaps the most well known case is that of Leamington Spa Railway Station. In fact, the station has been so plagued by ghostly activity that it now boasts its own supernatural liaison officer!

Rail travellers have reported seeing strange apparitions after purchasing tickets at the station, which was built in the late 1800s. In the upstairs office building, the staff has witnessed various creepy occurrences, with lights switching themselves off and on of their own accord, and doors slamming. Paperwork has also been thrown about poltergeist style, and drawers have been left open. Strange footsteps have also been heard in various parts of the office area.

A disused basement on Platform 3, where there is a partially sealed-off staircase that leads to nowhere, is the other area where much paranormal activity has been reported.

A nighttime security guard working at the station describes it as one of the most haunted places he has ever been to in his life. He says he sees spirits on both platforms, but believes that they are harmless ghosts with positive energy.

169. Tibbie Shiel's Inn

Set between two lochs and surrounded by breathtaking scenery, Tibbie Shiel's Inn is situated in Peebles, Scotland. In the 1800s, the inn was a popular haunt for many well-known literary figures, religious men and scholars. Amongst its famous clientele were Robert Louis Stevenson, Sir Walter Scott and James Hogg.

Formerly a cottage, the inn was opened in the early 1820s by an enterprising young lady called Isabella Shiel, who had recently become widowed and so needed some kind of income to pay her rent and put food on the table.

Tibbie Shiel died in 1878, and since her passing her cottage has undergone much renovation over the years to become an inn. But her ghost is said to still haunt her old business premises. People staying at the inn have reported sensing her presence as she pushes her way through the throng of customers to warm herself by the fire, which was always her favourite spot.

170. Edinburgh Castle

Some years ago, Time Magazine drew up a list of the ten most haunted places in the world, and included in that list was Edinburgh Castle. And it's not surprising either, for the castle has seen more than its fair share of hauntings over the years.

Among the many ghosts that have been seen and heard there is that of a headless drummer, who was first sighted in 1650.

Another phantom is Lady Glamis, who was accused of witchcraft in 1537 and was burned at the stake in front of her young son. She is said to stroll around the darkened halls of the castle.

And it's not only human ghosts that haunt the castle, for even animal spirits have been experienced by various people. For instance, a ghostly dog has been seen running through the misty graveyard.

Edinburgh Castle's long reputation for being home to so many spooks finally led to a major paranormal investigation in 2001, when an English doctor organised a group of 240 volunteers to spend 10 days in and around the castle. After the investigation of the castle's creepy, damp cellars, chambers and vaults was over, the conclusion reached was that the structure was most definitely a hotspot of paranormal activity. Much of the volunteers' experiences corresponded with those of previous sightings. Some of the team complained of being "groped" by invisible hands, while others experienced burning sensations and sudden drops in temperature. In addition, shadowy figures and a phantom in a leather apron were seen. The volunteers were not told by the organiser of the investigation which particular cells and vaults were noted for being haunted.

171. Blood Alley

Highway 93 - also known as 'Blood Alley' - runs through vast desert wilderness northwest from Wickenburg up to Hwy 40 near Kingman, east of the Nevada border, USA. The highway is called 'Blood Alley' because so many tragic deaths have occurred there over the years. The small white crosses that are dotted right along the highway's length bear sad testimony to this fact. In some spots, a cluster of crosses marks where an entire vehicle of passengers has died tragically.

In view of the highway's history of tragedies, it's therefore not surprising that the area is haunted by ghosts. For instance, a ghostly highwayman - described as being "six feet tall, dressed in black, and wearing a cowboy hat and boots" - was seen by a family as they were travelling along the highway late one night. The figure was holding a lantern in front of him, just above his head. From the lantern's glow, the family could discern an old-fashioned Black Harley parked just behind him. As the family passed the shadowy figure, the lantern's light went out, and he just disappeared into thin air.

172. The Five Bells Pub

In the centre of Cople, a small village near Bedford, stands The Five Bells Pub, which has a long history. Not surprisingly, a place with such a long history is bound to have the odd resident ghost or two, and this pub certainly does.

The ghost of a sailor has been seen sitting in a pew, which is situated in the corner near the fireplace. All of the people who have witnessed this apparition give the same description: he is elderly, with his grey hair tied in a pigtail, wears a hooped shirt and puttees, and smokes a grey pipe. This nautical spirit has been seen many times, by both staff and customers.

The Five Bells Pub dates from 1690. Its first licensee was Eliza Smith in 1729. The pub takes its name from the church dedicated to All Saints, situated just opposite.

173. Bedford Hospital

Bedford Hospital is a 400-bed district general hospital serving the residents of north and mid Bedfordshire. Dating back to 1897, it consists of a main site, which is also known as the South Wing, and Bedford Health Village, which is known as the North Wing and which used to be a workhouse back in the 1800s.

Just like many other hospitals in the UK with a history, Bedford Hospital also has a few resident ghosts.

In late 1972, a nurse on night duty was frightened by the apparition of a young girl walking slowly up the stairs and entering the corridor. The girl was described as tall, slender, quite pretty, and with short brown hair. She wore a long dress covered by a long white coat. This phantom girl was also seen by another staff nurse as she was unlocking the medicine trolley. Stunned with shock, the two nurses could only watch as the ghost glided into the toilet. The nurses expected her to come out of the toilet, but she never did. When one of them went into the toilet to investigate, she found nobody in there, just an unnaturally cold sensation.

Quite a few years later, more staff witnessed further paranormal activity in the hospital. They saw the spirit of a young woman in a long dress walking along the corridor before vanishing through the wall of a storeroom. Other members of staff have reported hearing the strange sound of footsteps sliding along the Shand Ward.

There is a story that a young girl of 23, who worked in the pathology department of the hospital, committed suicide there in the late 1960s.

In 2007, many of the old buildings of the North Wing were demolished and the site was reconstructed as the Bedford Health Village. Before this renovation work, a local paranormal group investigated Shire House, which used to be the old Bedford Workhouse. Accompanied by a security guard, one of the investigators took a tour of the old maternity unit, as he was born there. Walking along the 1950s part of the unit, they suddenly heard the voices of two people talking to each other in the upper part of the stairwell. When they went up to investigate, the conversation suddenly stopped, and when they investigated further, they were shocked to find that there was nobody in the corridor at all.

Even security staff working late in the building have experienced strange things. They have heard the eerie sound of footsteps, even though there was nobody else in the building other than them. Others have experienced unnatural cold sensations in various areas, especially at the top of the main stairs.

174. Carisbrooke Castle

Carisbrooke Castle stands in the village of Carisbrooke, near Newport, Isle of Wight. The castle is noted for being the place where Charles I was imprisoned, fourteen months before his execution in 1649.

The English Heritage runs the castle today, and it is always open to the public.

A number of ghosts are reported to haunt the castle. In the deep well, visitors have been frightened out of their wits by what appeared to be the ghostly face of Elizabeth Ruffin, who tragically drowned there.

The castle's moat has also been host to various ghostly apparitions, and is believed to be the most haunted area. The figure of a woman known as the Grey Lady, who wears a long cloak and who is accompanied by four hounds and a man dressed in brown, has been spotted here on many occasions. Also, the apparition of a large man in a long white gown has been witnessed near the moat. And a young woman was one day strolling along the moat when she was approached by a young man in a leather jacket. The man chatted with her for a few minutes, then suddenly vanished into thin air, without even ending the conversation.

175. The Miskin Manor Hotel

Situated in Miskin, near Cardiff, The Miskin Manor Hotel has quite an eventful and coloured history dating back to the 10th century. Surrounded by glorious expanses of Welsh countryside, Miskin Manor exudes an air of perfect peace and tranquillity, despite being only minutes away from the busy M4.

The Manor has quite a colourful and eventful history. The current house, however, was established in 1857, when the estate was purchased by David Williams, a popular Welsh philanthropist and bard. After two major fires - the first in 1922 and the second in 1952 - the house was restored and served as flats until 1985, when it was converted into a luxury hotel.

The most frequently reported spook at Miskin Manor is that of a ghostly lady, who appears mostly in the bar area. She seems quite harmless, and usually appears between the hours of midnight and 1.00 a.m. The hotel porter has often seen this apparition whilst relaxing in the bar with his cup of tea, around 1.40 a.m. He just sits there in silence, familiarity with this spirit obviously having rendered him impervious to the phenomena, watching her nebulous form gliding from the drawing room to the bar before slowly disappearing into thin air.

The woman is said to be a former resident of the house, who is just repeating a regular path that she once trod when she was alive. Where the bar stands today, there once was a staircase, so it seems that the ghostly lady is coming from the drawing room and ascending the stairs, just as she did when she lived there.

When psychic medium Norie Miles, accompanied by a team of researchers, investigated the Manor in June 2004, she and her group experienced a sudden and inexplicable change of atmosphere, at exactly the same time that the apparition was known to appear. Also, a heavy picture was lifted off the wall and thrown down onto the floor, right before their eyes. One might assume from this that the ghostly lady was thinking that just because the investigators could not actually see her, it didn't necessarily mean that she wasn't lurking around somewhere in the hotel!

176. The Haunted Cafe

At the Featherbed Rock Café in Seaham, County Durham, the spirit of a notorious serial killer is said to haunt the premises.

The ghost is said to be that of Mary Ann Cotton, who was Britain's first female serial killer and who lived in Seaham Harbour in the 19th Century, the period when she embarked on her heinous murder spree, using arsenic as a method of disposing of her victims. She was convicted of killing three of her four husbands, and one of her stepsons, but is believed to have murdered as many as 21 people. Cotton was executed at Durham Jail in March 1873. Her horrific crimes earned her the notorious name "The Black Widow".

The manager of the cafe, a former nurse, and her staff suspect that certain items - a baby's shawl, a postcard and even an oven - found in the North Terrace building have some relevance to the Victorian murderess.

The manager has reported experiencing various strange occurrences in the building. Things that she has left out have been mysteriously moved around. She and her staff have also heard sudden bangs in the kitchen. The manager also heard strange whispering in her ear. At first, she thought the whisperer was her daughter, but then she discovered the girl wasn't even in earshot.

The Featherbed Rock Café takes its name from coastal

rocks, situated just a short distance from the shop. A local paranormal group, on hearing about the strange incidents in the café, are planning to investigate the business.

As this book goes to print, filming work has just started on a new two-part ITV drama about the serial killer Mary Ann Cotton. The series will be called "Dark Angel", and will star the Downtown Abbey actress Joanne Froggart in the title role.

177. Haunted Lighthouses

It's not just old houses and crumbling castles that ghosts are noted for haunting. Sometimes, the spirits can be attracted to the towering majesty of lighthouses. Here are just a few examples.

The Owl's Head lighthouse in State Park, Maine, is open all the year round and offers breathtaking views of Penobscot Bay. But there is another breathtaking aspect about it, and breathtaking in a dark rather than a light sense. There is a trespassing ghost in the lighthouse. The young daughter of former keepers would often wake up her parents in the middle of the night and shout, "Fog's rolling in! Time to put the foghorn on!" The parents soon discovered the girl had an imaginary friend who looked like an old sea captain. The current inhabitants of the lighthouse have seen his footprints in the snow, alongside other ghostly impressions he has left, like polished brass and lowered thermostats.

The lighthouse deemed to be the most haunted one in America is the Point Lookout Lighthouse, in Scotland, Maryland. Visitors to the lighthouse have reported seeing the apparitions of both men and women. Doors open and close of their own accord. During the American Civil War, a hospital and a prison camp once stood on these grounds for wounded Confederate soldiers, so could these apparitions be those of the many hundreds of brave troops from that era?

The 78-foot Seul Choix Lighthouse, situated in Gulliver, Michigan, is said to be haunted by the spirit of one of its former keepers, a Captain Joseph Townsend. He died in the keeper's house in the early 1900s, and for months they could not inter his body due to the severity of the winter weather. Consequently, they had no option but to store his corpse in the basement. Maybe because his body was not laid to rest for such a long time that visitors and staff claim they have often got a whiff of the strong smell of cigars (Townsend was an inveterate cigar smoker) in various parts of the lighthouse. Other strange incidents witnessed include chairs in the adjoining museum's kitchen being moved around, and a mysterious man peeking through the windows.

At the Point Sur Lightstation in Big Sur, California, the ghost of a man dressed in a 19th-century keeper's uniform has been spotted inside the visitors' centre.

The Battery Point Lighthouse, in Crescent City, California, sits near downtown on a small peninsula. It has a resident ghost, which does seem pretty innocuous and playful. The phantom does mischievous things like set a rocking chair in motion and move a caretaker's bedroom slippers around in the dead of night. However, despite this entity's rather inoffensive actions, the cats do react rather guardedly whenever it appears. So is this ghost that of a dog or a child, or just a rather childish human being? Who knows?

The Saginaw River Rear Range Lighthouse, situated in Bay City, Michigan, has been the centre of some rather strange happenings. Cost Guard members who stayed there described hearing heavy footsteps on the iron staircase of the Rear Range Light's tower. When they went to investigate, there was nobody there. It is not known exactly whose ghost it is that is haunting the tower, but the lights were deactivated in the 1970s and nobody has lived in the building since.

In the AA Guide, South Stack Lighthouse, situated in Anglesey, on the north coast of Wales, scores very highly as one of the spookiest buildings in Great Britain, receiving a maxim 5 ghost rating for its spectral keeper, who seems to be permanently locked out in a storm. South Stack first opened in 1809, and was quite a peaceful place until 1825, when a fierce storm battered the area, destroying 200 ships, including the famous Royal Charter. The keeper at the time, a Jack Jones, was struck on the head by a piece of rock blown off the cliffs by a gust of wind. Though he managed to crawl over the bridge, he was found outside the door the next day, very badly injured. Jones sadly died two weeks later from his injuries. Legend has it that it's Jack's ghost you can hear desperately pounding on the lighthouse door at night, or tapping on its windows, in search of shelter from the storm. The lighthouse's ghostly reputation came to the attention of the Most Haunted production team, who visited the building a few years ago to conduct an investigation.

178. The Ghost Ship of Wales

Wales is arguably the most haunted country in the world. One classic Welsh ghost story is that of the so-called "haunted ship", namely The HMS Asp, which was just an ordinary surveying vessel.

These nautical hauntings occurred in the 1850s. Strange noises were heard coming from an empty cabin on the ship. Also, in the same cabin, the ghostly apparition of a female was often seen. This ghost would invariably frighten the life out of the sailors, and the ship's captain, who meticulously documented the phenomena, was even forced to try and keep his crew from holding a mutiny.

This ghost story first happened at Deeside, Flintshire, and ended at Pembroke Drive, where The Asp sailed to for repairs. Once the ship had docked, the entity disembarked. She strolled past a couple of dumbfounded sentries, who opened fire on her with their muskets, and disappeared permanently in a graveyard.

Nobody ever discovered the identity of the ghostly woman.

179. The Thing in Calico

Here is another very creepy ghost story that comes out of Wales. It was first documented in a book of True Ghost Stories, published in 1936.

On a lovely summer's night, the Reverend H Elwyn Thomas was strolling along a lonely road near a canal at Llangynidr, near Abergavenney, when he spotted a strange-looking figure standing a few yards away. Assuming he was a vagrant, Mr Thomas ventured to approach the man and speak to him. But, as it turned out, it was the worse thing he could have done.

The Reverend was confronted with the most hideous face he had ever seen on an old man: leaden-coloured skin tightly stretched over bone; lips bloodless and thin; half-open mouth devoid of teeth. Two piercing, glowing eyes, set deep in the hollow sockets, stared fixedly and perturbingly at Mr Thomas. And the figure's garb was every bit as odd as its countenance: two dirty strips of calico were wound around its emaciated frame, and nothing else.

Struck by fear, Mr Thomas turned and fled from the creepy-looking figure. And his fear was compounded when, glancing over his shoulder, he was shocked to see that the figure was following him! Gliding spectrally down the road, the apparition seemed hell bent on launching itself at him, as it gained ground rapidly.

Realising now that the figure chasing him was surely that

of a ghost, Mr Thomas eventually collapsed from nervous exhaustion. That ghost turned out to be that of a crazy old skinflint, who had died many years before. He had a tendency to dress himself in dirty old strips of calico - hence the title "The Thing in Calico" - and it was in this form that Mr Thomas had certainly seen him.

180. The Liverpool Banshee

At the top of the hill in Mount Pleasant, close to the Liverpool Metropolitan Cathedral, stands the once popular Irish Centre, which closed down in 1997 but is currently being considered for reopening in some form or other. Before it became the Irish Centre, the building was known as The Wellington Rooms, and in its day it was a popular hub for Liverpool's high society and elitist residents. Ship builders, slave traders and merchants all put money into the building to ensure its ongoing popularity.

The building is said to be haunted by an Irish Banshee (an appropriate ghost if any, considering the place's Irish history!). This entity has been seen many times, by both staff and visitors.

181. The Shopping Centre Ghost

In June 2016, a popular daily newspaper published a report about a busy shopping complex, which is said to be centre of some very eerie activity. The place in question, Silverburn Shopping Centre in Glasgow, is apparently being haunted by a mysterious woman in black period clothing. In the month of June 2016 alone, there have been at least four reported sightings of this terrifying entity by many customers. A Silverburn security guard has also encountered the phantom as he was just finishing his shift.

Managers of the centre have become so concerned about these reports that they have called in experts from Glasgow Paranormal Investigations to do a tour of the premises in the hope of finding out exactly who this ghostly lady is.

One theory being discussed by the Glasgow paranormal team is that construction work at Silverburn Shopping Centre, including the erection of a new cinema, may have disturbed some very restless spirits, which is a common thing in cases like this.

182. Cathedral House Hotel

Like the case of the Silverburn Shopping Centre ghost in the previous chapter, there is another building in Glasgow that has been the centre of some quite scary paranormal activity. The building in question is the Cathedral House Hotel.

The hotel was built in 1877, and is situated in one of the oldest areas in Glasgow, so naturally you would expect it to be plagued by the odd ghost or two. The building was used for many years as a rehabilitation centre for female prisoners nearby, and over the years there have been countless reports of phantom sightings, including ghostly children, who are often heard playing and shouting on the top floor. There is also a ghost that passes you on the stairway.

Paranormal teams investigating the building have reported witnessing light anomalies, furniture being moved around by unseen hands, and disembodied voices.

183. Tower Building, Liverpool

Liverpool's most haunted structure is said to be the Tower Building, situated in the middle of the city's seven original streets on The Strand. References to the site date as far back as 1256.

The daunting tower was once the borough gaol, and during the Napoleonic wars an estimated 4,000 French prisoners were incarcerated there, many of whom died under the most appalling conditions.

Residents of the building have reported hearing the sound of chains being dragged down the stairways. Others have seen distressing apparitions of emaciated souls chained to the walls. There have also been reports from other people of intense feelings of sadness in various parts of the building, and these feelings have become so oppressive at times that they have even caused those who've experienced them to flee from the building.

184. Cammell Laird Shipyard

In my hometown of Birkenhead, Cammell Laird is a world famous shipbuilding firm. It can boast quite an industrious and proud history, having launched over a thousand ships, among them HMS Ark Royal, HMS Prince of Wales and the RMS Mauretania.

As well as being famous for shipbuilding, Cammell Laird has become noted for being haunted. Various members of staff have reported seeing the ghostly apparition of a man dressed in blue overalls and a flat cap in the Construction Hall. Others have witnessed the appearance of an old lady in the corridor near the kitchen area.

Also, a number of shadowy figures have been seen in the corridors walking through walls into the adjoining rooms. Even the company's offices are said to be haunted by ex-Cammell Laird employees. Cold spots have also been experienced in various parts of the building.

Cammell Laird certainly has all the aspects one would normally associate with a haunted building: ghostly apparitions, strange noises, unexplained drops in temperature and oppressive feelings of unease.

The shipyard has been investigated by both local paranormal groups and also the crew of the TV show Most Haunted.

185. The Randy Monk

The Pig and Whistle Inn stands along the Newton Road (A381) near the village of Littlehempston, Devon. The inn is 400 years old, and is said to be haunted by a rather lecherous spirit in the form of a monk.

The story goes that a French monk from Buckfast Abbey had a rather steamy and illicit affair with the daughter of a local farmer at the Pig and Whistle. To this day, his ghost is said to haunt the Pig and Whistle, apparently waiting for his lover to turn up.

The randy monk has been nicknamed "Freddie". His phantom has been seen by customers in the bar area.

186. Wythenshawe Hall

The imposing Wythenshawe Hall stands five miles south from Manchester city centre. The half-timbered Tudor house was built by Robert Tatton in 1540, and remained in the family for nearly 400 years.

After being sold by Robert Henry Grenville Tatton to Ernest Simon in 1926, the former stately home was opened as a museum in the 1930s. However, due to spending cuts, the hall was closed to the public in 2010.

Wythenshawe Hall is reported to be haunted by a couple of ghosts. For example, a phantom known as The White Lady has been seen by petrified witnesses in the bedrooms and corridors of the hall. This woman is said to be the ghost of a former servant at the hall called Mary Webb, who was murdered by soldiers during the English Civil War.

Members of staff have also experienced the kind of paranormal activity normally attributed to a poltergeist.

Other people at the hall have witnessed strange bangs and crashes, ghostly footsteps, and even the occasional sound of musket fire. Also, a large tapestry suddenly flew from its place on the wall and landed on two terrified members of staff.

Even the library is said to have a resident ghost. Weird, unexplainable noises - dragging, shuffling sounds - have been heard in there from time to time. In addition, a number of odd photos have been taken in the library, showing unidentifiable figures, mists and orbs.

Frightened witnesses have also seen shadowy forms of monks in the grounds of Wythenshawe Hall.

187. The George and Pilgrim's Hotel

The George and Pilgrims' Hotel is a stone-faced Grade I listed building situated on Glastonbury's High Street. It was first opened in the 15th century to accommodate pilgrims to Glastonbury Abbey.

Not surprisingly, with the hotel being situated so close to the Abbey, it has become well known for having a ghostly monk haunting its floors. Various people have reported seeing this robed entity walking along the hotel's corridors, followed by the ghostly figure of a smartly dressed lady. The local story goes that these two were actually lovers.

There is another ghost that has been seen in the hotel: an apparition dressed in a blue sports jacket. This phantom is said to disappear into thin air whenever he is approached.

188. The Edenhall Country Hotel

The Edenhall Country Hotel is situated just a stone's throw away from the River Eden, near the village of Langwathby, Cumbria. Once known as Woodbine Cottage, parts of Edenhall Country Hotel date back to the 17th century.

A couple of resident ghosts have been seen in the hotel. In Room 4, a phantom female is frequently witnessed by shocked guests appearing in the reflection of the bathroom mirror. She sits on the edge of the bed, then vanishes into thin air.

And there is another female ghost haunting the hotel. This one is an old woman who has been seen by both guests and staff walking to a chair in the corner of the bar.

189. The Haunted Forest of Japan

A new horror movie has been released called The Forest, and whilst not many people may know it, this story is based on an actual haunted forest in Japan, called The Aokigahara (or The Haunted Suicide Forest of Death).

Situated at the foot of Mount Fuji, although The Aokigahara is one of Japan's most beautiful forests, it also has a dark side to it, for in the country's mythology, the place is said to be haunted by malevolent demons.

Many people believe that the ghosts - or yourei - of those abandoned by ubasute (a brutal form of euthanasia) and the mournful spirits of the suicidal linger in the woods. These souls are full of vengeful intent, their main aim being to harass any visitors to the forest, and to lure those who are sad and lost off the path.

If you should be unfortunate enough to become lost in the forest, you may be powerless to call for help, for the soil of the Suicide Forest is replete with magnetic iron, and this plays havoc with cell phones, compasses and similar forms of communication. However, there are some who believe that this interference is stark proof that supernatural entities really do lurk within the deep woods of the Aokigahara, always ready to affect human explorers in any malevolent way they can.

190. The Phantom Bus

In Cambridge Gardens, Notting Hill Gate, W11, London, there have been many reports over the years of sightings of a "Phantom Bus".

The ghostly bus was first seen back in 1934. In the early morning, a motorist was driving along Cambridge Gardens when, for some unknown reason, he suddenly swerved his car, crashed into a wall, and was instantly burnt alive as his vehicle burst into flames.

The inquest into his death produced witness statements testifying to the appearance of a phantom bus. These witnesses claimed to have seen this bus near the exact spot where the fatal crash occurred. They said that the bus could always be seen in the early hours of the morning (which was the time the crash had occurred), and described how frightened they were as this mysterious double-decker came speeding along the centre of the road, heading straight towards them. No driver was in the cab, and no lights were on. It was as if the vehicle was being driven by some strange invisible force.

The instant motorists knew they were heading for a collision with the bus, they would swerve out of its path, and as they did so, the bus would speed past them. Then, when they turned around to have a look at the bus, they were stunned to see that it had vanished into thin air!

This ghostly No. 7 double-decker bus was last seen in

Alan Toner

May 1990. However, as yet, nobody has come up with a reason why this phantom vehicle should haunt this particular stretch of road in Cambridge Gardens.

191. The Ghostly French Hitchhiker

On the 20th May 1981, on the Quartecanaux Bridge near Montpelier, France, around 11 o'clock at night, two couples were driving back home, after spending a pleasant day at the seaside, when they suddenly encountered a female hitchhiker who was headed for Montpelier. As it was so late in the evening and the woman was alone, the driver stopped the car, despite the fact that the vehicle only had room for four passengers.

The driver told the woman that they too were headed for Montpelier. She made no reply, but just nodded her head. The passengers made room for the woman to squeeze in to the back seat, where she sat between the two women.

There was a few moments' silence as the car proceeded on its way. Then, suddenly, the hitchhiker screamed out: "Look out for the turns, look out for the turns.

You're risking death!"

Startled by the woman's sudden outburst, the driver slowed down for the approaching bend. But he was further startled by more screams coming from the rear, this time from his friends, who had just experienced the sudden departure of the hitchhiker.

When the driver stopped the car, the couples jumped out and began an exhaustive search of the area in the hope of finding any trace of the woman. But she was nowhere to be found. She had just vanished as mysteriously as she had first appeared.

When they visited the local police station to report the incident, the Inspector initially didn't seem to give much credence to what they told him, and even accused them of wasting police time. However, he did listen carefully to their story, and although he was eventually won over by their sincerity, he could not offer a logical explanation for what they had just experienced, and so was unable to help them further.

192: The Ghostly Admiral

On 22nd June 1893, a British armada of ships was sailing through the Mediterranean, formed in two columns. Admiral Tyron led one column on the Victoria, while Admiral Markham led the other on the Camperdown. For some unknown reason, Admiral Tyron ordered the columns to turn in towards each other, creating an imminent danger of collision. Although both his officers and the crew on the Camperdown were scared and tried to have the order withdrawn, their protests fell on deaf ears.

As the Camperdown headed for the Victoria, Admiral Tyron seemed to realise the danger of his crazy decision and immediately ordered the ships to back off. But there was no going back now. The ships collided. As the Victoria started to sink, a surviving officer heard the admiral cry out that it was all his fault. Admiral Tyron went down with his ship and drowned.

At that very same moment, Lady Tyron was throwing a party at her London home. As the party was in full swing, the conversation suddenly fell silent as a figure in full naval uniform walked in. The unannounced visitor strolled right across the room, then vanished into thin air.

The visitor was identified as Admiral Tyron.

193: Ghostwatch – The Controversial TV Drama

Ghostwatch was a 90-minute controversial part drama-part reality BBC TV programme that was first aired on Halloween night 1992. Hosted by legendary chat show host Michael Parkinson, and assisted by Sarah Greene and Mike Smith (both of Blue Peter fame), the programme purported to be broadcasting from an actual haunted house in north London.

Although the show had been recorded many weeks before, it was presented as live television. As the supposedly "paranormal events" unfolded, the BBC switchboard was bombarded with thousands of calls from concerned – and spooked – viewers within an hour.

In reality, though, this pre-recorded mockumentary was just following a fictional script, and was probably the first of its kind in paving the way for the popularity of the similarly scripted paranormal shows we see on our TV screens today.

Basically, the general format of the show involved the manifestation of ghostly phenomena (e.g. poltergeist activity, strange noises etc.) in this reportedly haunted house, punctuated by telephone calls from terrified viewers. The main malevolent ghost supposedly responsible for all these disturbances was nicknamed "Pipes".

The whole thing culminated in these supernatural forces

apparently spreading to the television studio, where presenter Michael Parkinson started making incoherent guttural noises, giving the disturbing impression that he had been possessed by whatever entities had invaded his space.

While many viewers twigged on to the fact that the show was just a paranormal spoof, there were others who genuinely believed that it was real. And the show caused so much controversy that it even made the newspaper headlines the next day. Amid this entire furore, the BBC, not surprisingly, decided to distance itself from the programme.

Ghostwatch has never been reshown on British TV. However, there have been two UK home video releases: a special 10th Anniversary edition in 2002 on VHS and DVD, and a 101 Films release in 2011. In addition, a retrospective Documentary, Ghostwatch: Behind The Scenes, was released on DVD in 2013, featuring interviews with many of the cast and crew.

194. Isle of Wight Ghosts

The Isle of Wight is said to be the world's most haunted island. It is also known as the "Ghost Island" due to its reputation for being a paranormal hotspot.

All manner of ghosts and spirits are said to haunt the island - from ghostly monks to poltergeists – and, not surprisingly, the place regularly attracts many ghost hunters and paranormal groups from all corners of the globe. Even the Most Haunted team have been there, accompanied by top Liverpool medium Derek Acorah, and their paranormal experiences at Appuldurcombe House were filmed for their Living TV series.

Here are just a few of the ghostly goings-on on the Isle of Wight:

As I have just mentioned, Appuldurcombe House is something of a paranormal hotspot, and it's not just the Most Haunted team that have had experiences there.

This imposing mansion, with its 365 windows and 52 rooms, is now just a shell of its former self. But ghosts still haunt the dilapidated building. For example, a phantom carriage has been seen by different people. Also, dark shapes have been spotted flitting through the grounds. The sound of a baby's cry has also been heard, and unseen hands flip through the pages of the visitors' book.

Carisbrooke Castle has stood for more than nine centuries, and has held firm against many attacks. But all kinds of spirits still roam within its walls. In the Well House, the face of a dead girl, who drowned in the deep well there, has been spotted. In the castle grounds, a strange cloaked figure, walking four little lap dogs, has been witnessed. Other apparitions seen include Princess Elizabeth, the daughter of King Charles I, and a Victorian lady in grey.

The spot near the Hare and Hounds pub was the scene of a brutal murder in 1737, when woodcutter Micah Morey slaughtered his young grandson in cold blood. The killer's corpse was left to rot on the gibbet at Gallows Hill, close to the Hare and Hounds. The crossbeam of the gibbet, showing the date of his execution, can be seen in the pub. It is said that Morey's ghost can still be seen roaming around Gallows Hill, brandishing a large axe.

Knighton Gorges, Newchurch, is reputed to be Isle of Wight's most haunted place. The ghostly house is said to reappear every New Year's Eve, which brings people flocking to the area in their droves. Even though all that remains now of the Knighton Gorges manor house is a pair of weathered stone gateposts, its presence is still appreciably felt, for it has a bloody history of murder, suicide, hatred and madness. It also has various ghosts. Among the paranormal occurrences witnessed are a ghostly coach and horses, mysterious lights (attributed to poltergeist activity), strange laughter and music emanating from the house, and stone creatures seen on the gate pillars.

Arreton Manor is said to be haunted by the spirit of a young girl who was pushed from a window to her death. She is seen wearing a blue dress and crying "Mama, Mama."

Ventnor Botanic Gardens is said to be one of the most haunted places on the island. The Old Royal National Hospital, where hundreds of tuberculosis victims died, once stood here, and apparently their ghosts are still heard, groaning and weeping. Also, ghostly nurses in old-fashioned uniform have been seen walking around the gardens, and odours of ether have been sensed.

195. The Haunted Scottish Sweet Shop

In 2011 a news report appeared about a ghost haunting a village café in Cardross, Dunbartonshire, Scotland. This apparently friendly entity gets a kick out of moving sweet jars and other goodies around the tearoom at night. However, this playful ghost has been known to make the odd appearance during the day.

The proprietor of the café, Laura, believes that the phantom is that of an old woman, known by local folk as Nanny Goony. One evening, Laura was just locking up when suddenly a jar of lollipops was sent crashing to the floor. Laura decided to pick them up in the morning, but when she returned, the lollipops had been replaced in the jar and stood upright.

The other strange happenings in the shop include sweets being moved around by unseen hands, pictures falling off the wall, and crumbs appearing on freshly wiped tables. Laura has also heard the sound of legs moving under a table, but when she looked underneath, there was nobody there.

When Laura called in a local paranormal group to investigate, they told her that the ghostly occurrences bore all the signs of poltergeist activity. They believed that the entity haunting the café was a trapped soul who was attempting to relay a message to both the owner and her mum.

Alan Toner

Despite all these weird happenings, Laura says that she is not afraid of her resident phantom, as she deems her to be harmless and, actually, quite friendly, albeit a little mischievous. If, on the other hand, the ghost was really malevolent, then Laura says she would not stay in the place.

196. The Haunted Antique Chest

At Stanbury Manor, Cornwall, England, there is an old chest that is said to have been transported to this country with the Spanish Armada. The owner had purchased it from an antique shop, and the proprietor was glad to be rid of it, as he suspected that the chest was haunted.

The buyer placed the chest in the armoury of the manor house, and that's when strange things started to happen. Shortly after delivery, whilst walking through the armoury, the owner saw six guns, which had been secured to the wall with strong wire, suddenly fall to the floor. The weird thing was, neither the wire nor any of the fixings were broken.

On other occasion, the chest was moved to the bedroom, and on the same night, the owner was in the next room hanging pictures up on the wall when one of them fell and hit him on the head. It was as if the picture had just been moved by unseen hands.

Over the next few days, more pictures mysteriously fell from the wall. Falling pictures are, according to an old superstition, usually a signal of an impending death of either a family member or a friend. When the owner learned of the death of a relative a few days later, and saw that the pictures had suddenly stopped falling right after this bad news, it made him think whether there was any connection here as far as this old superstition was concerned.

The strange things surrounding the old antique chest even made the daily papers.

Another, and even more horrific, story involving the chest concerns a surgeon in the Midlands. Whilst staying with a friend, he noticed a large antique chest standing in the corner of his bedroom. His curiosity piqued about the chest's possible contents, he ventured to open the lid . . . and was immediately shocked to be confronted by the corpse of a man lying there with his throat cut. The shock caused the surgeon to lose his grip on the lid, and it fell closed. However, when he finally calmed down a bit and re-opened the lid, he was surprised to find that the chest was empty.

The following morning, he mentioned his horrific experience to his friend, who told him that a previous occupant of that bedroom had committed suicide in there, and the body had been found in the chest, covered in blood.

197. The Ghost of The Pink Lady

Over the years, many famous guests - from authors to even a president - have passed through the doors of the Grove Park Inn in Asheville, North Carolina. Among those guests is a ghost named "The Pink Lady".

This mysterious woman visited the Inn in the 1920s, and stayed as a guest in room 545. She wore a long, pink, flowing gown. Tragically, she lost her life there when she fell over the stone wall from the second floor. To this day, her spirit is said to haunt the Inn.

Various employees and guests claimed to have seen a strange pink mist, and even the actual ghost of the woman dressed in a pink gown, in various parts of the Inn.

The Pink Lady apparently has a bit of a soft spot for kids. For example, a doctor who once stayed at the Inn said that his children had described to him how they had loved playing with "the lady in the pink dress". Even her antics border on the childlike, as some guests have said that their feet have been playfully tickled at night. Also, the air-conditioning has been turned off and on, along with all the lights, and doors and windows have opened of their own accord.

But the phantom Pink Lady does not always act in the manner of a mischievous kid, for there have been times when she has adopted a more solicitous manner of behaviour. For instance, she once embraced a guest with all the affection of a loving relative. Another guest described how the lady held her hand when she became apprehensive.

Nobody really knows the true identity of The Pink Lady of Grove Park Inn. Some believe she may have been a debutante, while others think she was a scorned secret lover. Whoever she is, there is no doubt that she certainly has an incessant fixation for room 545.

198. The Ghost of Robin Williams

Robin Williams was a hugely popular American actor and comedian. He first rose to fame playing the space alien Mork in the TV sitcom Mork and Mindy (1978-82), before going on to star in such widely acclaimed films as Popeye (1980), The World According To Garp (1982) and Good Morning Vietnam (1987). His tragic suicide on the 11th August 2014, following a bout of severe depression, shocked the entertainment world.

Although the great actor has departed from the physical world, apparently his ghost lingers on in the California home where he died. The security staff has reported a series of strange incidents, such as pranks being played on them by an unseen presence and ghostly chuckling which, they believe, is from Williams himself. Also, when the security guards go into the house every few hours to check the alarm system, they find that the TV set has been mysteriously switched on. And on another occasion, a security team member entered the house and found that the TV had been switched to a comedy show starring the late Richard Pryor. The security insists that it would be impossible for anybody to enter the house without setting off the alarm.

A neighbour, on hearing of these strange incidents, said that all this was so characteristic of Robin, as he loved to play

Alan Toner

practical jokes.

199. The Ghost of Tommy Cooper

Fez-wearing comedian and magician Tommy Cooper, whose famous catch phrase was "Just like that", sadly died onstage in the middle of a live TV performance at Her Majesty's Theatre on 15th April 1984.

It is said that Cooper's ghost still haunts the stage on which he collapsed with a massive heart attack, as if he's intending to complete his act from beyond the grave to make up for the fatal interruption that cut it so tragically short that night.

In addition to the ghost of Tommy Cooper, there is another phantom haunting Her Majesty's Theatre in the form of famed Victorian Sir Herbert Beerbohm Tree, the venue's inaugural actor-manager. His apparition has been seen watching shows from a box, the back of the stalls and the wings.

In May 2016, Tommy Cooper was honoured with a blue plaque on his former West London home.

200. The Haunted Wardrobe

In October 2015, a news report appeared in a local Devon paper about a haunted wardrobe with an intricate Satanic head carving. This piece of furniture was said to be the cause of a string of weird happenings at two antique shops in Paignton's Winner Street.

Customers who viewed the wardrobe complained that they could not shut the doors, as if somebody - or some THING - was pushing it from the inside. They also said they could sense the presence of a little girl in the shop, and a strange coldness. The cupboard would also unlock itself, and the doors would swing open of their own accord.

These strange things started to happen soon after the proprietor of the Olden Ewe antique shop bought the spooky cupboard early in 2015. She paid £350 for it, but after all that she experienced with her new purchase, she soon began to wish she had never set eyes on it.

One of the staff working in the shop believes that the carved headpiece on the front of the cupboard may have come from the headboard of a bed. All the pieces comprising the cupboard date back to the early 20th century.

At another shop in Winner Street, The Yesteryears Antique, yet more paranormal occurrences were reported, around the same time as the ghostly happenings in the Olden Ewe shop. The co-owner of Yesteryears said that she often heard strange noises coming from the steps in the shop when nobody was there, and she claims to have seen a shadowy figure creeping up behind her. She believes that the figure may be the spirit of a woman who used to live on the premises many years ago, when the shop was a residential property.

Author's Note

If you enjoyed this book, I would really appreciate it if you could leave a review for it on Amazon.

You can also subscribe to my Newsletter at the following link:

http://bit.ly/2rDvlLB

Alan Toner
www.alantoner.com
www.trueghoststories.co.uk

Made in the USA
Monee, IL
30 July 2021